Composing Social Identity
in Written Language

Composing Social Identity in Written Language

Edited by

Donald L. Rubin
University of Georgia

LEA LAWRENCE ERLBAUM ASSOCIATES, PUBLISHERS
1995 Hillsdale, New Jersey   Hove, UK

Lawrence Erlbaum Associates, Inc., Publishers
365 Broadway
Hillsdale, New Jersey 07642

Cover design by Mairav Salomon-Dekel

Library of Congress Cataloging-in-Publication Data

Composing social identity in written language / edited by Donald L.
  Rubin.
      p.   cm.
  Includes bibliographical references and indexes.
  ISBN 0-8058-1383-7. — ISBN 0-8058-1384-5
  1. English language—Rhetoric—Study and teaching—Social aspects.
  2. English language—Style—Social aspects. 3. Authorship—Sex
  differences. 4. Identity (Psychology). 5. Group identity.
  I. Rubin, Donald L.
  PE1404.C6176 1995
  808'.042'07—dc20   94-28621
                                                            CIP

Books published by Lawrence Erlbaum Associates are printed on acid-free
paper, and their bindings are chosen for strength and durability.

Printed in the United States of America
10 9 8 7 6 5 4 3 2 1

FTW
AGY1230

DEDICATION

For many of us contributing to this volume, it was Gene Piché who invoked for us the fundamental laws of critical scholarship: "Beware of ideas sculpted in smoke" and "You can't just pull data out of your ears." It was Piché who encouraged in us the most catholic of reading—pursuing works across the widest range of disciplines, epistemologies, and genres—and who inculcated in us unrelenting prejudice only against shoddy work. It was Piché who imparted to us awe and faith in the palpable insistence of words well crafted to move minds. This volume is part of the intellectual legacy of Gene L. Piché.

Contents

CHAPTER ONE

Introduction:
Composing Social Identity

Donald L. Rubin
The University of Georgia

Theme for English B
by Langston Hughes[1]

The instructor said,

> *Go home and write*
> *a page tonight.*
> *And let that page come out of you—*
> *Then, it will be true.*

I wonder if it's that simple?

I am twenty-two, colored, born in Winston-Salem.
I went to school there, then Durham, then here
to this college on the hill above Harlem.
I am the only colored student in my class.
These steps from the hill lead down into Harlem,
through a park, then I cross St. Nicholas,
Eighth Avenue, Seventh, and I come to the Y,
the Harlem Branch Y, where I take the elevator
up to my room, sit down, and write this page:

It's not easy to know what is true for you or me
at twenty-two, my age. But I guess I'm what
I feel and see and hear, Harlem, I hear you:

---

[1]Reprinted from *Montage of a Dream Deferred*, 1951, by permission of Harold Ober Associates Incorporated.

hear you, hear me—we two—you, me, talk on this page.
(I hear New York, too.) Me—who?
Well, I like to eat, sleep, drink, and be in love.
I like to work, read, learn, and understand life.
I like a pipe for a Christmas present,
or records—Bessie, bop, or Bach.
I guess being colored doesn't make me *not* like
the same things other folks like who are other races.
So will my page be colored that I write?
Being me, it will not be white.
But it will be
a part of you, instructor.

You are white—
yet a part of me, as I am a part of you.
That's American.
Sometimes perhaps you don't want to be a part of me.
Nor do I often want to be a part of you.
But we are, that's true!
As I learn from you,
I guess you learn from me—
although you're older—and white—
and somewhat more free.

This is my page for English B.

"Will my page be colored that I write?" the writer queries. "I wonder if it's that simple?" Of course it is not that simple. The writer is so many things. His identity is multifaceted; ethnicity is but one dimension—albeit a crucial and salient dimension—of that identity. Consider for a moment this: In just now referring to the poem's student-writer as "he," I am (reflecting my reading process) ascribing gender identity. Am I justified in reading this writer as a man? I *believe* I am hearing a male voice in the poem, perhaps issuing from the brief and pithy sentences that are interspersed. Am I instead projecting the historical author's, that is, Langston Hughes', biological (if not psychological) gender onto the implied author of the poem? Or am I drawing my gender inference from something as simplistically stereotypical as the implied author's pipe-smoking persona?

The student-writer in the Hughes poem is justifiably perplexed by the complexity of defining identity ("It's not easy to know what is true for you or me . . ."). He recognizes that part of his identity arises from ethnic group membership ("Harlem, I hear you"). And he recognizes that affiliating with a social group implies otherness, implies a boundary that in this case separates the sensibilities of "coloreds" from "whites."

Yet the writer sees also that he belongs to multiple, overlapping communities ("I hear New York, too"). Some of these community memberships transcend differences among groups ("I guess being colored doesn't make me *not* like the same things other folks like who are other races"). Nor is the writer's identity some static entity; it evolves even as he interacts with his White instructor. Finally, in addition to being a collection of social affiliations, the writer is a unique individual who, *qua* individual, likes to "eat, drink, and be in love."

In "Theme for English B," Langston Hughes accents for us the key issues regarding social identity and writing. The remainder of this volume can be seen as an attempt to explicate those very issues. In doing so, the contributors to this volume will inevitably be examining some of the essential paradoxes of composing:

1. Writing is at once an individual and a cognitive process, and at the same time a social and a conventional practice.
2. Style is at once a function of the writer's idiosyncratic identity, and at the same time a function of the social matrix in which the writing and the writer are embedded.
3. Written language both reflects the writer's identity, and at the same time creates that identity.

TOWARD A SOCIAL STYLISTICS OF WRITING

Style Construed as Individuality or Intentionality

Influenced by the belletristic tradition, typical notions of style focus on the writer as an individual. The adage, attributed to Buffon, that "the style is the man" [sic] has guided stylisticians to consider style as an idiosyncratic reflection of an author's background and—especially—personality (e.g., Ohmann, 1962). The use of stylistic analysis to verify authorship of disputed texts reinforces the view of style as individualistic, much like a fingerprint.

One central issue in traditional stylistic analysis pertains to the role of intentionality in shaping the style of a work. On the one hand, if style is a mirror of deeply ingrained personality traits, then it lies beyond the author's focal awareness, and it is largely beyond the power of the author to alter. On the other hand, it is certain that skilled writers do make strategic decisions about wording, about what ideas to emphasize, about expressing deference, and the like. To distinguish unintentional clues or "leakage" about the writers' identity from intentional stylistic strategies, Louis Millic (1971) denoted the former as "stylistic option" and the latter as "rhetorical choice."

Style Construed as a Social Marker

No doubt a writer's individual identity (i.e., unique personality) is a major determinant of both stylistic options and rhetorical choices. But as we come to see writing, increasingly, as a social activity, we recognize that there is a social stylistics to written language as well. Stylistic options "leak" clues about writers' social identities. Rhetorical choices help writers construct the social identities they wish to project in given writing episodes. That is perhaps the most important theme of this volume of articles: Written language *reflects* or conveys a writer's social identity, but it also *constructs* or instantiates it.

Consider the following excerpts from a letter published in *The New York Times* (Pastre, 1991), written by a victim of a notorious crime against a family of tourists in New York City in 1991. Most likely the letter was subject to some professional editing, yet it illustrates the central principles of social stylistics:

> . . . My parents and I are French. We were visiting New York City when we were attacked by a thief . . . What do I do now? Do I scream in French or in English? I tried both. And then this nasty guy turned back and faced me, violence in his eyes. I could react against his threats and screaming, but when he grabbed this brick and hit my head with it, I could only disbelieve he would do it . . . I saw all this crowd of kids around me. They were between 12 and 18, maybe intrigued by this bleeding stranger screaming. Were they with me or against me? I feel bad now just to have had a doubt about it. They were black. They were from Harlem. And they were with me. And they were throwing bottles and cans at the nasty guy. I cannot explain the feelings and the emotion to see all of them helping me, the white, the stranger, the rich . . . I still like New York. I still like Harlem. He hurt my father and he could have killed me. Justice has to be done. Thank you.

As a matter of rhetorical choice, the writer explicitly reveals his ethnic identity as a White French person, as well as his social class (he's rich). These rhetorical choices certainly lend the letter a greater coherence than had the information been omitted. Notwithstanding those explicit revelations about social identity, the written language itself contains stylistic options that strongly mark this writer at least as a non-native writer/speaker of English. Experienced teachers of English as a second language will be familiar with the slightly off-idiom tone that results from expressions like "I could only disbelieve he would do it" or "had a doubt about it" (as opposed to "had *any* doubt" or "had doubt*s*").

In terms of organizational structure, the abrupt shift from "I still like Harlem" to "He hurt my father . . . Justice has to be done" seems like an odd rhetorical turn to American readers. Perhaps, though, it does issue from some characteristic trait of Gallic argumentation (Kaplan, 1966). In these respects, this piece of discourse deviates from standard edited English (SEE) and marks its author as other than a standard American. Most readers would agree, I am confident, that this social marking is both appropriate and forceful in this instance.

Socio-Stylistic Features as "Interference" in Writing

In the past, composition researchers as well as teachers have regarded stylistic markers of social identity in writing mainly as elements of *interference*. Some have claimed that nonstandard dialect interferes with writing (Wolfram & Whiteman, 1971), some have considered second-language interference in writing (Lay, 1975), and some have hypothesized that female-typical language may constitute another form of interference in writing (Smeltzer & Werbel, 1986).

This tendency to treat demographic markers in writing as sources of interference is predicated on the notion that communicative success and positive evaluation requires "unmarkedness" in discourse style, that is, requires conformity with the standard language forms (Banks, 1987). Voiceless, genderless, identity-less prose is the most desirable, according to this view. To be sure, deviance from SEE in the form of mechanical errors does undermine perceived quality of writing (e.g., Rafoth & Rubin, 1984).

Sociolinguistic Interference as a Reader Response. But the relationship between actual error and perceived error, and between actual social identity, and perceived social identity is not always straightforward. Error is very much in the mind of the beholder (Williams, 1982). In studies of speech evaluation, for example, listeners perceive error and identity according to their stereotyped expectations; if they are given false information that a speaker is non-native, they discern linguistic deviance, and their comprehension actually suffers (Rubin, 1992). Similarly, writing evaluators are not always accurate in discerning the actual social identities of writers. But if they decide (for any reason, plausible or not) that a particular writer is a member of a socially stigmatized group, then they are more likely to perceive the writing as nonstandard and error-laden (Piché, Rubin, Turner, & Michlin, 1978).

The locus of interference, therefore, lies at least as much in the readers' expectations of writers from certain social groups as in the writers' actual manner of marking social identity by using nonstandard forms.

One mind set, therefore, equates any social "deviance" with error in writing. A second point of view—perhaps a shade more humane—regards social markers as interference in the sense that they draw the reader's attention away from the intended effect of the message. The reader becomes distracted with supposedly irrelevant aspects of the writer's identity. According to this view, a writer's message has a better chance of affecting the reader if it is socially "unmarked," if the author is invisible. Richard Lloyd-Jones (1981) remarked in a not altogether disapproving tone that, "[O]ne can almost say that the objective of the schools is to acquaint all students with the blandest forms of English, the forms of least commitment, the forms of superficial order" (p. 174). In a like vein, a middle school teacher tells a student-writer:

> You are right that everyone will understand you if you say, "The Earth ain't nobody's personal property." But your readers will be so busy thinking about what kind of person you are to be saying, "ain't no," that they won't pay any attention to what you're really trying to get across to them.

The Myth of Socially Unmarked Style in Writing. Even this communication-based notion of social markers as interference is flawed, however. First, it is erroneous to suppose that the author can ever be invisible. True, the actual social identity of the historical author can be effaced. Such has often been the case of the woman writer who wishes to be taken seriously, to succeed commercially and critically (Heilbrun, 1988). But no text can be completely devoid of persona, without voice. Even a text composed collaboratively among members of a corporate entity—say an article published in *Morbidity and Mortality Weekly Reports*, to which authors' names may not be ascribed if they are employees of the U.S. Centers for Disease Control and Prevention—evokes some sense of authorship among readers. True, the constructed author's identity may well be disembodied from any corporeal individual. Indeed, that is the avowed objective of many professional writers: to become proficient in projecting a consistent organizational identity in their writing.

Second, it is a myth that any style can achieve unmarkedness. What linguists and stylisticians sometimes call "unmarked forms" are really just normative forms, that is, representing social and political prestige (Banks, 1987; Penelope, 1990). Use of SEE is *not* unmarked. If it does not always signal membership in the dominant culture, at very least SEE marks acceptance of, aspiration to, and complicity with mainstream definitions of status. (See Rubin, Goodrum, & Hall, 1990, for a critique of the notion of interference from an instructional perspective.)

Socio-Stylistic Features as Markers of Affiliation or Accommodation in Writing

The Obligatory Nature of Socio-Stylistic Marking in Writing. The claim here, then, is that writing style is never devoid of social marking, never really unmarked. It is useful, therefore, to think of writers as selecting (by virtue of some obligatory sociolinguistic rule) from among socio-stylistic variants and thereby projecting a social identity. Conversely, readers construe author identity based on their associations with socially distributed features of language and discourse. This view presumes that stylistic variants that may be more or less referentially equivalent may yet carry with them differing social presuppositions (Keenan, 1971).

In speech, if I call you *tu* instead of *vous,* I am presupposing (whether rightly or wrongly) high solidarity and low power differential between us (Brown & Gilman, 1960). If I speak to you in the local rural dialect rather than in the dialect of national literacy, I am accentuating that aspect of my identity that is more communal and less cosmopolitan (Blom & Gumperz, 1972). If I am an educated South African and I insist on speaking to you in Afrikaans instead of in English, I may be asserting the salience of my ethnic identity.

In writing, as well as in speech, I convey my social identity by selecting from among stylistic variants. For example, Serbian resistance to Romanization of its Cyrillic orthography during the former Yugoslav regime (see Fishman, 1988) can in retrospect be seen as a harbinger of the nationalistic aspirations that fuel the tragic Balkan wars of the 1990s. In a less obvious fashion, I may signal or invoke my social identity as a first-language literate in Spanish by writing long sentences with little punctuation (see Rubin et al., 1990). Or I may project my identity as an inner-city African American by writing, "It [as opposed to 'there'] is one more reason why I support this plan" (Farr & Daniels, 1986). Or I may convey a male gender role orientation by writing a description that catalogues and enumerates objects—"In this room there are three tables forming a partial horseshoe shape. Each table has four chairs"—rather than writing a more holistic and relational description.

When I say that I "select" from among stylistic variants in order to convey social identity in writing, my language seems to imply some kind of deliberate, calculated text manipulation. Sometimes, of course, that may be the case. The writer may be exercising—in Millic's (1971) terms—a rhetorical choice. Thus a novelist may deliberately incorporate linguistic or rhetorical devices that unambiguously signal her ethnic or national background (Li, 1992). Student-writers sometimes do the same. When asked to produce a descriptive writing sample in response to a standard pictorial prompt first used by the National Assessment of Educational Progress, one fourth-grader from inner-city Milwaukee began, "Mean old wrinkled up white lady . . ." Clearly racial identity was salient to this youngster, and it is not difficult to discern hers.

Style as Social Accommodation. Most often, however, marking social identity in writing is more subtle, and oftentimes quite below the focal awareness of the writer—a matter of stylistic option (Millic, 1971). Speech accommodation theory (Giles, Mulac, Bradac, & Johnson, 1987) provides a useful perspective on this process. When conversational partners perceive themselves to be similar one to the other, their speech patterns tend to converge. Generally the lower status individual moves further toward the prestige form, but the prestige form speaker also does display some shift in the direction of the lower status language patterns. When conversational partners perceive themselves to be more different one to the other than alike, then they tend to accentuate those stylistic features that distinguish them. Generally this all happens quite automatically.

Research in the tradition of speech accommodation theory finds this linguistic convergence or divergence operating with quite a range of discourse features (Giles et al., 1987). Bilingual speakers may switch from one distinct language to another (say Flemish vs. Walloon in Belgium) in order to either construct a common identity or in the alterative to construct an alien identity. But stylistic convergence and divergence can also occur in use of paralinguistic features like speech rate, or in phonological features like postvocalic /-r/ deletion.

Speakers are often unaware that they are modifying their speech in these less dramatic ways, but—what is particularly interesting for educators concerned with encouraging students to use dominant culture (i.e., standard) language forms—awareness is somewhat greater for language divergence than for convergence (Sachdev & Bourhis, 1990). In other words, people sometimes expend considerable effort in marshalling language to create and maintain a minority culture identity. Linguistic resistance does not arise from ignorance of standard forms; to the contrary, maintaining nonstandard forms often entails considerable language awareness.

Affiliation and Alienation Enacted Stylistically. The principles explicated by speech accommodation theory thus link social affinity with language convergence and conversely link social alienation with language divergence. These principles help explain why some students from minority speech communities have little difficulty producing SEE whereas other students of similar sociocultural backgrounds fail to do so regardless of hours upon hours of instructional drill. It seems certain, for example, that most children we might classify as typically nonstandard dialect speakers in fact are quite capable of producing standard English forms. We can hear them doing so when they are role-playing school talk, for example (Gleason, 1973).

So the "barrier" to SEE use among many minority group students is probably not ignorance, and probably cannot be eliminated by any amount of traditional instruction in mechanics and usage. Instead, the "barrier" is a matter of social identification.

In one set of interviews (Garner & Rubin, 1986), by way of illustration, some members of an African-American attorney's guild indicated that they had acquired SEE fairly effortlessly, with little focal awareness of what they were doing. It seems that many of them had simply disassociated SEE from any ethnic or racial meaning. Some even disputed the existence of any ethnic dialects. They did not admit the existence of a Black English vernacular (BEV). They construed writing in SEE as a matter of identification with the legal profession and with the mainstream of society, and for them it entailed no alienation from inner-city African-American roots.[2]

CONSTRUCTING SOCIAL IDENTITY IN WRITING

A socio-stylistics of writing, therefore, would regard a writer's selection from among varying patterns of discourse as an act of social identification. Even when I write in perfect SEE, I am not eliminating social markers. Rather, I am adopting a stylistic stance that identifies me with the values and beliefs of an educated, mainstream culture discourse community. Native Chinese speaker Fan Shen (1989) reflected:

> . . . I found that learning to compose in English is not an isolated classroom activity, but a social and cultural experience. The rules of English composition encapsulate values that are absent in, or sometimes contradictory to, the values of other societies (in my case, China). Therefore, learning the rules of English composition is, to a certain extent, learning the values of Anglo-American society. (p. 460)

Social Identity as a Construction

An Interactional Perspective on Social Identity. That characterization suggests that I do not *have* a social identity as I might "have" a particular texture of hair or even as I might "have" acquired a particular tattoo. Hair texture and tattoos are attributes. But an identity is something I *enact* (Collier & Thomas, 1988). Identity is dynamic (Hecht, 1993), and it is something that is presented and re-presented, constructed and reconstructed in interaction (including in written communication). Banks (1987) captured this point with respect to ethnic identity. He stated, "[this perspective] allows ethnicity to 'float' upon the instant of interaction, requiring it to be neither objective and historical nor hidden and psychological. Ethnicity becomes what ethnicity does interactionally" (p. 175).

---

[2]Of course some deviance in writing is probably a function of nothing more significant than care-lessness. Many students of all social backgrounds simply "could care less" about their writing. Their errors reflect distraction and mental absenteeism. It is important to distinguish the etiology of care-less background noise from any systematic effects of social identity. Sometimes the outcomes appear similar. In the case of minority writers, however, background levels of error production that might remain unnoticed among mainstream students can trigger socially stigmatized judgments.

Several demonstrations all point to social identity as something enacted through symbolic interaction. As a preliminary, it is interesting to observe that people change their social identities with a certain degree of fluidity. For example, people who might have once considered themselves Jamaicans in their native land, may transform themselves into more generic "West Indians" when they come to mingle with other immigrant groups in the United States and find the new identity to be more functional (Waters, 1990). Conversely, gross labels like "Asian American" can break down as people find that more discrete social categories like "Filipino American" better serve their needs, at least in certain contexts (Magner, 1993). In a related matter, recent census reports in the United States show increases in Native American populations that cannot be accounted for by birth rates. People who 10 years previously saw themselves as Anglo/Europeans now construe themselves to be Native Americans.

Social Identity as a Fluid Entity. In part, such dynamism in defining and redefining social identity may be due to the fact that social identities are developmental for each individual. That is, people go through stages in acquiring a sense of themselves as culturally defined beings (Helms, 1990). On a more macroscopic level, it seems to be a recurring historical pattern for cultural entities to proliferate at some times (e.g., the emergence of Sikh as an ethnic category separate from Hindu), and to consolidate at others (e.g., the forced consolidation of Pauite, Wasco, and Warm Springs Native Americans into a single Warm Springs "tribe"). So cultural categories are themselves dynamic (Horowitz, 1975); boundaries between cultures may be more or less plastic at various times in history.

Social Identity Self-Appropriated as Well as Other-Ascribed. A person's social identity has long been regarded by social psychologists as a function of two factors: (a) the social category that others ascribe to the individual and (b) the individual's own sense of affiliation to one "reference group" or another (see Gudykunst & Kim, 1988; Horowitz, 1975). Radical lesbian Jill Johnston (quoted in Kitzinger, 1989) expressed the point concisely: "Identity is what you can say you are according to what they say you can be" (p. 82).

Social identity, then, is to some degree imposed by others and to some degree embraced by the self. It is to some degree a function of what people conventionally regard as "a Jew" or "a Latino" or "a German" or "a woman" or "an educated person." It is to another degree a function of one's own construction of "my affinity with Jewishness at this time" or "my wish to identify with La Raza at this time" or "my appropriation of a sense of German-ness" or "the degree of female-ness of my gender role orientation" or "my current feelings of authority with respect to this topic and this audience."

The notion that writers construct their social identities in texts according to their own sense of affiliation bears some resemblance to Bartholomae's (1985) notion of appropriating roles. Bartholomae noted that undergraduates in freshman composition classes are told to write from the stance of membership in an academic community. Yet they are not members (and may not even wish to apply for the dubious honor), do not possess authority, and have but little expertise about the literary genres, the historical epochs, or the sociological principles about which they are typically asked to write. The successful freshman writers write *as if* they were members of an academic community. They appropriate that role and its associated style.

Social identity, then, is complex in several respects. One's own sense of self as defined by group membership can wax and wane. The very social categories to which we may even potentially belong may shift in number and definition. Social identity is something that is ascribed to us by others. And social identity is something that we appropriate for ourselves. Together, these factors render the socio-stylistics of writing a much more interesting enterprise than simply correlating linguistic markers with demographic traits of writers.

Cultural Identity and Authenticity in Writing. Consider, for example, the issue of authentic voice in writing. If a woman writes a story, does her biological gender perforce qualify the piece into the corpus of women's literature? That proposal smacks of essentialism (Graves, 1993). Is it possible, therefore, for a man to write in a female voice, for a man to author women's literature? (See Moore, 1992, and discussion thereof later in this chapter.) Various forms of computer-mediated communication now do provide writers an opportunity to try out whatever gender personae they wish (see, e.g., the thread regarding Multi-User Dungeons on COMSERVE's Gender List in early December of 1992). A number of "cross-communicators" in these forums conclude that it is indeed possible to textually construct for oneself a gender identity that other participants seem to accept as quite authentic. As evidence of authentic female voice, these computer communicators offer the fact that they are often the targets of sexually harassing responses.

In a parallel fashion, readers are periodically embarrassed by the revelation that some favorite author has been a cultural imposter. Such was the case of the well-loved account of Native American youth, *The Education of Little Tree*. As it happens, the book was composed by a White man who had been associated with racist and fascist causes (Gates, 1991). The author appropriated a Native-American identity and textualized it superbly. Readers reciprocated by ascribing to the author a social identity consistent with the text, if not with the man.

The writer's social identity, therefore, need have little to do with heredity (though, to be sure, demographic traits do map onto social identity with considerable fidelity in most cases). It is rather a construction in text that writers instantiate and that readers reify (see discussion of the audience's role in creating the author in Enos, 1990, and in Phelps, 1990). The articles collected in this book treat three types of identity: ethnolinguistic, gender, and role-relational. Whichever of these social identities is being treated, however, it is important to recognize that it is ultimately a social construction, jointly erected by writer and reader.

COMPOSING ETHNOLINGUISTIC IDENTITY

Dialect and Writing

Nowhere, it seems, is the notion of interference so deeply and uncritically rooted as in accounts of "dialect interference" in writing. In the public mind, and even in the minds of many educators, nonstandardness in speech is inextricably and causally linked to nonstandardness in writing. Carol Reed, then of the National Institute of Education, wrote in 1981:

> Clearly the most significant problem facing the college English teacher today is what to do about the results of what has been a consistent failure on the part of our inner-city grade schools and secondary schools to impart standard English literacy skills to those Black students in the basic composition course whose primary mode of oral communication is Black English Vernacular. (p. 142)

Even careful and insightful analysts like Mina Shaughnessy (1977) presumed that writing errors like lack of subject/verb concord were attributable to oral dialect patterns.

And yet the preponderance of empirical evidence on the matter compels the conclusion that speakers of BEV—the most extensively studied nonstandard dialect—do not write just as they speak (see reviews in Farr & Daniels, 1986; Hartwell, 1980; Rubin, 1979). The incidence of nonstandard features in the writing of African Americans is much lower than in their speech, and not much different in kind or in quantity than nonstandard features appearing in the writing of mainstream culture students. To be sure, a small number of studies (e.g., Epes, 1985) do seem to offer evidence of direct impact of BEV on written language. But one of the more recent empirical studies of this issue (Zeni & Thomas, 1990) found that when social class and writing achievement were held constant, few ethnic differences appeared. "Dialect is simply not a problem for most [African-American writers]; for others it is a problem, but not the main problem . . . We conclude, first of all, that premature or primary stress on dialect and error is counterproductive" (Zeni & Thomas, 1990, p. 25).

In "Stylistic Variation in Vernacular Black English and the Teaching of College Composition" (chapter 2 of this volume), Michael Linn provides some explanation for the fact that the written language of nonstandard dialect speakers does not usually mirror their oral language. The key, Linn reminds us, is to recognize that variability lies at the heart of language use. Dialects are known to function according to variable rules. In addition to variation at the levels of morphophonemic and syntactic constructions, Linn continues, competent communicators vary their rhetorical styles to accommodate to differing audience demands in high- or low-context situations. Messages need to be more explicit and organized when readers cannot be presumed to share much contextual information with writers. Teachers can encourage speakers of Black English vernacular to build upon their skills in code switching.

Orality and Ethnolinguistic Style in Writing

Most explications of ethnic style in writing—whether focused on narrow dialect interference or on broader rhetorical strategies—presume that stylistic features marking social identity in writing are somehow a residue of the features that characteristically mark social identity in speech (e.g., Ball, 1992; Farr & Janda, 1985; see also chapters 2 and 11 of this volume). This notion of oral-based style influencing writing style is no doubt a fruitful avenue for understanding the source of social markers in writing. Yet a number of cautions are in order when pursuing that line of reasoning (see discussion in Rubin et al., 1990):

1. Written style is never isomorphic with oral style; not even very early writers write just as they speak.
2. By the same token, style is not wholly determined by the mode of composition; speech performances vary in the degree to which they incorporate literacy-based elements, and writing varies in the degree to which it manifests oral-based elements.
3. Oral-based style is not the exclusive province of minority culture writers; writers from all backgrounds vary the ratio of conversationality in their writing depending on author–audience role relations.

Taking these considerations into account, Rosalind Horowitz (chapter 3 of this volume) examines oral influences in writings from several ethnic groups. In "Orality in Literacy: The Uses of Speech in Written Language by Bilingual and Bicultural Writers," Horowitz follows Halliday (1987) in taking a deliberately *functional* approach to oral features in writing. (For a more structural/formal approach to a similar set of issues, see Haynes, 1992.) Thus, for example, Horowitz shows one elementary school boy from a Mexican-

American community writing a line of dialogue as a means of launching into more extended prose. And in another example, Martin Luther King, Jr., is shown to appropriate oral formulae familiar to his audience into his own productions. Horowitz takes the position that to call such appropriation "plagiarism" is an inappropriate ethnocentric response. Instead, Horowitz regards the dependency of writing on orality to be a source of strength for many minority culture writers. Adopting that position, she argues, is critical for educators who face the challenge of enhancing literacy among an increasingly multicultural clientele.

Contrastive Rhetoric

By including examples of Spanish-dominant youngsters, Yiddish-speaking immigrants, and African-American orators, Horowitz's chapter points to certain similarities among the composing of nonstandard dialect speakers and second-language speakers. (To be sure, there are very dramatic dissimilarities that ought not be ignored. No doubt phonological, morphological, and syntactic interference exerts more profound and persistent impact on the written style of non-native speakers. See, e.g., Garcia, 1975.) Particularly when non-native speakers are writing in English as a second language (ESL), it is evident that they are in the business of negotiating social identity through style, just as are speakers of nonstandard dialects. Recall, as an example, the French crime victim's letter to *The New York Times* presented earlier in this chapter.

The field of contrastive rhetoric (Kaplan, 1966; see review in Leki, 1991) arose in response to an increasing need to understand factors affecting the writing of ESL speakers. From the outset, this perspective emphasized cultural differences in thought patterns and the manner in which these may manifest themselves as broad rhetorical patterns of organization and argumentation in writing (Kaplan, 1966). Thus, for example, Matalene (1985) concluded that because of deeply acculturated reverence for ancestors and authority, Chinese writers avoid the kind of original discovery and unique expression that Western writing teachers typically seek to inculcate.

Work in contrastive rhetoric is quite compatible with the notion of socio-stylistic construction of identity that this book develops. Some formulations of contrastive rhetoric point directly to issues of identity formation. Hinds (1987) working in Japanese, Zellermeyer (1988) working in Hebrew, and Scollon and Scollon (1981) working in Athapaskan, for example, independently evolved notions of culture-typical rhetorical styles embodying particular relations between authors and readers. In each of these cultures discourse norms dictate that significant amounts of information are to be left for readers to infer for themselves. An Athapaskan persuader, by way of illustration, will list evidence, but considers it rude indeed to explicitly tell an interlocutor what conclusion to draw from it. In such a culture, when one does adopt a highly explicit style, one is creating a distant, nonfamiliar persona.

Other aspects of contrastive rhetoric have more indirect—but nonetheless significant—implications for the ways people construct social identity. For example, Arabic prose (or English prose composed by Arabic speakers) is sometimes characterized as florid, full of high diction and superlatives. This has been linked to the pervasive influence of Qu'aranic style on Arabic expression (Almany & Alwan, 1982). An Arabic writer reconstructs her affiliation with Qu'aranic traditions and values each time she enacts this florid style. Even mundane variations in syntax and morphology may bear social meaning. One must be cautious of interposing questionable cognitive or value-driven interpretations on culture-typical language patterns. Nevertheless, if a Hispanic writer composes markedly loose and loosely punctuated sentences in English, then one can still safely conclude that this writer is displaying her comfort with native-language patterns. In that sense, at least, her syntax expresses her cultural identity.

In "Examining Syntactic Variation Across Three English-Speaking Nationalities Through a Multifeature/Multidimensional Approach" (chapter 4 of this volume), Ulla Connor compares texts written by American, British, and New Zealander writers. Because all writers are native English speakers, this study differs from most in the contrastive rhetoric paradigm. In a sense, this study represents a uniquely pure test of the effects of cultural identity on discourse, for in this case nationality is not confounded with language difference.

Connor focuses on two dimensions of style: (a) interactive versus edited text and (b) abstract versus situated content (see Biber, 1988). As might be expected on the basis of culture typical value structures such as those proposed by Hofstede (1984), Americans wrote in a style that was significantly more interactive and less abstract. One of the more interesting results here is that American composition teachers actually appeared to prefer the British and New Zealander writing styles. This finding reminds us that members of certain speech communities (usually low-prestige communities) may very well maintain culture-typical norms in terms of language production, and yet subscribe to culture-alien norms in terms of language evaluation (Labov, 1972). The term *linguistic self-hatred* is surely too strong for the phenomenon Connor demonstrates here, yet it is useful to mark that cultural identity in production is not always matched by cultural identity in evaluation.

Studies of contrastive rhetoric focus on texts, specifically on the ways in which cultural characteristics are instantiated in linguistic and discourse structures. Less common are related comparative studies that focus on the ways in which cultural characteristics affect the *processes* by which texts are composed. In "Social Dimensions of Second-Language Writing Instruction: Peer Response Groups as Cultural Context" (chapter 5 of this volume), Gayle

Nelson and Joan Carson (with Ned Danison and Linda Gajdusek) consider just such an issue of cultural identity and composing process. Nelson and Carson begin from the position that composing is a social behavior. By establishing peer response groups in their classrooms, writing teachers acknowledge and cultivate the sense of writing as social. One might expect that students from highly collectivistic cultures would function especially well in peer response writing groups. And yet it is commonly observed that this expectation often does not hold true. Nelson and Carson propose a hypothesis accounting for the depressed participation of many students from collectivistic cultures in writing groups. These students' lack of comfort may arise from goals and procedures that are more addressed toward improving individual writing performance than toward enhancing group performance.

To explore this hypothesis, Nelson and Carson observed and interviewed native Chinese speakers who were enrolled in an ESL writing class employing peer response groups. Through strategies like indirection, silence, and formulaic complementing, these Chinese students demonstrated a greater concern for maintaining group harmony than for providing incisive feedback to individuals. Of particular interest, Nelson and Carson note that the Chinese students were well aware of the Western construction of peer response groups, that is, that their purpose is to provide criticism to individuals. Although aware of it, the Chinese students simply did not subscribe to what was for them a culture-alien construction.

COMPOSING GENDER IDENTITY

To invoke the term *gender*, as opposed to *sex*, is to presuppose that the essential factors that categorize one person as female and another as male are socially constructed (Kessler & McKenna, 1978). Gender is a psychosocial construct, and not simply a matter of biological contingency. We acknowledge this notion when we speak of gender in a verblike sense: "doing gender" or "gendered identities" (e.g., West & Zimmerman, 1991).

Writing is an important mode of action by which people en-gender themselves. One way in which writing functions as a vehicle for constructing gender is by enabling writers to reflect upon and eventually reform the gender roles they assume in their lives. Thus, for example, a group of Bahamian women prisoners collaborate on a consciousness-raising letter addressed to Bahamian men (Fiore & Elsasser, 1981). Writing instruction in both traditional (Morahan, 1981) and nontraditional (Cooper, 1989) settings can profitably center on gender identity as a topical locus for student writing projects. In a related manner, writers who have achieved a degree of gender awareness can deliberately experiment with prose style to construct new gender identities. By stretching writing conventions, one can simultaneously stretch gender role conventions (Bridwell-Bowles, 1992; Penelope, 1990; Zawacki, 1992).

Another way in which writing constructs gender is more a matter of rhetorical option than rhetorical choice (Millic, 1971). That is, by more or less naively favoring certain gender-typical stylistic features, a writer assumes a gendered identity along some continuum of female-to-male voice. Identifying those stylistic features, verifying their distribution by gender, determining their effect on readers' perceptions of writers' gender identity, and eventually determining their impact on readers' judgments of composition quality—these types of inquiries constitute the major thrusts of research on gender and writing. The body of theory and research addressing these issues of gender-typical style in writing has been well reviewed elsewhere (see Annas, 1987; Rubin & Greene, 1992; see also chapters 6 and 8 of this volume).

Gender as a Determinant of Style

Although the theoretical underpinnings for presuming that men write differently than women are compelling, the findings of various empirical studies are by no means unequivocal. Rubin and Greene (1992), for example, found that only a small number of the stylistic features expected to differentiate women's writing from men's actually did so. And in at least one instance men showed a higher incidence of a female-typed feature than did women. On the other hand, Mulac, Studley, and Blau (1990) identified a constellation of features that strongly discriminated between the writing of boys and girls.

One explanation for disparate findings may lie in the disparate stylistic features selected for analysis. The gender-distinctive features found by Mulac et al. (1990), for example, do not appear deeply rooted in social or psychological accounts of gender. A number of studies in gendered language production are liable to the criticism that they are mired in syntactic and lexical levels of analysis, whereas the most important gender differences in writing may reside in larger issues of discourse structure or use. Studies of *oral* communication and gender have for some time recognized the limitations relying exclusively on structural—as opposed to functional—linguistic analyses (Kramer, Thorne & Henley, 1978). Thus, in the domain of writing, Johnson and Roen (1992) examined written peer critiques for gender differences in the use of compliments.

In "Gender and Language Variation in Written Communication" (chapter 6 of this volume), Duane Roen, Chere Hansen, and Valentina Abordonado extend functionally oriented analyses of gender and writing. For example, each script is assigned a holistic "ways of knowing" score. And rather than merely tabulating grammatically marked hedges, the authors consider how writers use those hedges to modify relations with their readers. This analysis of hedges is based on Brown and Levinson's (1978) face theory. Thus, by way of illustration, one category captures "hedging threats to other's negative face."

Contextual factors like genre no doubt account for substantial variation in the incidence of gender-typical style. In particular, formal argumentative writing seems to exhibit fewer female-typical markers than does informal/expressive writing (see Rubin & Greene, 1992). A number of feminist scholars claim that formal, conventional, argumentative essays are essentially androcentric (e.g., Gearhart, 1979). According to this position, these androcentric forms require women to contort their discourse to conform to alien values and modes of thinking.

Presumably, then, more spontaneous writing ought to exhibit greater gender differences than do more highly edited texts. It is worth noting that results reported by Mulac and associates (1990)—which do indicate widespread gender differences—are derived from informal, extemporaneous compositions. Perhaps, then, the nature of revision differs for men and women. For women, unlike for men, revision may involve monitoring and "denaturing" gender-typed language. In "The Suppressed Voice Hypothesis in Women's Writing: Effects of Revision on Gender-Typical Style" (chapter 7 of this volume), Kathryn Greene and I address exactly that question. Spontaneous first drafts produced by men and women are compared with their revised, final drafts. This study also attempts to consider the impact of psychological gender schema—reflecting in some sense writers' own constructions of their gender roles—in addition to a typical dichotomous notion of biological gender.

Impact of Writer Gender on Readers

It is a common experience for readers to hear gendered voice in an author's work (see my introductory remark about the Langston Hughes poem). One hears an unambiguous (even caricatured) male voice in reading Norman Mailer or Ernest Hemingway. Eudora Welty and Margaret Atwood, on the other hand, write in female voices. But what of George Eliot and others like her (see Heilbrun, 1988)—females adopting male *noms de plume?* An Ayn Rand is an even more significant case—a female writer adopting a clear male voice.

It is not at all surprising that it is more difficult to find clear cases of males adopting either female voices or female pseudonyms. But Dinty W. Moore (1992) recounted his curious experience in having his work included in a published collection of works by American women writers. Apparently the editors never directly asked Mr. Moore about his biological sex. The gender of his writing, in contrast, was manifestly female. My point is that the biological gender of the historical author is not equivalent to the readers' representation of the imagined author's gender. Readers construct gender identities for writers.

In analyzing readers' gender constructions of writers, we are squarely acknowledging that gender is a dependent variable as well as an independent variable—an effect as well as a cause—in studies of discourse (Rakow, 1986). As yet, little reliable information links particular discourse features with readers' impressions of writer gender. Considerable evidence is available, however, to demonstrate that readers (of student papers, at any rate) are surprisingly inaccurate in inferring actual writer gender. Readers do no better than a coin flip in guessing writer gender (Mulac et al., 1985; Roen, 1992; Roulis, 1990).

The interesting paradox is that even though readers are unable to accurately identify writer gender, they do reliably evaluate female-written compositions differently than male-written compositions. More specifically, raters typically evaluate female-written compositions more positively than those written by males (see chapter 6 of this volume).

In "Gendered Voice in Composing, Gendered Voice in Evaluating: Gender and the Assessment of Writing Quality" (chapter 7 of this volume), Eleni Roulis sets out to deliberately ascertain the role of gender identification in the evaluation of student writing. Accordingly, teachers read boys' and girls' argumentative essays under one of three conditions: (a) with no explicit gender identification, (b) with correct gender identification, or (c) with incorrect gender identification. Roulis analyzes teachers' ratings on sets of scales relating to perceptions of the writers and to the rhetorical stances of the writers. She also analyzes the speech act illocutionary force of the comments teachers wrote upon the student papers. Essentially the results confirm the potency of gender-typical linguistic cues in triggering judgments of the student writers along gender-typed dimensions. Thus, by way of illustration, female writers were perceived as more aesthetically oriented than their male counterparts, whereas male writers were perceived as more dynamic. Girls were seen as adopting a more cooperative rhetorical stance.

By and large, these gender-typed responses were more dependent on language style than on explicit gender identification of the writers. Roulis also tests whether these patterns of responses hold true for female raters as well as for male. She concludes that male and female teachers tend to adopt different styles of response to student papers. For example, female teachers tend to offer editing suggestions, whereas male teachers are more likely to write evaluative judgments on student papers.

COMPOSING WRITER–AUDIENCE ROLE RELATIONS

In this essay, I have been proposing a dynamic view of social identity. Your social identity is not some permanently affixed brand or tattoo that you might sometimes cover up, but never erase. Instead, your social identity is more like a musical note, played as middle C in this context, but B-flat in that one. And like a musical note, your social identity comes into being only in the enactment of it. You can enact your identity, again like a musical note, in quite variable ways—with greater or lesser intensity, slightly different timbre, and so on. Sometimes listeners hear the same note you hear yourself playing, and sometimes they hear only the note they expect to hear from you. This dynamic view is not the way most of people are used to thinking of ethnicity or nationality or sex.

On the other hand, it is quite natural to think of writers' relations to their audiences as an aspect of their social identity that is variable in just this fashion. As a competent writer, you shift your stance toward your potential readers (one might wish to reserve the term *readership* to refer to potential readers) with considerable fluidity, depending at once on your purpose and on your sense of who your readers may be (Rubin, 1984).

At the heart of Aristotelian rhetoric is the notion that rhetors adapt their messages to their audiences. Among the most potent strategies for adaptation, Aristotle and his heirs would claim, are those involving the presentation of the rhetor's personal ethos. One establishes credibility for a given audience by establishing subject matter expertise, but in another situation the best route to credibility might be to establish one's similarity (identification) with the audience.

The Nature of the Audience Construct

The Aristotelian prototype of agonistic discourse—within which the notion of audience adaptation is most prominently embedded—has suffered withering attack on many fronts for at least the last half-century. Most interesting from the perspective of constructivist theories have been critiques that problematize the very concept of audience. In his watershed article, "The Writer's Audience is Always a Fiction," Ong (1975) proposed that writers presuppose particular audience characteristics through style, and that a written work bids a reader to adopt the presupposed audience stance. Rather than adapting to some given audience, then, writers fictionalize—read "construct"—audiences that conform to parameters of their own selection. As Ede and Lunsford (1984) developed this idea, writers *invoke* audiences, not merely *address* them.

Audience as a Cognitive Entity. Under the fictionalize/invoke paradigm, audience becomes something transacted between writers and readers. Writers presuppose a particular social identity vis-à-vis their audiences, and the cooperative and competent reader reads as if the role fit. For example, I write a paragraph in which I presuppose an audience that is only vaguely aware of Walter Ong's (1975) work. You, in fact, may be eminently aware of Ong's contributions (perhaps you *are* Walter Ong reading this chapter). Nevertheless, as you read you will take the role that I have constructed for you, else you will find the reading very frustrating indeed. If you are a knowledgeable reader, and yet agree to abide by the audience role I have constructed for you, your response to the paragraph will not be one of enlightenment (you already stand in the light), but perhaps of journeypersonlike appreciation.

Audience as Discourse Community. A more radically social (as opposed to cognitive) turn to constructivism might regard audience as neither invoked nor addressed, but rather as constituted in social convention (e.g., Bartholomae, 1985; cf. Harris, 1989). One reads an article in *Harpers* in the manner in which a community of educated, concerned, progressive aesthetes read. One reads an article in *Mad Magazine* the way a community of puerile, prurient, and nonreflective preadolescents read. Rafoth (1988) proposed that the concept of speech community might, in the end, be of more utility than the concept of audience.

The audience-cum-discourse community position places a great burden on the notion of genre (see Swales, 1990). If genre is regarded as a set of highly conventionalized parameters for composing a specific type of work (say, a *Mad Magazine* parody of a Hollywood film, or an insert for an FDA-approved prescription drug), then the writer's role relation with the audience is rather narrowly determined by the genre itself. In writing an appellate brief, by way of illustration, attorneys possess a certain degree of latitude in devising argumentative strategies and in inventing arguments to fulfill those strategies (Stratman, 1990). But the genre of appellate brief requires attorneys to adopt a particular constellation of role relations vis-à-vis the tribunal: deferential and nonmanipulative, yet assertive and evaluative.

Audience as Simultaneously Social and Cognitive—But in Varying Balance. In fact, the roles that writers construct in relation to their audiences can never be wholly socially constructed and instantiated in genre conventions. Nor is it likely that writers are very often free to fictionalize audiences at will, with complete disregard for actual, embodied readers (Tomlinson, 1990). Indeed, recent theory and research regarding writer–audience role relations (see, e.g., Bonk, 1990; Brandt, 1992; Flower et al., 1990; Nystrand, 1990; see also various works collected in Kirsch & Roen, 1990) collectively suggest at least two dimensions along which differing conceptions of audience vary. These dimensions are (a) the ontology of audience—what kind of entity *is* an audience?—and (b) the epistemology of audience—how does a writer come to *know* (in one sense or another) an audience?

Differing positions regarding the ontological status of audience can be ordered, as follows, generally from audience as an addressable entity to audience as an authorial element that is invocable by text as much as by the historical author:

1. The classical perspective: The audience is comprised of flesh and blood, individuated readers, about which an author makes inferences.
2. The social-organizational perspective: The audience is some corporate entity (AT&T, the Kenneth Burke Society, etc.) that takes on qualities other than the sum of its individual members.
3. The marketing perspective: The audience is a readership, defined in terms of fairly stable factors (e.g., demographic, educational) that mark individuals as potential readers.
4. The social constructionist perspective: The audience is a discourse community defined in terms of largely tacit conventions for texts.
5. The virtualist perspective: The audience is a fiction (i.e., ideal reader, mock reader, second persona) which the writer mentally represents and textually instantiates, and which is only contingently isomorphic to the people who actually read the text.
6. The reader-response perspective: The audience is itself a kind of collaborator, constructing the text in the process of reading it, and even constructing the author, such that no text can have a fixed audience, nor a fixed author.

Differing positions regarding the epistemology of audience—not at all independent of ontological positions, of course—can likewise be ordered, as follows, from those that posit authors as audience analysts to those that regard authors as audience constructors:

1. The direct knowledge approach: Authors know about their audiences what they directly observe or what they are explicitly told.
2. The role-taking approach: Authors know about their audiences what they infer by trying to see the world from the perspective of those audiences.
3. The organizational induction approach: The author receives more or less deliberate initiation into rules and norms and stylebooks for addressing some corporate audience.
4. The demographic category approach: The author uses demographic generalizations to represent the particular audience.
5. The community socialization approach: Authors tacitly assimilate norms and practices of a discourse community by virtue of extended literate participation in that community.
6. The don't-ask-that-question approach: Under the most radical virtualist and reader-response perspectives, authors never come to *know* an audience because audiences are purely constructed entities.

To take seriously and perhaps extend Phelps' (1990) proposal for a "pluralist" notion of audience, we need to appreciate that in any given writing episode, we may treat audience on several different ontological perspectives, and we may depend on several different epistemological approaches. Thus, for example, if I am writing a letter to some academic dean in order to apply for a position, I recognize that some embodied individual will indeed take action based, in part, on the effects of my discourse. And perhaps I query my cronies who are more familiar with that particular dean about her background and preferences. On the other hand, I know that my letter will be read not only by the person to whom it is formally addressed, but also by several individuals in the organization to which I am applying. Therefore I need to project myself in a manner that indicates I am a peer, competent to fully participate in that organizational life.

At the same time, I will to some degree construct in my writing an ideal audience. That is, I will project a role into which I invite my readers to step. So I will presuppose a degree of intimacy with the kinds of accomplishments I wish admired (perhaps through the judicious use of acronyms—we "insiders" of course do not need to spell them out to each other). And I will let slide an occasional glimpse of conviviality and solidarity (perhaps by using a contraction where a contraction'd not be expected). I hope my actual audience will cooperate by at least reading as if this convivial role relation truly obtained between us. And in inscribing this relational presupposition in text, I can possibly bring the actuality to pass in the domain of interpersonal affect.

Developmental Factors

Early research on children's development of audience adaptation in writing was much influenced by Piagetian genetic epistemology (see extensive review in Bonk, 1990). It presumed that children's rhetorical skills were limited in large measure by the level of social perspective taking possible at each "stage" of cognitive development. In more recent years, theories of cognitive development have themselves taken a more distinctly social turn, and maturation is no longer widely regarded as some autonomous, preprogrammed engine of growth.

Instead, social contexts—the contexts of the immediate interactions as well as the broader social milieu in which a child is acculturated—are seen as driving development in social meaning making (Wertsch, 1985). For example, rather than just asking how writing skill is dependent on social cognitive status, we might well ask how a particular set of writing experiences enhances social-inferential skills. Or we might ask how a particular type of writing assignment promotes social cognitive processes during that particular discourse production episode.

To this point, however, there is no empirical research that explores the reciprocal nature of relations between writing and social cognition. The body of research that does exist on this topic, however, is subject to review by Marion Crowhurst in "The Developmental Stylistics of Young Writers' Communicative Intentions" (chapter 9 of this volume). In this chapter, Crowhurst concludes that much of that body of research underestimates children's abilities to perceive the role of their audiences. Crowhurst enumerates several conditions that enhance the match between children's abilities in this domain and our ability to accurately discern it. One such condition is the use of "real rather than imagined audiences." If this is so, then it suggests a need to conduct research regarding the developmental point at which children are likely to move from an exclusively classic perspective on audience to integrate a virtualist perspective.

In a like vein, Crowhurst concludes that researchers have often underestimated children's abilities to adopt varying communicative purposes with regard to their audiences. Standard writing curricula are sequenced such that younger children's writing is often limited to description and narration. Argumentative or persuasive writing has generally been regarded as suitable only for adolescents. Crowhurst demonstrates, however, that even when children misread argumentative writing prompts, they may nonetheless display sophisticated knowledge of what it means to adopt a persuasive stance toward an other.

Interactions Among Elements of Social Identity

Mature writers, then, eventually develop the ability to textually construct role relations with audiences whom they in some degree analyze and in some degree invent. The research on audience adaptation focuses on such role relations as elder–younger, informed–naive, petitioner–authority, and persuader–persuadee. But it would be a gross oversimplification were we to fail to interconnect these audience adaptation processes with the processes of social identification described in earlier sections of this chapter. In the dynamic space of socio-stylistics, writers compose their ethnolinguistic or gender identities *in conjunction with the rhetorical exigences presented by their audiences.*

Historically, female writers have typically been permitted to project only those gender identities that did not offend or threaten the audience of primary authority—conservative White males (Heilbrun, 1988; Kitzinger, 1989). More recently, feminist writers have taken it upon themselves to construct different audiences, audiences with greater ambition for gender-role diversity. Writers like Julia Penelope or bell hooks presuppose such audiences in their deliberate stylistic efforts to move away from language patterns they identify as paternalistic. By the same stylistic devices as they compose a relation with their audiences, Penelope and hooks and others create unmistakable gender identities for themselves—empowered, critical, female.

In "Ultimatum and Negotiation: Gender Differences in Student Writing" (chapter 10 of this volume), Kathryn Heltne Swanson explores the conjunction between writer gender and audience awareness. In this study, Swanson operates from a research tradition that uses social cognitive complexity as an index of audience awareness activity. As predicted by gender-role theories that posit women as more relational and interpersonally attuned than men, the study found that women exhibited higher levels of this social cognitive status. Moreover in regulative writing tasks, females were more likely than their male counterparts to adopt a negotiative stance ("rhetorical message design logic").

In short, Swanson's chapter supports the rather strong position that women's characteristic writing styles result not merely from presumably socialized gender-typical discourse patterns. Rather female writers' preference for collaborative and non-face-threatening styles (see chapter 6 of this volume) may actually result from especially high levels of social cognitive activity.

As gender identity interacts with writer–audience role relations, so does ethnolinguistic identity. Clear cases emerge from stories of oppressed groups developing indigenous literacies to promote their people's ethnolinguistic survival. For example, the dissemination of Sequoyah's Cherokee syllabary during the 1830s created a readership whose ethnolinguistic identity was reinforced in each literate encounter (Walker, 1981). Writers who chose to write in Cherokee—whether publicly in the *Cherokee Phoenix* or privately in personal correspondence—surely established their own ethnolinguistic identities through that choice of writing system. At the same time, they established a relation of ethnolinguistic solidarity with the audience they addressed or invented. (Presumably writers may also choose to use culture-typical patterns in order to signal "other-ness," when demarcating themselves off from an audience of differing ethnic identity. That is no doubt why Bureau of Indian Affairs officials decided they could not tolerate the spread of Cherokee literacy.)

Teresa Redd, in "Untapped Resources: 'Styling' in Black Students' Writing for Black Audiences" (chapter 11 of this volume), charts the interaction between ethnolinguistic identity and audience adaptation among contemporary African-American college students. Redd analyzes essays for occurrences of oral-based rhetorical devices (see chapter 3 of this volume) such as exaggerated language, aphorism, and word play. Redd's chapter is part of a growing trend that emphasizes rhetorical strategies, rather than more microscopic dialect patterns, as the most important locus of social identity in African Americans' written composition (see, e.g., Ball, 1992; Linn, 1975; Zeni & Thomas, 1990; see also chapter 2 of this volume).

The key contribution of Redd's chapter here, however, is to link together the issues of ethnic identity on the one hand with author–audience role identity on the other. Previous researchers (e.g., Rubin, 1979) have noted the infrequency of culture-specific markers in the writing of Black English vernacular speakers. Redd hypothesizes that this relative paucity of dialect markers could be an artifact of audience. The writers in these studies were generally producing prose for mainstream readers; they may have simply been adapting appropriately for outgroup members.

Redd's participants wrote for both White and African-American audiences. About half of them engaged in African-American-typical "styling" only for their African-American audiences; compositions directed to White readers were stylistically more conventional.

In addition to assigning the race of the audience, Redd inquired of writers what additional elements of their audience the writers themselves had constructed. Some had projected "racist Whites," others "conservative African Americans." These virtual aspects of the audiences, invented by the writers, also exerted an impact on use of African-American discourse patterns.

More to the point, in Redd's view, is the fact that culture-typical stylistic devices constitute a powerful rhetorical resource that African-American writers can draw on regardless of the audience they happen to be addressing. As Hughes wrote in *Theme for English B* with which this chapter begins, ". . . let that page come out of you . . . Then it will be true."

But then, recall, Hughes stops to reflect, "I wonder if it's that easy."

These processes of writers and readers inscribing and ascribing group membership, constructing and construing role relations, composing social identity—they are not at all "easy" matters to explain. But far from interfering with effective written expression, the socio-stylistics of writing are essential resources for enriching written discourse.

REFERENCES

Almany, A. J., & Alwan, A. J. (1982). *Communicating with the Arabs.* Prospect Heights, IL: Waveland Press.

Annas, P. J. (1987). Silences: Feminist language research and the teaching of writing. In C. Caywood & G. Overing (Eds.), *Teaching writing: Pedagogy, gender, and equity* (pp. 3–18). Albany: State University of New York Press.

Ball, A. F. (1992). Cultural preference and the expository writing of African American adolescents. *Written Communication, 9,* 501–532.

Banks, S. P. (1987). Achieving "unmarkedness" in organizational discourse: A praxis perspective on ethnolinguistic identity. *Journal of Language and Social Psychology, 6,* 171–189.

Bartholomae, D. (1985). Inventing the university. In M. Rose (Ed.), *When a writer can't write* (pp. 134–165). New York: Guilford.

Biber, D. (1988). *Variation across speech and writing.* New York: Cambridge University Press.

Blom, J., & Gumperz, J. J. (1972). Social meaning and linguistic structure: Code switching in Norway. In J. J. Gumperz & D. Hymes (Eds.), *New directions in sociolinguistics* (pp. 407–434). New York: Holt, Rinehart & Winston.

Bonk, C. J. (1990). A synthesis of social cognition and writing research. *Written Communication, 7,* 136–163.

Brandt, D. (1992). The cognitive as the social: An ethnomethodological approach to writing process research. *Written Communication, 9,* 315–355.

Bridwell-Bowles, L. (1992). Discourse and diversity: Experimental writing within the academy. *College Composition and Communication, 43,* 349–368.

Brown, P., & Levinson, S. (1978). Universals in language usage: Politeness phenomena. In E. N. Goody (Ed.), *Questions and politeness* (pp. 56–289). New York: Cambridge University Press.

Brown, R., & Gilman, A. (1960). The pronouns of power and solidarity. In T. Sebeok (Ed.), *Style in language* (pp. 253–276). Cambridge, MA: MIT Press.

Collier, M. J., & Thomas, M. (1988). Cultural identity: An interpretive perspective. In Y. Y. Kim & W. B. Gudykunst (Eds.), *Theories in intercultural communication* (pp. 99–122). Beverly Hills, CA: Sage.

Cooper, M. M. (1989). Women's ways of writing. In M. M. Cooper & M. Holzman (Eds.), *Writing as social action* (pp. 141–156). Portsmouth, NH: Boynton/Cook.

Ede, L., & Lunsford, A. (1984). Audience addressed/audience invoked: The role of audience in composition theory and pedagogy. *College Composition and Communication, 35,* 140–154.

Enos, T. (1990). "An eternal golden braid": Rhetor as audience, audience as rhetor. In G. Kirsch & D. Roen (Eds.), *A sense of audience in written communication* (pp. 99–114). Newbury Park, CA: Sage.

Epes, M. (1985). Tracing errors to their sources: A study of the encoding processes of adult basic writers. *Journal of Basic Writing, 4*(1), 4–33.

Farr, M., & Daniels, H. (1986). *Language diversity and writing instruction.* New York and Urbana, IL: ERIC/Institute for Urban and Minority Education and National Council of Teachers of English.

Farr, M., & Janda, M. A. (1985). Basic writing students: Investigating oral and written language. *Research in the Teaching of English, 19,* 62–83.

Fiore, K., & Elsasser, N. (1981). Through writing we transform our world: Third world women and literacy. *Humanities in Society, 20,* 395–418.

Fishman, J. (1988). Ethnocultural issues in the creation, substitution, and revision of writing systems. In B. Rafoth & D. Rubin (Eds.), *The social construction of written communication* (pp. 273–286). Norwood, NJ: Ablex.

Flower, L., Stein, V., Ackerman, J., Kantz, M. J., McCormick, K., & Peck, W. C. (1990). *Reading-to-write: Exploring a cognitive and social process.* New York: Oxford University Press.

Garcia, R. L. (1975). A linguistic frame of reference for critiquing Chicano compositions. *College English, 37,* 184–188.

Garner, T., & Rubin, D. L. (1986). Middle class black attorneys' perceptions of dialect and style shifting. *Journal of Language and Social Psychology, 5,* 33–48.

Gates, H. L., Jr. (1991, November 24). "Authenticity," or the lesson of Little Tree. *The New York Times Book Review,* pp. 1, 26–30.

Gearhart, S. M. (1979). The womanization of rhetoric. *Women's Studies International Quarterly, 2,* 195–201.

Giles, H., Mulac, A., Bradac, J., & Johnson, P. (1987). Speech accommodation theory: The first decade and beyond. In M. McLauglin (Ed.), *Communication yearbook 10* (pp. 13–48). Beverly Hills, CA: Sage.

Gleason, J. (1973). Code-switching in children's language. In T. E. Moore (Ed.), *Cognitive development and the acquisition of language* (pp. 159–167). New York: Academic.

Graves, H. B. (1993). Regrinding the lens of gender: Problematizing "writing as a woman." *Written Communication, 10,* 139–163.

Gudykunst, W., & Kim, Y. Y. (1988). *Communicating with strangers* (2nd ed.). New York: McGraw Hill.

Halliday, M. A. K. (1987). Properties of spoken and written language. In R. Horowitz & S. J. Samuels (Eds.), *Comprehending oral and written language* (pp. 55–82). San Diego: Academic Press.

Harris, J. (1989). The idea of community in the study of writing. *College Composition and Communication, 40,* 11–22.

Hartwell, P. (1980). Dialect interference in writing: A critical view. *Research in the Teaching of English, 14,* 101–118.

Haynes, L. A. (1992). The development of speaking/writing variability in narratives of non-native English speakers. *Issues in Applied Linguistics, 3,* 43–68.

Hecht, M. L. (1993). A research odyssey: Toward the development of a communication theory of identity. *Communication Monographs, 60,* 76–82.

Heilbrun, C. (1988). *Writing a woman's life.* New York: Ballantine.

Helms, J. (1990). Toward a model of white racial identity development. In J. Helms (Ed.), *Black and white racial identity* (pp. 49–66). New York: Greenwood.

Hinds, J. (1987). Reader versus writer responsibility: A new typology. In U. Connor & R. Kaplan (Eds.), *Writing across languages: Analysis of L2 texts.* Reading, MA: Addison-Wesley.

Hofstede, G. (1984). *Culture's consequences: International differences in work-related values.* Beverly Hills, CA: Sage.

Horowitz, D. L. (1975). Ethnic identity. In N. Glazer & D. Moynihan (Eds.), *Ethnicity* (pp. 111–140). Cambridge, MA: Harvard University Press.

Johnson, D. M., & Roen, D. H. (1992). Complimenting and involvement in peer reviews: Gender variation. *Language in Society, 21,* 27–57.

Kaplan, R. B. (1966). Cultural thought patterns in intercultural education. *Language Learning, 14,* 1–20.

Keenan, E. (1971). Two kinds of presupposition in natural language. In C. Fillmore & D. Langendon (Eds.), *Studies in linguistic semantics* (pp. 45–52). New York: Holt, Rinehart & Winston.

Kessler, S., & McKenna, W. M. (1978). *Gender: An ethnomethodological approach.* Chicago: University of Chicago Press.

Kirsch, G., & Roen, D. H. (Eds.). (1990). *A sense of audience in written communication.* Newbury Park, CA: Sage.

Kitzinger, C. (1989). Liberal humanism as an ideology of social control: The regulation of lesbian identities. In J. Shotter & K. Gergen (Eds.), *Texts of identity* (pp. 82–98). London: Sage.

Kramer, C., Thorne, B., & Henley, N. (1978). Perspectives on language and communication. *Signs: Journal of Women and Culture in Society, 3,* 638–651.

Labov, W. (1972). *Sociolinguistic patterns.* Philadelphia: University of Pennsylvania Press.

Lay, N. D. (1975). Chinese language interference in written English. *Journal of Basic Writing, 1,* 50–61.

Leki, I. (1991). Twenty-five years of contrastive rhetoric: Text analysis and writing pedagogies. *TESOL Quarterly, 25,* 123–143.

Li, D. L. (1992). Filiative and affiliative textualization in Chinese American literature. In J. Trimmer & T. Warnock (Eds.), *Understanding others: Cultural and cross-cultural studies and the teaching of literature* (pp. 177–199). Urbana, IL: National Council of Teachers of English.

Linn, M. (1975). Black rhetorical patterns and the teaching of composition. *College Composition and Communication, 26,* 149–153.

Lloyd-Jones, R. (1981). Rhetorical choices in writing. In C. Frederikson & J. Dominic (Eds.), *Writing: Process, development and communication* (pp. 169–176). Hillsdale, NJ: Ablex.

Magner, D. K. (1993, February 10). Colleges faulted for not considering differences in Asian-American groups. *The Chronicle of Higher Education*, pp. A32–A34.

Matalene, C. (1985). Contrastive rhetoric: An American writing teacher in China. *College English, 47*, 789–808.

Millic, L. (1971). Rhetorical choice and stylistic option. In S. Chatman (Ed.), *Literary style* (pp. 77–87). Cambridge, England: Oxford University Press.

Moore, D. W. (1992, December 6). Gender de plume. *The New York Times Magazine*, pp. 28, 30.

Morahan, S. (1981). *A woman's place: Rhetoric and readings for composing yourself and your prose.* Albany: State University of New York Press.

Mulac, A., Studley, L. B., & Blau, S. (1990). The gender-linked language effect in primary and secondary students' impromptu essays. *Sex Roles, 23*, 439–469.

Nystrand, M. (1990). Sharing words: The effects of readers on developing writers. *Written Communication, 7*, 3–24.

Ohmann, R. (1962). *Shaw: The style and the man.* Middletown, CT: Wesleyan University Press.

Ong, W. S. J. (1975). The writer's audience is always a fiction. *PMLA, 90*, 9–21.

Pastre, J. (1991, July 15). "They were throwing bottles and cans at the nasty guy." *The New York Times*, p. A14.

Penelope, J. (1990). *Speaking freely: Unlearning the lies of the fathers' tongues.* New York: Pergamon.

Phelps, L. W. (1990). Audience and authorship: The disappearing boundary. In G. Kirsch & D. Roen (Eds.), *A sense of audience in written communication* (pp. 153–174). Newbury Park, CA: Sage.

Piché, G. L, Rubin, D. L., Turner, L. J., & Michlin, M. L. (1978). Effects of non-standard dialect features in written compositions on teachers' subjective evaluations of students and composition quality. *Research in the Teaching of English, 12*, 107–118.

Rafoth, B. A. (1988). Discourse community: Where writers, readers, and texts come together. In B. Rafoth & D. Rubin (Eds.), *The social construction of written communication* (pp. 131–146). Norwood, NJ: Ablex.

Rafoth, B., & Rubin, D. L. (1984). The impact of content and mechanics on judgements of writing quality. *Written Communication, 1*, 446–458.

Rakow, L. F. (1986). Rethinking gender research in communication. *Journal of Communication, 15*, 11–26.

Reed, C. E. (1981). Teaching teachers about teaching writing to students from varied linguistic, social and cultural groups. In M. Farr Whiteman (Ed.), *Variation in writing: Functional and linguistic-cultural differences* (pp. 139–152). Hillsdale, NJ: Ablex.

Roen, D. H. (1992). Gender and teacher response to student writing. In N. M. McCracken & B. C. Appleby (Eds.), *Gender issues in the teaching of English* (pp. 126–141). Portsmouth, NH: Boynton/Cook.

Roulis, E. (1990). *The relative effect of a gender-linked language effect and a sex role stereotype effect on readers' responses to male and female argumentative-persuasive writing.* Unpublished doctoral dissertation, University of Minnesota, Minneapolis.

Rubin, D. L. (1979). The myth of dialect interference in writing. *Arizona English Bulletin, 21*(3), 55–72.

Rubin, D. L. (1984). The effect of communicative context on style in writing. In A. Pellegrini & T. Yawkey (Eds.), *The development of oral and written language: Readings in applied and developmental psycholinguistics* (pp. 213–232). Totowa, NJ: Ablex.

Rubin, D. L. (1992). Nonlanguage factors affecting undergraduates' judgments of non-native English speaking teaching assistants. *Research in Higher Education, 33*, 511–531.

Rubin, D. L., Goodrum, R., & Hall, B. (1990). Orality, oral-based culture, and the academic writing of ESL learners. *Issues in Applied Linguistics, 1*, 56–76.

Rubin, D. L., & Greene, K. (1992). Gender-typical style in written language. *Research in the Teaching of English, 26*, 7–40.

Sachdev, I., & Bourhis, R. Y. (1990). Language and social identification. In D. Abrams & M. A. Hogg (Eds.), *Social identity theory* (pp. 211–229). New York: Springer-Verlag.

Scollon, R., & Scollon, A. (1981). *Narrative, literacy, and face in interethnic communication.* Norwood, NJ: Ablex.

Shaughnessy, M. (1977). *Errors and expectations.* New York: Oxford University Press.

Shen, F. (1989). The classroom and the wider culture: Identity as a key to learning English composition. *College Composition and Communication, 40*, 459–466.

Smeltzer, L., & Werbel, J. (1986). Gender differences in managerial communication: Fact or folklinguistics? *Journal of Business Communication, 23*, 41–50.

Stratman, J. F. (1990). Theories of the appellate court brief: Implications for judges and attorneys. In G. Kirsch & D. Roen (Eds.), *A sense of audience in written communication* (pp. 115–139). Newbury Park, CA: Sage.

Swales, J. (1990). *Genre analysis: English in academic and research settings.* Cambridge, England: Cambridge University Press.

Tomlinson, B. (1990). Ong may be wrong: Negotiating with nonfictional readers. In G. Kirsch & D. Roen (Eds.), *A sense of audience in written communication* (pp. 85–94). Newbury Park, CA: Sage.

Walker, W. (1981). Native American writing systems. In C. A. Ferguson & S. B. Heath (Eds.), *Language in the USA* (pp. 145–174). Cambridge, England: Cambridge University Press.

Waters, M. C. (1990). *Ethnic options: Choosing identities in America.* Berkeley: University of California Press.

West, C., & Zimmerman, D. H. (1991). Doing gender. In J. Lorber & S. A. Farrell (Eds.), *The social construction of gender* (pp. 13–37). Newbury Park, CA: Sage.

Wertsch, J. (1985). *Culture, communication, and cognition: Vygotskian perspectives.* Cambridge, England: Cambridge University Press.

Williams, J. (1982). The phenomenology of error. *College Composition and Communication, 32*, 152–168.

Wolfram, W., & Whiteman, M. (1971). The role of dialect interference in composition. *Florida FL Reporter, 9*(1), 2, 34–38, 59.

Zawacki, T. M. (1992). Recomposing as a woman: An essay in a different voice. *College Composition and Communication, 43*, 32–39.

Zellermeyer, M. (1988). An analysis of oral and literate texts: Two types of reader-writer relationships in Hebrew and English. In B. Rafoth & D. Rubin (Eds.), *The social construction of written communication* (pp. 287–303). Norwood, NJ: Ablex.

Zeni, J., & Thomas, J. K. (1990). Suburban African-American basic writing, grades 7–12: A text analysis. *Journal of Basic Writing, 9*(2), 15–39.

PART ONE

COMPOSING ETHNOLINGUISTIC IDENTITY

Stylistic Variation in Vernacular Black English and the Teaching of College Composition

Michael D. Linn
University of Minnesota, Duluth

The 1992 video tape of the Rodney King beating, the verdict of the White Los Angeles police officers, and the subsequent riots, once again riveted the attention of the nation on the plight of the poor, especially inner-city African Americans. One had to wonder whether any genuine progress in race relations had been made since the assassination of Martin Luther King. In fact, there is much to suggest that the last 12 years have been a move backwards in race relations, because poverty, violence, and alienation in the inner city have increased. A kinder, gentler nation does not seem to have emerged.

However, there is continued, genuine concern for the plight of those forced to live in the inner city. Since the 1960s, linguists, rhetoricians, and educators have been trying to alleviate the conditions of African-American students through enlightened education. Unfortunately, all too often, even with well-meaning intentions, success has been minimal. Certainly the position of College Composition and Communication expressed in *The Students' Right to Their Own Language* (1974) was such a well-intentioned act. But it is questionable how much it has helped. On the one hand, no one can or should prevent any group from using its own dialect. To do so would require an elimination of that group. It is preposterous to even seriously propose it. On the other hand, this policy has often been interpreted to mean that the teacher should do nothing and that anything should be allowed in the classroom. This also seems an unworkable solution to an important and complex problem. The intent of this policy statement was noble in its attempt to extend the bounds of racial tolerance into the classroom; the results have not lived up to expectations.

Yet, I personally believe that the spirit behind this policy contains one of the elements necessary for effectively teaching inner-city African-American students: the acceptance of them as people who deserve understanding and who need positive reinforcement. As Glenda Gill (1992) stated, "What the teacher can do is to be helpful to those who make efforts, who attend class regularly, who seem sincere, and who try. . . . Many serious hard working African Americans are relegated to the ash-heap, and teachers can help by providing them with positive reinforcement" (p. 226). A second, and just as important, element to effectively teach students at risk is to learn about their linguistic and rhetorical systems in order to bridge the gap between their oral tradition and the written system demanded for obtaining a college education. Because Gill did such a thorough job of explaining the reasons for and methods of providing positive reinforcement for African-American students, I do not go into those reasons or methods here. Instead I first look at some of the linguistic patterns of Black English vernacular (hereafter called BEV) that differ from standard edited English (hereafter called SEE). Next I examine BEV from the standpoint of rhetoric, with special attention to high-context and low-context discourse. Then I offer some reflections about teaching strategies.

LINGUISTIC PATTERNS

In the Langston Hughes (1939) novel, *Simple Takes a Wife*, the narrator asks Simple, "Why do you sometimes say, 'I were' and at other times, 'I was'?" Simple responds with the commonsense statement: "Because sometimes I *were* and sometimes I *was*. . . . I was at Niagara Falls and I were at the Grand Canyon—since that were in the distant past. I was more recently at Niagara Falls."

"I see [the narrator responds]. *Was* is more immediate. *Were* is way back yonder."

"Somewhatly right. But not being colleged like you, I do not speak like I came from the North" (pp. 38–39).

Because of the linguistic analyses of BEV brought about by the desire to "college" African Americans, English teachers are now aware that BEV differs from SEE in grammatical structures such as lack of agreement between subject and verb (*They runs home*), copula deletion (*He tall*), and absence of the {Z} possessive morpheme (*The boy hat*) and in phonological variants such as consonant cluster reduction (*desk* pronounced as *des*), the substitution of alveolar stops for dental fricatives (*three* pronounced as *tree* and *the* pronounced as *da*), and the monophthongalization of /ay/ and /aw/ diphthongs (*find* and *found* both pronounced as *fond*). Because there is not room to discuss all of the grammatical features of BEV, this is all that is said about them here. Anyone desiring to know more about this aspect of BEV should consult any of the numerous studies of it. Particularly informative are Baugh (1983, 1988), Fasold (1981), Feagin (1979), Labov (1970a, 1970b, 1972, 1983), Smitherman (1984), and Wolfram (1969, 1974, 1991).

However, paying too much attention to the grammatical and phonological features of BEV gives a distorted view of the African-American speech community. Such a lack of perspective can lead too easily to the idea that "street talk" is the primary, or perhaps the only, style that African-American youths have. As a result, when a teacher notices dialect interference between BEV and SEE, he or she considers the student to have a ghettoese mentality. The danger in such stereotyping is that it often leads to the dehumanization of students and to the self-fulfilling prophecy.

Work by Ferguson (1959) and Brown and Gilman (1960) has established that speakers in any community control various styles of language and switch according to whom they are speaking. The African-American community, like any speech community, is not limited to a single style of speech. The type of language used in bars or on the street is different than that used in church or school. However, for speakers of BEV, this can be a problem when switching from street speech to school speech, as Baugh (1983) pointed out:

> . . . both because of the question of group loyalty from within and because of social and economic pressures from without the vernacular black community. I remember several occasions as a child when we would tease boys who spoke standard English, calling them sissies and exerting other forms of peer pressure or exclusion. (pp. 55–56)

Yet it is also necessary for teachers to keep in mind that the college freshman, simply by being in college, is what Labov (1972) would call a "lame" so that "he inevitably [has] acquired an ability to shift towards the standard language and has [had] more occasion to do so" (Labov, 1972, p. 257). However, even in the peer-centered street culture, there is a wide variety of styles. Richard Wright (1975) described his experience growing up in Washington, DC:

> Our peer group behaviors were one of a variety in which it was important to demonstrate competence. In addition to "vernacular" . . . we engaged in a variety of natural interactions with community people in which other varieties of a more standard [speech] were called for. (pp. 194–195)

Wright emphasized that being able to skillfully manipulate a more elaborate language on certain appropriate occasions received the vocal approval of peer-group members.

This shifting between registers helps to produce inherent variability. Most features that characterize BEV fluctuate so that they can be quantified, that is their occurrence can be stated by frequency of occurrence. For instance, Wolfram (1969) found that the absence of agreement between subject and verb occurred 74.3% of the time and absence of the possessive {-Z} morpheme occurred 30.1% of the time among working-class men. A few features, such as iterative *BE* are qualitative features and cannot be quantified because there are no comparable forms in SEE. However, for the composition teacher, it is the quantitative features that create the major grammatical problems. Because these features are variable in their speech, some variation can be expected to be transferred to writing. The teacher needs to be aware of the variable features of BEV so that they do not treat them as careless mistakes.

However, the relationship between spoken language and written language is more complicated than a simple direct transfer. All students when learning to write make mistakes that are not predictable on the basis of their speech. For instance there is a higher frequency of the absence of verbal and plural *-s* in the writing of White elementary students than in the writing of elementary African-American students. "This pattern would hardly be predicted on the basis of the spoken language, since the white speakers do not have appreciable levels of suffix *-s* absence in their speech" (Wolfram, 1991, p. 258). This pattern comes as a surprise because we would normally expect fewer socially stigmatized features in the formal context of a written school essay than in spoken language. Yet this pattern of suffix absence in writing also occurs with final consonant cluster reduction with the *-ed* in forms such as *miss* for *missed* much more frequently than in forms where the final consonant clusters are part of the same morpheme such as *mis* for *mist*. This reversal of what is found in spoken language where White students have fewer absent *-s*'s than do African-American students is explained by Farr-Whiteman (as quoted in Wolfram, 1991): "These features (plural *-s*, verbal *-s*, and consonant *-ed*) seem to be omitted in writing at least partly *because* they are inflectional suffixes" (p. 259). As with most inflectional endings in English, they are redundant so the word can stand without them. Words such as *mis* for *mist* cannot stand alone without confusion, but *miss* can stand alone as a whole word whether or not the *-ed* is added. As Wolfram pointed out, "All writers of English, regardless of their native dialect, seem to reveal instances of suffix omission in the process of learning the written form of the language" (p. 260). By the time middle-class White students come to college, they have written enough papers that this absence of inflectional endings is no longer a problem, but for many inner-city students, the use of inflectional endings is still in the variable stage. Sometimes they occur and sometimes they do not. It is this inherent variability that causes the problem for the composition teacher.

Because these students come to college with variable rules and inexperience in writing college-type papers, their papers are inconsistent with respect to grammar. Characteristic features of BEV are sometimes present and sometimes absent in the same paper and sometimes even in the same sentence. The teacher's reaction and attitude to these quantifiable or variable characteristics of BEV are a determining factor in the success or failure of the composition student. It is important for the teacher to remember that these inconsistencies are the result of inherent variability in BEV and part of the process of learning to write, not necessarily laziness or carelessness on the part of the student. A feature undergoing language change begins with variation; and when the change goes to completion, it becomes categorical or loses its variation (see Labov, 1980). It is the teacher's job to speed up this process of language change as students move from informal oral street language to SEE, which requires the categorical rules of formal English.

In helping students master appropriate usage as they move from informal to formal settings, teachers must be aware that when there is variation in linguistic rules, different social values are attached to each variant (see Linn & Piché, 1982). A major problem associated with teachers' negative reactions toward the students' street speech and writing is that often the students feel guilty for having it, and yet they do not always know what caused the negative response. What the composition teacher must do is to make the African-American student understand that the use of SEE variants does not necessitate a rejection of the street culture in favor of White middle-class culture.

To do this, teachers need to be aware of students' verbal codes and make the students aware that they are trying to aid them in developing a formal written style of SEE that will extend their communication network, not change or eradicate their oral street code. BEV speakers are quite verbal and have a keen sense of oral communication. However, their speech and stylistic patterns differ markedly from those of their college composition teachers.

RHETORICAL AND STYLISTIC PATTERNS

First and foremost, as Kochman (1981) points out, ". . . black style is more self conscious, more expressive, more assertive, more aggressive, and more focused on the individual than is the style of the larger society of which blacks are a part" (p. 130). The function of verbal games such as shucking, rapping, and signifying demonstrate the African-American style with its emphasis on performance and audience participation. Because the purpose of these games is to demonstrate individual style, to assert oneself, and to arouse emotions in others, the language needs powerful images and must be indisputably the performer's own. The speaker performs in a high-context setting, one where there is a high degree of shared knowledge, experience, and background information.

But in composition classes, individualistic African-American street style is likely to get the students into trouble. College composition teachers expect students to adapt themselves to fit within the classroom's framework and for everyone to do the same writing assignments. In addition, street African Americans are used to performing in high-context situations and do well when there is a shared familiarity with the situation and the people in it.

Unfortunately, the composition classroom is a low-context environment, one with a low degree of shared knowledge and experience. The shared knowledge between the professor and the inner-city student can be non-existent. For a composition program to be effective, it must develop students' abilities to communicate effectively in low-context environments. Because such a writing situation prohibits the students from depending on shared information and relying on nonverbal cues that are characteristic of the peer-group street culture, the teacher needs to help students learn to communicate ideas without depending on shared knowledge. In this way, it is much like helping students move from what Joos (1961) described as casual style to formal style. One of the most difficult tasks for the students is to learn when and how much background information to include in their writing when communicating outside their peer group to the larger English-speaking world.

If African-American students are to learn how to control the low-context writing style demanded in the college composition classroom, they must learn to avoid the intrusive *I* and the subjective individual approach to their material. As they grow up, African Americans present their material as advocates and show that they care passionately about it. In this way, their oratory is like that of most oral cultures. As Walter Ong (1967) pointed out in oral cultures, "The orator's stance, passionate involvement in his material and feeling that there was an adversary at large, was standard equipment provided by formal education for man's confrontation with the world" (p. 225).

As they perform on the street, every African-American storyteller creates a world of his own in which he is the master of the situation; he directs the heroes' lives. He achieves control of the situation by means of what Abrahams (1970) called the "intrusive I" (p. 58). (See also Cleary & Linn, 1993.) Throughout the narratives there is usually a close relationship between the hero of the story and the teller of the tale. Because the verbal performance is done in first person, the narrator can maintain a complete identification with his hero. It is this close identification and personalization of the story that is referred to as the intrusive I. The subjective nature and performance qualities of various types of African-American street oratory patterns have been adequately described so they are not presented here. Those interested in studying them should consult Abrahams (1974), Kochman (1972), Kernan (1971), and Linn (1975).

In contrast, college writing students are trained to relate to their material as presenters, not as advocates. There is the belief that the truth and other merits of a written composition should be intrinsic to the idea itself. The truth is in the idea itself. How deeply the writer cares about a subject is irrelevant to its fundamental value and should not influence the writing. As pointed out by Kochman (1981):

> This view—the separation of truth and belief—is heavily influenced by what whites understand of the scientific method, where the goal is to achieve a stance of neutral objectivity with regard to the truth that is "out there": a truth that is not to be possessed or created but, rather, discovered. Whites believe that caring about one's own ideas, like the infatuation of scientists with their own hypotheses, will make them less receptive to opposing ideas and consequently prevent them from discovering the real truth. (p. 21)

Thus the incoming African-American students, who have grown up being passionately involved with their arguments, must learn the rhetoric and stylistics of presenting ideas as though they were completely objective and impartial and that the ideas had an objective life of their own.

The following two passages demonstrate how Martin Luther King, Jr. was able to vary his style to fit high- as well as low-context situations. The first passage, part of his "I Have a Dream" speech, was written for a high-context situation. It was delivered at the Lincoln Memorial during the Freedom March on Washington, DC, in August 1963. It is similar to a dry bones sermon in the African-American church. Everyone in the audience already knew King's dream and supported it or they would not have been there:

> I say to you today, my friends, even though we face the difficulties of today and tomorrow, I still have a dream. It is a dream rooted in the American Dream. It is a dream that one day this nation will rise up and live out the true meaning of its creed: "We hold these truths to be self evident, that all men are created equal." I have a dream that one day, on the hills of Georgia, the sons of former slaves and the sons of former slave owners will be able to sit down together at the table of brotherhood. I have a dream that one day even in the state of Mississippi, a state sweltering with the heat of oppression, will be transformed into an oasis of freedom and justice. I have a dream that my four little children will one day live in a nation where they will not be judged by the color of their skin, but by the content of their character. (quoted from Lester, 1974, p. 72)

The primary purpose of King's speech is to provide an emotional release and at the same time to provide a rallying point for the demonstration. It capitalizes on a high-context situation by recalling common knowledge—the difficulties and the frustrations of the moment—to unify the crowd. Yet it also offers hope for tomorrow. Like a dry bones sermon, it has the theme that the conflict and conditions in the African-American community under which African Americans are forced to live are a result of "the man's" attempt to keep African Americans down. As Grace Sims Holt (1972) points out, "one of the goals of the dry bones sermon is to supplant the inhuman white authority with religious black authority, where white authority is declared unjust and unchristian and the authority of the black church is declared the only just authority for black people" (p. 202). Like a dry bones sermon, King's speech has functioned as a unifying force to bridge class lines and overcome divisive factionalism.

"I Have a Dream" carries King's personal style. The *I* is Martin Luther King, Jr. and the speech is focused on *his* dream. It is a great performance that involves the audience. It is filled with powerful images: "deeply rooted in the American dream," "a desert state sweltering with the heat of injustice," and "transformed into an oasis of freedom and justice."

Much of the powerful impact of the speech results from the repetition of "I have a dream." It drives home to the audience that justice, equality, and brotherhood among all people, and especially African Americans, is a dream today, but it might become a reality tomorrow if the establishment (The Man) can be overcome. Although it may be a reality tomorrow, today it is still only a dream. It is by means of this repetition that King is able to unify the audience while bringing home the meaning of his speech. "I Have a Dream" is a beautiful example of the high-context street oratory enlarged to a general audience.

As beautiful and as effective as this passage is—and much of it is poetry, complete with alliteration ("a state sweltering") and metaphor ("an oasis of brotherhood")—it is not the type of writing that is demanded in college composition courses. It is too personally stylized, it is too high-context, and it is expressed too passionately. Because it is presented to a group that shares a common set of premises and worldview, it does not need to develop a logical argument, defend a thesis, or present new information. Most of the speech, like a dry bones sermon, is based on the shared experiences and values of the recent march to Washington against racial discrimination and an unexpressed distrust of the justice system, as it currently exists, to provide the American Dream for African Americans.

The style that makes it the great, memorable work that it is prevents it from being the type that is accepted in the college composition classroom. It lacks a clear-cut thesis statement. The paragraphs do not have supporting arguments. There is too much repetition of "I have a dream." The ideas are not presented with neutral scientific objectivity. The rich descriptive phrases, the lack of sentence variety (too much parallelism), and the faulty paragraph structure are all elements that college students are expected to avoid in their themes. However, it is the effective passionate personalization of the speech that would be most criticized. In type, if not in quality, King's speech is the kind of writing that many inner-city African-American freshmen turn in for their first work.

In contrast to the "I Have a Dream" speech, the second example of King's writing is the type that is demanded in the composition classroom. As opposed to the high-context style of "I Have a Dream," "Testament of Hope" (King's last published essay, which appeared in the January 1969 issue of *Playboy*) is a low-context one:

> Whenever I am asked my opinion of the current state of the civil rights movement, I am forced to pause: it is not easy to describe a crisis so profound that it has caused the most powerful nation in the world to stagger in confusion and bewilderment. Today's problems are so acute because the tragic evasions and defaults of several centuries have accumulated to disastrous proportions. The luxury of a leisurely approach to urgent solutions—the ease of gradualism—was forfeited by ignoring the issues for too long. The nation waited until the black man was explosive with fury before stirring itself even to partial concern. Confronted now with the interrelated problems of war, inflation, urban decay, white backlash, and a climate of violence, it is *forced* to address itself to race relations and poverty and it is tragically unprepared. What might once have been a series of separate problems now merge into a social crises of almost stupefying complexity. (p. 174)

Immediately King begins to fill in background information. He tells why he is writing. He does not use the metaphorical language of his first passage. All of the beautiful parallelism of the first passage is absent. Instead, he develops his argument in a straightforward, objective, dispassionate manner. He leaves nothing for the reader to assume. In the remaining part of the passage, he demonstrates how war, inflation, urban decay, White backlash, and a climate of violence are interrelated and how race relations and poverty are part of the same social crisis. The intrusive *I* is not present, nor is the passionate presentation. The plight of the civil rights movement is described in an objective, dispassionate style. Technically, it is a marvelous example of the type of writing that is expected from college students. It fits the formal, low-context criteria valued in the college classroom.

Although is it easy to see the influence of African-American language on King's two speeches, there is also the parallel with classical Greek rhetoric. And considering King's education, there is probably a direct influence. King's "I Have a Dream" speech is an example of what Aristotle referred to as epidiectic or ceremonial rhetoric. Ministers are trained in this type of oratory in seminary. Even today many sermons and homilies exemplify this type of rhetorical mode. A key feature of this type of speech is the recognizable pep-talk aspect. It is designed to raise people's spirit and to make them feel good about themselves.

The second passage, "Testament of Hope," has no pep-talk aspect to it. Instead, it is a variation of forensic rhetoric that is concerned with establishing facts and interpreting them. In this article, King is concerned with piling up the facts to convince his audience of the need for addressing racial grievances. Yet unlike the Athenian high-context orations, King's essay maintains the detached tenor of academic writing.

In aiding the student's move from the high-context, intimate, personal vernacular style to the low-context, formal, objective, classroom style, composition teachers need to be aware of the inherent variability involved in the acquisition of a new stylistic and grammatical level of usage. As students first begin mastering the low-context writing style, they will exhibit different styles and grammatical inconsistencies in the same paper, and sometimes even in the same sentence. However, as the formal writing system becomes internalized, the stylistic, as well as grammatical variation, should disappear and the usage should become invariant. Inconsistent usage should disappear. Because developing the low-context written style involves a functional shift to one set of grammatical rules that are categorical, it is more efficient and effective to treat the grammatical differences between BEV and SEE as a set of stylistic features dependent on a formal code instead of separate items. To do this, composition teachers need to explain and demonstrate how low-context situations and formal English are linked.

In moving to low-context situations, the teacher needs to be aware that in street culture, the words themselves are not as important as the context in which they are used. It is the social setting and the style of delivery that determine the meaning. For example, the term *bad* can signify negative qualities as in "He's a bad man" or positive qualities as "He's a *baáad* man," depending on the intonation and stress. Teachers should not make the mistake of looking at the individual words, phrases, or grammatical units to determine the verbal ability of their students. It is essential to consider the social setting, frame of reference, and context to determine their verbal dexterity. By failing to understand the verbal patterns of their students, teachers make it difficult for African-American students to succeed in school. Early in their educational experience, African-American children learn that if they write as they talk, teachers will consider their work inadequate. For this reason, most African-American inner-city students have developed a phobia against writing by the time they reach college and are often convinced that they cannot write.

TEACHING STRATEGIES

As Glenda E. Gill (1992) demonstrates, positive reinforcement is essential. But it is not enough. Students also need practical, concrete advice to aid them in acquiring the formal, low-context, classroom SEE. Teachers in college need to demonstrate the difference between formal, low-context, impersonal style on the one hand, and informal, high-context style on the other. Then they need to show when each should be used. By doing these things, teachers can effectively help students make the transition to college writing. To do this, the teacher must be explicit about the characteristics of both styles and the context where each should be used. Also, students need to know that they have the right to maintain BEV, which is important for them to do. The teacher is only helping them to expand their perception of the world by extending their communication network to include formal, low-context English.

Because most inner-city students are already familiar with oral perform-ances, I found it quite effective to begin with a skit or short play to be produced in front of the class. To get the class started, I divide the class into groups of four or five students. Each group has to write and produce their own work. In group work the students interact with each other so that a certain camaraderie develops, making the classroom a less threatening place. Because inner-city students are familiar with performance techniques and gamesmanship, they often take the lead. Later in the term, I divide the students into new groups and have them write a group essay. Again, it should be read to the class so that the students know that they have an audience other than the teacher. By having the students work together, the first essay is less threatening and there is immediate feedback with the better students tutoring the poorer students. Sometimes one or two students will do most of the work, but that does not matter at this stage of the semester. The better writers help the weaker ones. Students with writing blocks can observe how the better students go about writing their papers. The group theme is especially effective in integrated classrooms when White and Af-rican-American students work together. Because the African-American stu-dents do not share a similar background with their classmates, they learn the necessity of filling in background information. Also, the teacher does not appear as direct threat, but a resource person. Because students familiar with the oral tradition are familiar with personal narratives, this type of writing makes a good first individually written paper. It allows students to relate personally to the material, even to use the intrusive *I.*

By beginning a writing course with themes based on rhetorical patterns from the oral culture, students start with familiar patterns, allowing the composition teacher to build upon skills they already possess. However, students need to get beyond the high-context style. They need to begin writing in the low-context style and to begin developing analytical reasoning skills. Thomas J. Farrell developed an instructional method that he used with remarkable success when he was teaching African-American students. Be-cause college students need to be able to discuss both sides of controversial subjects, he assigned his students to library research some controversial public policy debate. They had to find two well-developed articles that argued for a particular course of action and others that argued against that same action. Then he would have his students write summaries of one article in favor of and one article opposed to a particular course of action. Next he would outline the basic elements of an oration as they were taught for centuries in the Western tradition of rhetoric, stressing the standard refutation of the adversarial position that comes before the conclusion of the oration. After completing the discussion of the oratorical tradition, the students would write a position paper on the issue that they had researched. Because they had examined both sides of the issue, they could state both the adversarial position and argue against it. Finally, the students would summarize the main points of their arguments and make their conclusions. This type of exercise is especially effective in moving students from high-context to low-context situations because they are researching something with which they are not familiar. In addition, they are forced to relate to their material as presenters instead of advocates as they summarize the two opposing points of view.

CONCLUSIONS

Studies have show that concentrating on isolated spelling and traditional grammar drills has little or no effect on student writing unless the drills are personalized (see Cleary & Lund, 1989). However, this does not mean that spelling and grammar are not important. College-level writing needs to be free of nonstandard spelling and grammar. What needs to be done is to individualize the lessons and to make them relevant to the individual students. Richard Van De Weghe (1983) offered just such a method. He outlined a method in which students use logs to keep track or their nonstandard spellings and grammar so that they only have to learn items with which they themselves have trouble. I have found his system to work well.

Showing students how to modify grammatical and stylistic usage is important, but the teacher needs to do more. It is necessary to show the students where and why SEE rules differ from their street speech. As Simple tells the narrator, "Neither *is* or *are* reduces expenses. Funerals and formals is both high, so what difference do it make." Teachers can make a difference. They can reduce the pressure and the anxiety their students feel and make their students feel that learning SEE does make a difference. To do this, teachers need a two-pronged attach. On the one hand they need to provide some positive reinforcement and validate their students. On the other hand, good intentions are not enough. Teachers also need to effectively teach their students how to augment their high-context street talk with standard edited English. In this way teachers can begin fulfilling the promise of the CCCC's resolution on "The Students' Right to Their Own Language."

ACKNOWLEDGMENTS

I would like to thank Thomas J. Farrell for his excellent reading and the many helpful comments that he made on this chapter.

REFERENCES

Abrahams, R. D. (1970). *Deep down in the jungle: Negro narrative folklore from the streets of Philadelphia* (rev. ed.). Chicago: Aldine.

Abrahams, R. D. (1974). Black talking in the streets. In R. Bauman & J. Sherzer (Eds.), *Explorations in the ethnography of speaking* (pp. 240–262). New York: Cambridge University Press.

Baugh, J. (1983). *Black street speech: Its history, structure and survival.* Austin: University of Texas Press.

Baugh, J. (1988). Language and race: Some implication for linguistic science. In F. J. Newmeyer (Ed.), *Language: The socio-cultural context; Linguistics: The Cambridge survey* (Vol. 4, pp. 64–74). New York: Cambridge University Press.

Brown, R., & Gilman, A. (1960). Pronouns of power and solidarity. In T. Sebeok (Ed.), *Style in language* (pp. 235–276). Cambridge, MA: MIT Press.

Cleary, L. M., & Linn, M. D. (Eds.). (1993). *Linguistics for teachers.* New York: McGraw-Hill.

Cleary, L. M., & Lund, N. (1989). Debunking some myths about traditional grammar. *Minnesota English Journal, 19,* 1–8.

Fasold, R. W. (1981). The relation between black and white speech in the South. *American Speech, 56,* 163–189.

Feagin, C. (1979). *Variation and change in Alabama English.* Washington, DC: Georgetown University Press.

Ferguson, C. (1959). Diglossia. *Word, 15,* 325–340.

Gill, G. E. (1992). The African American student: At risk. *College Composition and Communication, 43,* 225–230.

Holt, G. S. (1972). Stylin outta the black pulpit. In T. Kochman (Ed.), *Rappin' and stylin' out: Communication in urban black America* (p. 202). Urbana: University of Illinois Press.

Hughes, L. (1939). *Simple takes a wife.* New York: Simon & Schuster.

Joos, M. (1961). *The five clocks.* New York: Harcourt Brace.

Kernan, C. M. (1971). *Language behavior in a black urban community* (Monograph of Language-Behavior Research Laboratory, No. 2). Berkeley: University of California Press.

King, M. L. (1969, January). A testament of hope. *Playboy,* pp. 174–236.

Kochman, T. (Ed.). (1972). *Rappin' and stylin' out: Communication in urban black America.* Urbana: University of Illinois Press.

Kochman, T. (1981). *Black and white styles in conflict.* Chicago: University of Chicago Press.

Labov, W. (1970a). The logic of nonstandard English. In J. E. Alatis (Ed.), *Georgetown monograph series on languages and linguistics* (Vol. 22, pp. 1–44). Washington, DC: Georgetown University Press.

Labov, W. (1970b). *The study of nonstandard English.* Champaign, IL: National Council of Teachers.

Labov, W. (1972). *Language in the inner city: Studies in Black English vernacular.* Philadelphia: University of Pennsylvania Press.

Labov, W. (1980). The social origins of sound change. In W. Labov (Ed.), *Locating language in time and space* (pp. 251–265). New York: Academic Press.

Labov, W. (1983). Recognizing Black English in the classroom. In J. Chambers, Jr. (Ed.), *Black English: Educational equity and the law* (pp. 20–55). Ann Arbor, MI: Karoma Publishers.

Lester, J. D. (1974). *Patterns for composition.* Dubuque, IA: Brown.

Linn, M. D. (1975). Black rhetorical patterns and the teaching of composition. *College Composition and Communication, 26,* 149–153.

Linn, M. D., & Piché, G. L. (1982). Black and white adolescent and preadolescent attitudes toward Black English. *Research in the Teaching of English, 16,* 53–72.

Ong, W. S. J. (1967). *The presence of the word.* New York: Houghton Mifflin, Clarion.

Smitherman, G. (1984). Black language as power. In C. Kramarae, M. Schultz, & W. O. Barr (Eds.), *Language and power* (pp. 101–115). Newbury Park, CA: Sage.

Students' right to their own language. (1974). *College Composition and Communication, 25* [Special Issue].

Van de Weghe, R. (1983). Grammar and spelling logs. In C. Carter (Ed.), *Non-native and non-standard dialect students* (pp. 101–105). Urbana, IL: National Council of Teachers of English.

Wolfram, W. (1969). *A sociolinguistic description of Detroit Negro speech.* Washington, DC: Center for Applied Linguistics.

Wolfram, W. (1974). The relationship of Southern white speech to vernacular Black English. *American Speech, 50,* 498–527.

Wolfram, W. (1991). *Dialects and American English.* Englewood Cliffs, NJ: Prentice-Hall.

Wright, R. (1975). Black English. *Language in Society, 4,* 194–195.

CHAPTER THREE

Orality in Literacy:
The Uses of Speech in
Written Language by
Bilingual and Bicultural Writers

Rosalind Horowitz
The University of Texas-San Antonio

At a literacy conference, a woman rushed across the room to talk to me about her reading of one of my published papers. After going through the motions of politely telling me that she had enjoyed the article, she proceeded to tell me that she found me to be exactly what she had expected. I was surprised to hear that, somehow, my writing had conveyed a distinct image. Numerous questions flashed across my mind: Did the publication really reflect my identity? Did it reveal certain aspects of my social and cultural worlds? Did the text really represent me so vividly that the reader had created a memorable portrait? Since that exchange, I have often reflected about how authors reveal an identity, whether they intend to or not, (whether one ever has full control of such matters), and how one achieves this through elements of formal, academic, written language that one would think, by their very nature, would create some objectivity and distance between writer and reader.

This chapter examines uses of speech in written language while addressing the presentation of social and cultural identity in writing. The view that I elaborate upon is that the use of speech in writing is a frequent occurrence in essays by skilled writers as well as by those developing as writers and particularly by bilingual and bicultural writers. Although sometimes construed as ill-formed, mismatched language or interferences, the use of speech in writing may be a positive and even rich contribution to the writing and social development of a writer. Moreover, I submit, in keeping with this volume, that through the use of speech in writing, a social identity oftentimes is shaped and reshaped and, ultimately, finds expression. Speech in writing need not signal the need for remediation. It may reflect social and cultural aspects of a writer and may be developed as an effective linguistic strategy with increased practice in writing.

Although research on oral–written contrasts is growing, and I believe is needed, what has been studied less often, the subject of this chapter, is how speech enters into and is used *in* writing. The commingling of speech and writing in written communication has been treated in the research literature and seems to be an agreed-upon phenomenon. Nevertheless, it has been rarely investigated in real-world sociocultural settings or through real-world samples of a bilingual's writing.

More specifically, it is timely that we understand how oral-like language, particularly conversational styles of speech, come to play a role in written text, academic discourse among bilingual and bicultural groups. Bilinguals and biculturals use oral language, be it at home or in the peer group, that may enter (for a variety of reasons) the written language required by schools. Our understanding of the mingling of oral and written language will influence the way in which we teach writing and reading to them. It may also influence the way we contribute to these students' social and cultural development.

In this chapter, I try to accomplish three tasks. First, I examine ways in which orallike language and strategies are expressed in writing and social identity is expressed through these strategies. I am specifically fascinated with the intricacies of what happens to the person and the discourse when a writer moves from a first language—unplanned, conversational discourse and culturally based language—to communication in a second language, the formal, academic written language of the text genres used in schools.

Second, I discuss samples of discourse from African-American, Jewish, and Hispanic-American communities, communities in which I have taught and lived. I provide illustrations and analysis of the uses of speech in writing produced by these bilingual and bicultural composers of text. Where appropriate, I show the intertextuality of written language—whereby oral text becomes linked to or enters in written text.

Third, I discuss the implications of these analyses and raise questions that I think are critical for the teaching of writing in today's schools.

THEORETICAL BACKGROUND

Theoretical work on language and cognition has contributed to my belief that the writing act involves the dramatic performance of an individual—is a dialogue that gets formed and translated on to paper. Voices that we have heard or used surface and enter into the writing. Dialogues that we have had with friends or colleagues, arguments that we have expressed on a topic, aloud with others or for just self, consciously or unconsciously, surface.

In the past decade, however, sufficient evidence has accumulated to show that writing is not just a dramatic conversation put on paper. Writing is *not* simply speech written down as Leonard Bloomfield proposed in 1933—although some written compositions by beginning and basic writers appear as if this were the conceptualization guiding the writing. Study of discourse styles has shown that written and spoken language differ in significant respects. We know that written and spoken language use different kinds of vocabulary, syntax, rhetorical structures, and represent different kinds of processes of production and perspectives (Biber, 1988, 1991; Chafe, 1986; Chafe & Danielewicz, 1987; Danielewicz & Chafe, 1985; de Beaugrande, 1983; Einhorn, 1978; Olson, 1993, 1994; Ong, 1982; Tannen, 1988). Writing and speaking result in qualitatively different kinds of interpretations and meaning systems (Halliday, 1987; Olson, 1990). They serve different functions for both author and reader (Halliday, 1987; Horowitz & Samuels, 1987; Shuy, 1985; Tannen, 1982, 1983, 1989). They may also employ different social models and situational representations (Bizzel, 1986).

In writing, decisions are made about what speech to include, to give rhetorical prominence, to place in the background, or to conceal. Writing entails more than a psychological presentation of self in everyday life on paper (Goffman, 1959); it is a distinctly social- and cultural-psychological act (Bruner, 1991). Uses of oral strategies and culturally based styles of speech in writing may be uniquely pronounced among bilinguals, or students for whom English is a second language, and among biculturals, who belong to more than one significant culture and have processed texts of these cultures (Kaplan, 1987; Zellermayer, 1988). Moreover, through the use of speech in writing, texts and social identities take shape, concurrently, and bilinguals may establish footing in written communication.

Decisions about voice are relevant to writing as well as to speaking. Should voice be—as Walker Gibson demonstrated in 1966 in his discussion of modern American prose styles—tough, sweet, or stuffy? The voice and personality of the performer set the stage for the quality of reciprocity and the relationships that will evolve between author and reader. Clearly, voice selection occurs in speech, and this has been discussed in the speech literature. It is less apparent, but accurate to say, voice selection occurs also in writing—and that voice is discovered and illocutionary force processed in reading and the "listening" to text.

Some theoretical work substantiates such claims. Mikhail Bakhtin demonstrated the value of analyzing communication in terms of social situations. He viewed voice, in speech and writing, as utterances with particular speaking personality and speaking consciousness. James Wertsch (1991) discussed in *Voices of the Mind: A Sociocultural Approach to Mediated Action* how Bakhtin's notion of voice includes more than vocal-auditory signals. Rather, Bakhtin was concerned with a speaking subject's "perspective, conceptual horizon, intention, and world view" (p. 51). For Bakhtin, "voices always exist in a social milieu; there is no such thing as a voice that exists in total isolation from other voices" (pp. 51–52). Consequently, Bakhtin proposed that an addressee and the addressee's voice are essential and influential in both developing and achieving what he termed "addressivity" and communicative meaning (p. 53).

Voice plays a role in the formation and the processing of discourse style. In the book *Style: Toward Clarity and Grace*, Joseph M. Williams (1990) said the following about voice:

> . . . when we stand back from the details of subjects, agents, passives, nominalizations, topics and stress, when we listen to our prose, we should hear something beyond sheer clarity and coherence. We should hear a voice . . . I suspect that we all speak in many voices . . . The problem is to hear the voice you are projecting and to change it when you want to. That's no more false than choosing how you dress, how you behave, how you live. (p. 79)

A number of questions follow that warrant exploration and that we can only begin to touch upon in this chapter. What are the markers of voice? What creates the effect of orality in literacy, for example, speech in written language? In what ways do oral and written language mingle and develop across age and cultural group? How should the use of speech styles in writing be viewed by composition experts and teachers? And when might speech style be used to create a positive effect or sound in text (as it can serve that purpose)?

SAMPLES OF DISCOURSE STYLES

Samples of Conversational Speech and Written Language Contrasted

To begin the aforementioned inquiry, I sought examples of persuasive discourse strategies and styles. As part of previously reported research (Horowitz, 1990, 1992), I obtained samples of conversational speech and written language from each subject in order to understand both intraindividual and intercultural differences in the production and presentation of each. Some such comparisons have been made of the speech and writing of adult subjects, and some attention has been given to the role of instruction in children's development from conversation to composition (Bereiter & Scardamalia, 1981). However, only a small number of comparisons of the speech and writing of school-age subjects have begun to appear in the literature (Erftmier & Dyson, 1986; Pellegrini, Galda, & Rubin, 1984; Shuman, 1986; Temple, Wu, & Snow, 1991).

I chose, in one study, 7-year-old children as my subjects. As for cultural context, the children lived in a rural community in South Texas. Some were Mexican-American. The ranch and country lifestyle these children grow up in is far removed from the formal school context of the town. The teachers noted that the children exhibited rural speech patterns and cultural experiences that were different than those used and treated in the school. I was interested in the linguistic and macrostructural differences between their speech and writing, their view of audience, their use of arguments accordingly to match that audience, and the social-cultural features of the discourse.

Students were asked, prior to a Christmas holiday to convince mom or dad, an intimate target audience, to buy them a Snoopy Sno Cone Machine. A videotape of a television commercial about the Snoopy Sno Cone Machine was presented prior to the oral task and again prior to the written task. A tape recorder was used to record the speech, and two prompts (following work of Scardamalia, Bereiter, & Goelman, 1982) were used in both the oral and written task to encourage the children to sustain their discourse. Scardamalia et al. found discoordination in writing results from lack of external signals to keep the child-writer going and that this could be altered by introducing prompts. They argued that children's compositions are equivalent to single conversational turns, with quantity of writing low because of no incentive to keep going. The student may stop writing, as if taking a turn in a conversation, and wait for a response. We used a prompt at two intervals each time language production stopped, asking the subject to "tell more" about what they were saying or writing. The prompts were effective in generating more discourse. The written and oral tasks were administered to the children in counterbalanced order.

The following text represents Billie Jo's oral production:

Billie Jo's Spoken Version

Well . . . I was coming home last time. I want to see if I can . . . Mom, can I have a . . . what's that thing? [E: Snoopy Sno Cone Machine.] Snoopy Sno Cone Machine. Now what? and . . . "No." But why not, please! "No. Why can't you buy it?" Because I don't got no money. [prompt #1] Because I wanted to play with . . . me and my brother can make some snow cones and we wouldn't give one to Jeremy and give my little brother some and me and my big brother some and he wanted to keep it. That's all [prompt #2] Can't I go over to my grandma's and get some money from her? "No, because she's at work." Do you . . . uh . . . go . . . uh "Why don't you go . . . to the . . . to um go see Daddy . . . see if he can." All right. We got some? Our brother. We went up to . . . where my Dad works I mean, we got some money and we can buy a Snoopy Sno Cone Machine.

For Billie Jo's writing, see Fig. 3.1.

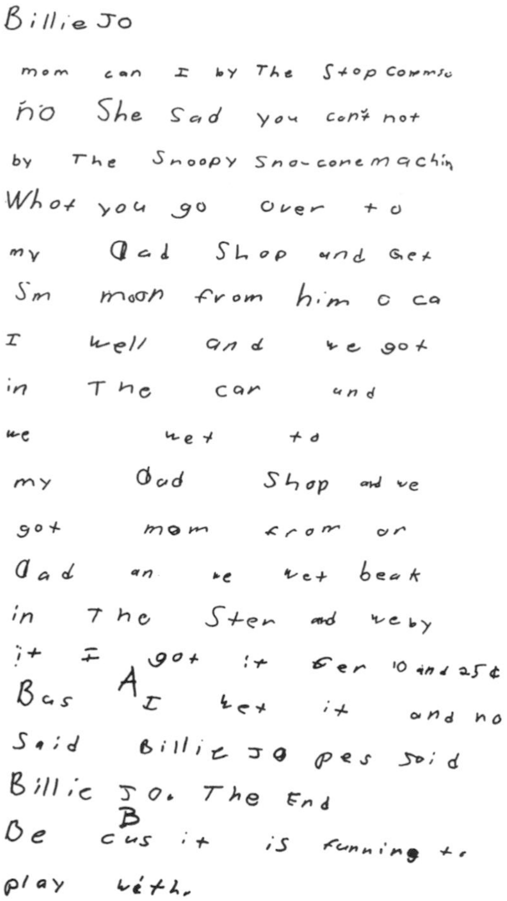

Billie Jo

mom can I by The Stop Commso
no She Sad you cont not
by The Snoopy Sno-cone machin
What you go Over to
my Dad Shop and Get
Sm moon from him o ca
I well and ve got
in The car and
we vet to
my Dad Shop and ve
got mom from or
Dad an ve vet beak
in The Sten and veby
it I got it fer 10 and 25¢
Bus A I bet it and no
Said Billie Jo pes soid
Billie Jo. The End
Be cus it is funning to
play with.

A. FIRST PROMPT
B. SECOND PROMPT

FIG. 3.1. Billie Jo's written production.

It is significant that Billie Jo used conversational dialogue as a vehicle for initiating his written discourse. Eventually, he turned his written persuasion into a coherent story and convinced his mother to go off to his father's shop for money. His persuasion is a narrative presented as a series of steps that resulted in his mother agreeing to purchase the Snoopy Sno Cone Machine. His oral language sample, in contrast, is less developed than the writing, with many starts and restarts, incomplete sentences, and less structure and cohesion than the text. Billie Jo made a topic shift each time he was prompted in speech. But in writing, the topical unit was longer; prompting has relatively little impact on topical structure in the writing condition. Billie Jo also used speech in an exploratory way to find a topic he could eventually sustain. In the written performance, he exploited the topical invention work that had been accomplished first in speech.

Several of the students produced, in speech as well as in writing, dramatic two-way dialogues—between themselves and a parent—although no mention was ever made in the instructions to create a drama or to role-play a parent interacting with the child. This trait suggests the influence of dialogue and oral language on writing. Some linguists have characterized dialogue and oral language as the foundation of written language and as a prerequisite for writing; others are not convinced of its priority or prerequisite nature (cf. Flores, 1992).

The next samples demonstrate Angie's creation of a superb drama in speech and in writing:

Angie's Oral Production

Mom, can I have a Snoopy Sno Cone Machine? [prompt #1] I guess I can think of something. "I don't think we got enough money right now." Please, Mom? "Angie, I told you before. No." Please mother? [prompt #2] Mother, have I been good? "I don't know, Angie, let's see. If you don't stop bothering me about that Snoopy Sno Cone Machine, you won't get it. You stop bugging me, start being good and making your bed and putting your clothes on, maybe I will. Like yesterday, you didn't get up and you didn't make your bed, and you didn't get your clothes on right, and you almost was late, so if you start getting up, putting your clothes on, and making your bed, I'll see about getting you the Snoopy Sno Cone Machine." But Mom . . . last year I had one and it broke. But Daddy won't let me have another one this year. And he said I could have one last year. "Angie, I said maybe. If you start getting up and making your bed, and putting your clothes on. Now stop bugging me about it, or you won't get it." Please, Mom? "Angie, stop bugging me!" Mom, Mother. "Angie, stop bugging me!" I'll stop bugging you if you get me the Snoopy Sno Cone Machine. "I won't get it for you if you don't stop bugging me." Please, Mom? "O.K., I'll get it for you. But you have to promise me one thing. If it breaks like last year, you ain't never gonna get one again. Is that understood?" Yes, Mother.

Angie's Written Production

Mom can I have a snop snow coon mushes. noWedont have a nafe mune to by you one but mom how come becaus I said. I think I shode becaus I think I been good for ones. And ded said I cood last year but I dint get one. becaus mine brock last year and I want a nuth one. becaus I been good.

Angie produced one of the longest oral samples in the study, 259 words long, and considerably more words in her oral sample than in her written communication. She produced organized, cohesive, conversational speech. She showed great skill in role-playing her mother as well as in expressing her own point of view. In the oral communication, she used two distinct voices, appropriate for each interlocutor, one to represent herself and the other her mother, with control of pitch, stress on key words, and intonation and pauses to suit each. Angie's written language, in contrast, is short. It does not yet contain quotation marks to signify speakers or voices, nor does she know how to represent tone or pitch in writing. The written version is, however, more concise as we would expect of writing.

An additional example of dialogue in writing appeared in the writing of Matthew, one of the Mexican-American students in this sample:

Matthew's Written Production

Mom, please, would you buy me a Snoopy Sno Cone Machine? I'll do everything I could to make money so I can buy it. I'll take out the trash and everything. Please would you buy it for me if I earn enough money? I'll clean up the rooms and make the beds. And do everything I can. Please. I like snow cones. I spell good.

Matthew's argument that he addressed to his mother consists of a list of trades, common in 6- and 7-year-olds' speech from mainstream culture children as well. Note that Matthew employed cause and effect structures, more advanced than many of the writing samples we received.

It is instructive to compare the written and oral compositions of Marilyn, another Mexican-American student.

Marilyn's Oral Production

I want a snow . . . a snow flake machine and um . . . buy one bag of ice and a little cup and a spoon. Get another one and um . . . and if I broke the spoon, get another one. And um . . . and if my friends throws the cup it's hard to buy a new one. [prompt #1] So I can share with my friends and my cousin, my uncle. My uncle might want some. And um . . . take it to my teacher . . . and where ever I go take it. To my daddy's grandma. She lives in Albuquerque. We might go Monday. And um . . . [prompt #2] Because I like it. It's fun. We can get a blanket, put on the grass and we, I could get it and my sister could get ice, cups and we'll start eating it up. And . . . that's all I can know.

Marilyn's Written Production

I what a snow com mchen. I think my sister want sum. and I think my want sum to and my mom. and my cusend and my friend. And we cud play out sid whet my friend. and I think my grnmom what sum to. and my ucel to. the End. be one I think my genu want sum to and gdel and lulu the becus my rend cud play what it and my cusen and one my dest frend. and my ant to. and my DaD grmom frend and my Techer to and the ces to. the End.

Marilyn produced 99 words in her written version with an extended list of family members (sister, mom, cousin, grandmom, uncle, aunt, and dad) and friends who would use the Sno Cone Machine. This discourse seems to overuse the conjunction *and* and shows much other repetition, as it proclaims generosity toward so many family members. The argument's warrant rests on the number of potential users, a reflection of Marilyn's sense of family and friends as powerful reasons for buying the Snoopy toy. The oral version is 137 words, longer than the written, as we would expect. Although the oral text is less complete in terms of the list of relationships (it does not include mom or dad, perhaps assumed), it however does include still another extended family member, "Daddy's grandma." Horowitz (1990) described and illustrated a system for categorizing levels of persuasive complexity for this sample of oral and written discourse.

Speech Strategies in Writing

What, then, is speech in writing, for at least 7-year-olds? The previous children's writing samples provide excellent examples of unplanned, instinctive speechlike language in writing. These writing samples use linguistic strategies to express an involvement in the task and spontaneity that is characteristic of childlike speech to an intimate target audience. Use of hyperbole, hedges, and quick and numerous topic shifts discussed by the linguist Wallace Chafe (1986), as characteristic of speech, were present in so many of the writing samples that we analyzed.

This research impressed upon me the need for developmental research. I asked under what conditions does conversational speechlike language enter the page as the 7-year-old writer matures and becomes an adult or expert in a given field? What are the features of speech that are acceptable and even desirable in mature writing? In what ways can oral strategies be most effective in particular genres in conveying a message that is believable and moving?

Examples of intentional use of speech in writing may be found in advertisements, usually accompanied with flashy pictorial images. These writers are skillful in conversing with readers and in introducing speechlike language in writing. As I was writing this chapter, I stopped to open my mail. I was being persuaded to shop at one of the regional department stores in the Southwest. Supported by a photograph of a suntanned, shirtless man, the text used poetrylike speech geared to male values but indirectly appealing to female readers:

The fragrance
of Heros.
Powerful.
Sensual.
. . .
For the man
who believes

in himself
—and his team.
Join his club.

We do not write in these forms. Nor do we talk in these forms. Each advertisement contained single words or short phrases set up so that these would be followed by vocal pauses and a breathy reading of the text. Walker Gilbson (1966) would call this the classic Sweet Talk. The impact of the advertisements is grounded in the writers' skill at using the oral aspects of intimate, indirect language to create a captivating image and seductive arguments. Speech in writing can produce quite powerful imagery through what is said—but also not said.

The task of producing speech in writing is not simple. Teachers cannot just say, "Write as you talk." De Beaugrande (1983) argued that we cannot use features of speech—that is, pauses, hesitations, and errors—in the same way in writing or to evaluate the writing. He contends some speech features are actually disruptive and damaging if incorporated into writing. The samples of speech he collected from University of Florida freshmen contain *redundancies* (fillers, repeated words, simple restarts, and restatements), *inconsistencies* (revised restarts, shifts, and nonagreements) and *approximations* (vagueness in reference, co-reference, and pronominalizations). Although acceptable in speech, these are unacceptable when included in college writing assignments.

The New Bilingual and Bicultural Populations

Examination of speech styles in writing becomes more intriguing when one considers the vast range of bilingual and bicultural speech styles in our world. Bruner, in fact, recently called for a cultural psychology (see *Acts of Meaning*, 1990) to address these issues of culture. His ideas, I believe, are important for writing research. Comparisons between ethnic conversational speech and academic writing have been limited in the orality-literacy literature, and studies of speech in writing also have been rather limited when one considers basic writers who are biculturals (Bizzel, 1986), yet are desperately needed. Further, examples of speech styles in writing, which reflect social and cultural aspects of human development, need to be identifiable by teachers, understood, and appropriately guided.

William Zinsser, author of the best seller *On Writing Well* (1980), indicated "... every writer must approach his subject in a manner that most naturally suits what he is writing about and who he is" (p. 69). Zinsser illustrated cultural speech in writing by drawing from the lead of an article by Richard Burton, the actor, on the topic of rugby. Zinsser noted that the second sentence is one of the longest he had ever seen but that it is under control and noted ". . . it sounds very Welsh, and if that's how Welshmen talk it's how they ought to write" (p. 69). See the following:

> It's difficult for me to know where to start with rugby. I come from a fanatically rugby-conscious Welsh miner's family, know so much about it, have read so much about it, have heard with delight so many massive lies and stupendous exaggerations about it and have contributed my own fair share, and five of my six brothers played it, one with some distinction, and I mean I even knew a Welsh woman from Taibach who before a home match at Aberavon would drop goals from around 40 yards with either foot to entertain the crowd, and her name, I remember, was Annie Mort and she wore sturdy shoes, the kind one reads about in books as "sensible," though the recipient of a kick from one of Annie's shoes would have been not so much sensible as insensible, and I even knew a chap called Five-Cush Cannon who won the sixth replay of a cup final (the previous five encounters having ended with the scores 0–0, 0–0, 0–0, 0–0, 0–0, including extra time) by throwing the ball over the bar from a scrum 10 yards out in a deep fog and claiming a dropped goal. And getting it. (Zinsser, 1980, p. 69)

The text contains loose, conjoined clauses that string along one after another. The vocabulary is such that one can imagine the words spoken informally with the rhythm of talk—to a keen listener. The second sentence is indeed long. We typically would not write it. But with proper pauses, intonation, and stress on the right words, one can easily imagine this being spoken in the context of face-to-face communication.

Although some ethnic styles of speech in writing seem to secure wide-spread appeal, many culturally influenced incidents of speech in writing are criticized as improper and the speaker's ideas devalued. Bilingual and bicultural speakers and writers are often judged harshly because attitudes toward languages are confounded with attitudes toward the users of the language. As a result, monolinguals may hold negative views of bilingual and bicultural traits such as code switching and cultural expressions (Grosjean, 1982; Rodriguez, 1982; Rose, 1989). As Maxine Greene (1993) so effectively stated:

> There have always been newcomers in this country; there have always been strangers. There have always been young persons in our classrooms we did not, could not see or hear. In recent years, however, invisibility has been refused on many sides. Old silences have been shattered; long-repressed voices are making themselves heard. Yes, we are in search of what John Dewey called "the Great Community" but, at once, we are challenged as never before to confront plurality and multiplicity. (p. 13)

Demographers have repeatedly reported that minorities will represent at least half of the population in schools in the next century and that this population will be largely Hispanic. Many of these children, Mexican-Americans, Puerto Ricans, Cubans, and South and Central Americans, come from two-culture families where there are intermarriages and more than one speech style may be used in the home.

Children growing up in two cultures in the 1990s encounter new challenges not faced by children growing up in one culture or by those who grew up in two cultures at the turn of the century. (See later discussion of Yiddish in this chapter.) For example, one researcher, Amado Padilla (1993), noted that often the offspring of intercultural marriages neither identify with nor care to assimilate into mainstream American culture. More so, these children opt to identify with a new unique culture that is a mixture of both parents' cultures. There may be cognitive and social gains in the combination, however, that are seldom elaborated upon in literature on ethnic minorities and bilingual and bicultural populations.

Padilla (1993) analyzed the unique roles played out in the oral discourse of bilingual and bicultural children. These children learn to be translators of the symbols they are exposed to—for themselves and their parents. The skill of translating from one language system into another is a higher order metacognitive skill than processing one language; it usually goes untapped and unappreciated in education. In addition, some children become what Padilla characterized as skillful "navigators" and/or "negotiators" between two cultures. But he also suggested the possibility of a negative result. Some children who are negotiators may retreat into their culture and language as a way of coping with the difficulties of being ethnic minority or of adapting to American cultures at large. Padilla indicated that ethnic preference and high ethnic loyalty emerge particularly among lower income and less educated minorities. Sometimes there is a fossilization of culture, and sometimes parents hold on to the culture in a way they perceive is that of the old country, but their understanding of this past-life culture is out of date and no longer accurate. Still, other children, with the help of school and family, may become biliterate in addition to being bilingual and bicultural (Hornberger, 1989). In such cases, they may have access to multiple positive variations in the way oral and written styles of each language are combined in discourse.

USES OF ORAL TRADITION AND SPEECH IN WRITTEN LANGUAGE

As we consider bilingual, bicultural, and biliterate writers, knowledge of oral historical precedents, social experiences, and cultural contexts from which they come, speak, and compose can be valuable.

I turn now to examples of speech in written language drawing from African-American, Jewish, and Hispanic-American communities.

Samples of Speech in Writing from Sermons
in the African-American Community

Uses of an oral tradition and oral-like strategies in written language can be found in the writings of Martin Luther King, Jr. (See also chapter 2 of this volume.) *The Wall Street Journal* (Waldman, 1990) and *The Washington Post* (Balz, 1990) reported that Stanford scholars had discovered that Martin Luther King, Jr. plagiarized graduate essays and his doctoral dissertation (see related discussion by Linn in chapter 2 of this volume). Since then much hullabaloo has emerged regarding the accuracy of this claim. Did he really plagiarize? How do we know? And what does it mean for our interpretation of Martin Luther King, Jr.? Discussion has even ensued about whether he can or should still be regarded as a hero.

Keith D. Miller (1993), an English professor at Arizona State University, and the son of a minister, presented the argument that "legally forbidden to read and write, slaves created a highly oral religious culture that treated songs and sermons as shared wealth, not private property . . . During and after slavery, African-American folk preachers gained stature by merging their identities with earlier authoritative bearers of the word" (p. A60). Miller argued that Martin Luther King used language from this oral tradition—one that rarely acknowledged sources. According to Miller, it would be highly ethnocentric to devalue this cultural practice.

In *Voice of Deliverance: The Language of Martin Luther King Jr. and Its Sources*, Miller (1992) traced King's sermon themes, illustrations, questions, and metaphors. More significantly for the purpose of this chapter, Miller also traced sources of King's voice, as expressed through the cadence and rhythm of speeches, to precedents in King's oral-based culture or print by other influential African-American clergy.

For example, the well-known essay, "Letter from Birmingham Jail," was originally written for *Christian Century*, with eventually nearly a million copies circulated among churches. Miller (1992) argued that although the structure of this essay was unlike King's other discourse, reflecting his study of Euro-American philosophy and classical persuasion, "Letter" also manifested familiar influences of the African-American folk pulpit. Further, it was written under trying conditions, when King entered Birmingham jail, with no notes or examples to draw from—except memory. Yet there is a strong resemblance to other sources. King drew from George Kelsey, his professor at Morehouse College. Kelsey is identified by Miller as writing:

> [S]egregation is morally wrong and sinful. It is established on pride, hatred, and falsehood. It is unbrotherly and impersonal. Two segregated souls never meet in God . . . To use the words of Martin Buber, segregation substitutes "I-it" relationship for the "I-thou" relationship and ends up relegating persons to the status of things. (p. 166)

Miller then argued that Martin Luther King "distilled this analysis" in "Letter from a Birmingham Jail": "Segregation, to use the terminology of . . . Martin Buber, substitutes an 'I-it' relationship for the 'I-thou' relationship and ends up relegating persons to the status of things" (p. 166).

Another example of what might be ethnocentrically termed plagiarism appears in King's "I Have a Dream" speech. Miller (1992) referred to this example as "voice merging" and noted that King borrowed a voice sometimes to merge with his and to give a powerful effect to his remarks. In "I Have a Dream," he drew from the Old Testament prophet Amos:

> There are those who are asking the devotees of civil rights, "When will you be satisfied?" We can never be satisfied as long as the Negro is the victim of unspeakable horrors of police brutality. We cannot be satisfied as long as our bodies . . . cannot find lodging in the motels of the highways or the hotels of the cities . . . No . . . we will not be satisfied until justice rolls down like waters and righteousness like a mighty stream. (quoted in Miller, 1992, p. 143)

Miller (1992) contended that the "we" of the last sentence calls forward a famous exhortation from the Old Testament prophet—referring to Amos' cries, "Let justice roll down like waters and righteousness like a mighty stream!" King merges his voice with Amos' personae, as he does with other Biblical figures later on (Miller, 1992, p. 143) and achieves the voice of the old—with his new text.

In an opinion piece published in *The Chronicle of Higher Education*, Miller (1993) called for two standards and the acceptance of this orally based culture's use of discourse. Fiery reactions appeared in later issues of *The Chronicle*. For example, Irving Louis Horowitz (1993) vehemently rejected Miller's proposal. Horowitz argued that it is such a call for a double standard that ultimately undermines Martin Luther King, Jr. Several critics argued King needed to adhere to academic-research standards, not those of his oral tradition.

The debate has continued to escalate. More is at stake here than Martin Luther King Jr.'s heroic stature. In May 1993, additional articles on plagiarism appeared that asked questions about orality in literacy (Magner, 1993a, 1993b, 1993c). What impact does an oral tradition and concomitant oral-like language have on a writer's choices and actions in writing? What is the unit of written language to be treated as plagiarism? Are we to be concerned with paragraphs, sentences, phrases, vocabulary choices? Under what conditions is a given unit of language to be regarded as plagiarism? Stephen Oates, a professor of history, has produced writings that have been questioned by the American Historical Society and several other scholarly groups because of his use, not of sentences or paragraphs of language, but of mostly short phrases believed to have been taken from other written historical sources and used in his historical accounts (Magner, 1993c).

Complaining: Uses of Conversational Speech in Writing by Speakers of Yiddish

Oral traditions and rituals have also played an important role in the Jewish community and its speech (Tannen, 1981a, 1981b, 1981c, 1983) and writing styles (Katriel, 1990; Zellermayer, 1988).

One form of conversational speech that has received recent attention in discourse literature and in the American and Israeli-Jewish community is the use of *complaining*. In fact, complaining has recently been viewed as a unique form of discourse, a ritual worthy of analysis. For example, the genre of letters to advice columnists has been studied by discourse analysts (see Kruez & Graesser, 1993) to understand the reasoning and assumptions behind questions posed and advice sought while one complains.

Katriel (1990) characterized a form of complaining, referred to as "griping," as a verbal ritual that serves a variety of purposes. It builds solidarity, a sense of community and support for the Israeli who is struggling to survive in the bureaucracy of the country—and is practiced during Friday-evening gatherings frequent in Israel among family and close friends.

At the turn of the century, complaining—in the form of conversational speech—entered into writing, on the pages of *The Jewish Daily Forward*, a Yiddish language newspaper. Especially interesting from a discourse analytic perspective is the section of the *Forward* that carried letters to an advisor by immigrants to the New World. From 1881 to 1925, 2,650,000 Jewish immigrants managed to come to America from Eastern Europe. Often they were fleeing from the pogroms in Russia and Rumania and from poverty and persecution. America became known as the "Goldenerland," "the new land of milk and honey" and the "place for equality for all." The Yiddish language used by immigrants in America received extensive description and analysis by Joshua Fishman (1965). His more recent work (1990) discusses the decline in use of Yiddish, at least among secular speakers, and means for reversing this language shift.

The Forward was a working man's and woman's newspaper, and was designed to serve as a vehicle to help the Eastern European Jewish immigrants resolve the psychological and cultural dilemmas that they faced—on a daily basis. Even the news coverage was geared to help them survive work, family, religious, and ethical and moral issues, as they adapted to American life. One of the most popular sections was "A Bintel Brief"—which may be translated as "a bundle of letters." Abraham Cahan, its editor, described how these letters represented speech from the heart:

> People often need the opportunity to be able to pour out their heavy-laden hearts. Among our immigrant masses this need was very marked. Hundreds of thousands of people, torn from their homes and their dear ones, were lonely souls who thirsted for expression, who wanted to hear an opinion,

who wanted advice in solving their weighty problems. The 'Bintel Brief'
created just this opportunity for them. (Metzker, 1971, p. 13)

The relationship between author of a letter and the editor of "A Bintel Brief"
was characterized by some of the letter writers in the following ways: "You
are the only one whom I can trust and to whom I can pour out my heart . . .";
"As a reader of the *Forverts* since 1910, when the big cloakmakers' strike took
place, I appeal to you for advice, and I will do as you tell me . . ."; "I know
that no one can advise me as well as you can . . ." (Metzker, 1971, p. 16)

These letters, in my estimation, represented a unique genre of speech
written down. They were favorite topics of conversation and debate in my
family, as well as within the community in which I was raised. In many
cases, like dialogue journals, fashionable in schools today, they defined the
relationship and the roles to be played out by writer and reader and bridged
the oral and written (see Staton & Shuy, 1988; Staton, Shuy, Payton, & Reed,
1988). The letters also depicted the complex problems and roles of the
Jewish-American immigrant in ways that were soothing to the authors and
convincing for the readers.

Some of the letters in the "Bintel Brief" addressed an editor who was
sitting in their imaginary living roomlike theater, taking it all in word for
word; for example, "My husband reads the *Forward*, but where does he
read it? In the barbershop where he goes all the time with those other card
players. Let him see this letter!"

By the same token, some letters represented intergenerational religious
conflicts and asked for advice in an intimate way one would ask a cherished
friend: "Is it a sin to use face powder? Shouldn't a girl look beautiful? My
father does not want me to use face powder. Is it a sin?"

The immigrant Yiddish genre humorist, Harry Golden, who contributed
the forward to Metzker's (1971) book, also used a talklike style. His text
contains clauses—only sometimes marked by punctuation—analogous to
the intonation units of speech that carry the flow of information. According
to Wallace Chafe (1986), spoken language is produced in a "series of spurts"
or "intonation units" that are imperfectly represented by punctuation marks
in writing. In the following sample, the clauses create the effect of a mel-
ancholy talk (the slashes are mine and represent the pauses that I make
when I read this aloud and turn it into speech):

> In the ghettos of New York,/ the crotchety maiden aunt,/ Grandmother and
> Grandfather,/ the wild-eyed high school boy/ who had just begun to study
> Marx,/ Uncle Boris from uptown/ and the boarder/ who studied Spinoza and
> Shakespeare until late at night/ every night—/ all sat at the same table/ and
> shared the same bread,/ soup,/ and potatoes./ (Metzker, 1971, p. 22)

The "Bintel Brief" letters are varied and difficult to analyze. They are
filled with code-switching, conversational strategies used in speech, expres-

sions of intimacy, and the kinds of anguish we only talk in private dialogues. One caveat is in order. The examples that I have provided here from Metzker (1971) should be understood to be English translations of Yiddish letters. As is the case in any translation, they may not carry the full expressions that the original author intended and probably picturesquely expressed in Yiddish.

Uses of Speech in Writing from Hispanic-American Communities

Many Hispanic-American children grow up in two cultures. Until the beginning of this century, few individuals immigrated from Mexico to the United States. However, between 1910 and 1920 there was a sudden large influx of Mexican immigrants—about 1 million (Grosjean, 1982). The intermarriage rate among minorities has increased significantly, with more than a million Hispanic Americans and non-Hispanics intermarrying. This has resulted in at least a third of Hispanic-American children coming from essentially two-culture homes. This biculturalism has profound effects on U.S. society and on the transformation of various regions (see, Phaneuf, 1993; Phelon, 1993).

Communication in these homes is often bilingual—in Spanish and English. As I have witnessed in San Antonio, Texas, some children move from the environs and the language styles of their protective homes to the more formal academic languages of the city and the school system. We have much to learn about the experiences encountered moving across these worlds and functioning as an effective speaker and writer in both worlds.

Hispanic-American children face the challenges of holding on to their first language, Spanish, or shifting to the mainstream language and its uses in various new contexts, or utilizing some combination of both. Richard Rodriguez, author of *Hunger of Memory* (1982), described his inner conflicts when home and school were in psychological opposition, rather than in cooperation. Rodriguez wrote that nuns from the school he attended visited his parents one Saturday morning when he was in first grade and asked his parents to encourage their children to practice English at home. Their misguided goal was the eradication of Spanish as a home language. Rodriguez indicated the change that ensued as English became the language of the home:

> The special feeling of closeness at home was diminished . . . We remained a loving family, but one greatly changed. No longer so close . . . [there] was a new quiet at home. The family's quiet was partly due to the fact, as we children learned more and more English, we shared fewer and fewer words with our parents . . . [At dinner] my father at the other end of the table would chew and chew at his food, while he stared over the heads of his children. (pp. 22—23)

The dramatic switch is analyzed by Goldenberg (1993) as unusually sudden, surprising, and with far-reaching demoralizing implications for school and home. Giving up the language was clearly giving up a precious family bond.

As a researcher at The University of Texas at San Antonio, I have been interested in the language development of the Hispanic-American children in the urban schools. Over 60% of San Antonio is Hispanic-American and in some schools most of the children, 95%, are Mexican-American, with Spanish as their first language. Many are the children of parents who have come from Mexico.

One of my students, Brett Jeffries, teaches in such a largely Hispanic-American school. Sixty-eight percent of the students in his school are Mexican-American. His sixth-graders are reading and writing on the average at about the fourth-grade level. Brett asked his students to provide an autobiographical account of family rituals and traditions with appropriate drawings to match. Tapping into their memories, these students enthusiastically prepared narrativelike texts, which were historical accounts, of their family customs and routines over special holidays. Autobiography has been recently receiving attention as a particularly powerful and socially revealing genre (see Bruner, 1990; Bruner & Weisser, 1991). As one reflects on one's life, a story takes shape and some kind of unity and cohesion is established for the text, but also about one's life and social identity. Such was the case of the written narrative reports that we received.

I provide some examples of conversational strategies used by Mexican-American sixth-graders, in written discourse, as they describe family gatherings and their social role and relationship to other members of their Hispanic-American family. One function of speech or writing is to define role relationships (Robinson, 1972):

Melissa's Favorite Ritual

On my birthday the way we celebrate is my mom buys me a pinata and a cake and she invites relatives and friends. During the party all of the adults sit down and talk and all of the kids run around and play games. After the kids have hit the pinata they sing Happy Birthday to me then we eat cake, and I open my presents after everyone goes home we go to bed and then the next day we wake up and have a cleaning party That is what we do on my birthday.

Yesena's Family Reunions

Every other year in August or in September we have a family reunion. Of course, we invite all of our relatives and sometimes say the same thing "Oh well I don't know if we can make it." Then the reunion is here and we're only expecting about 500 people and more less 700 people showed up. When

I saw them I thought to myself "Wow" I have a lot of relatives. So, after while some of the kids and myself started too meet each other and our families.

Melissa's writing has limited conventional punctuation. Still it does capture the sound of speech. Pauses are to be inferred by the reader in a continuous speech rather than to be determined by signal words linking clauses. Similarly, Edelsky (1986) found three general patterns in the development of bilingual children's use of links between clauses. First, no links; then, use of *and* between most clauses; finally, the use of *and* with a variety of other links.

Yessena's text is more standardized. It uses quotation marks to indicate speech in writing and capitalization, other punctuation, and complete sentences that are closer to conventional written language than is Melissa's. Still, Yessena's style retains colloquial expression. The text uses hyperbole; I doubt there were 700 people at the family reunion, but speech allows one to exaggerate. In an Earth Day composition (see Fig. 3.2), Marcus the author directly talks to an audience with, "You can do something. . . ." At the same time, he presents a persuasive text that conforms even more closely to academic formal style.

Marcus' writing directly addresses the reader-audience: "You can do something about it." Marcus' artwork (see Fig. 3.3) is unusually detailed and vividly represents the impact of the tree. Despite this considerable speech in writing, Marcus' text exhibits strong cohesion (e.g., repeating the theme of tree planting, appropriate use of *but*), inclusion of rudimentary evidence, and also a rudimentary problem-solution structure. All of this presages the qualities of academic prose.

My San Antonio Literacy Project (SALP) designed in conjunction with Project SER (Spanish for "to be"), a project in one of the poorest school districts in Texas, allowed me to study the writing of 9th-graders "at risk" of dropping out of school. Many, though not all, of the participants were Hispanic-American. The teens were asked to write letters to their parents about their conflicts, and these were published in the August 1989 edition of the SER magazine, *Asking Questions/Finding Answers.*

The letters seem to include the kind of authentic language that teens often do not put in writing in schools. The head of Project SER, Dennis Poplin, has been skillful in helping these students openly express their feelings in writing. These letters appeared in the student magazine prefaced with the following:

TEEN'S LETTERS TO PARENTS

THESE ARE A FEW OF THE THINGS WE'VE BEEN TALKING ABOUT
BUT ARE AFRAID TO SAY TO YOU. THE PARENT!!

Consider the following two letters, fairly typical of what appeared in the magazine:

Marcus
Per2 5-10-93

Every Earth day I plant a
tree. I have a little help getting
the tree. But I do most of it.
Earth Day is about taking
care of the place where you
live. We are destroying the
rain forest every minute to make
land for cows. The cows are
used for ham burger meat.
but I plant a tree to replace
the ones that died for cows.
It is the end of another
Earth day and trees are still
dying. You can do something
about it plant trees, and
Recycle things dont throw
things away that can be
recycled. Dont buy stuff
that harms the earth.
You can save the earth dont
put it off you can make a
diffrence.

FIG. 3.2. Marcus writes about Earth Day.

From The Unknown Son

Dear Parents,

Parents Hmm, when I think about you, I just can't stand it. Sometimes I want
to tell you something but I know I can't do it. Often, you treat my brothers
and sisters differently. You never tell me you care. I can tell you do by your
actions but I would like to hear it from you once in a while. I am proud of
you and want you to be proud of me. See it's not that I hate you It's just that
we live differently. Deep down I really care. Do you care about me?

Love,
The Unknown Son

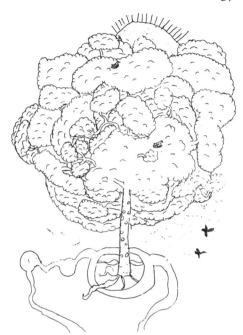

FIG. 3.3. Marcus' artwork accompanying his Earth Day composition.

From The Unknown Daughter

Dear Parents,

Well, first of all I think you're cool. But sometimes when I want to go out, you have a heart attack. You start asking me stuff like "Why do you want to go out" and "What time will you be back" I hate it when grown ups try to take care of me. It's not like I'm going to be gone forever! You should know how well I'm doing in school. I guess you don't trust me for some reason. . . . Finally, stop embarrassing me. When I'm outside, you yell at me from three houses down. That's something that ticks me off! . . . ."Amargo" means that Dad is always at home bored. He wants me to be that way. He wants me to do things that guys do such as: Cut the yard, trim the trees, do brick work, and many other chores. One day, he made me work on the roof. How embarrassing when my friends walked by. Some times you make me feel like a guy because of the way you treat me. So please trust me a little more and think about it when you might embarrass me.

Sincerely yours,
The Unknown Daughter

Both of these texts manifest teen conversationallike speech (a real teen-ager talking to a real parent) but in writing. The examples of frustration are real for these students and the page represents those feelings. Both letters use first and second person. The Unknown Son, in addition, uses speech "fillers" like *see*, and even the paralinguistic *hmm*. In the Unknown Daughter's letter, truncated sentences represent the actual language of angry speech, and active verbs are used to convey disgust and the desire for immediate change. I believe that it is the act of writing that ultimately brings the tormented adolescent's concerns and speech to consciousness and, I hope, resolution.

CONCLUSION

In summary, I have provided real-world samples of uses of conversationlike speech found in written language produced by bilingual and bicultural writers and ethnic minorities. The chapter highlights a number of distinct features of this speech in writing:

1. *Informal, Colloquial Language.* A number of the oral discourse samples that we examined, produced by 7-year-olds, contained colloquial expressions, repetitions, reductions of lexical choices (e.g., *going to* changed to *gonna*) or syntax, some expressed through starts and restarts, unexpected topic shifts, incompleteness of ideas, and sometimes vernacular forms of language. These oral patterns also surfaced in the writing of these students, as well as others—sometimes to the detriment of the writing, but sometimes to its advantage.

2. *Dialogue in Writing.* Some of the writings included in this chapter contain dialogue, actual speech (presented as quotations), paraphrases of talk exchanges (e.g., Angie's two-way dialogue reflecting her model of talk with her mother), questions to the audience-reader (e.g., the "Bintel Briefs," "My husband reads the *Forward*, but where does he read it?"), and cues for a privatelike reciprocity between writer and reader (e.g., characteristic of Yiddish letters to the *Forward*).

3. *Code Switching.* In the samples presented here, we have only two examples of code switching where there is interjection of Spanish lexical items in English writing (see reference to *pinata*, in Melissa's writing and *Amargo* in the Unknown Daughter's). In San Antonio public and private schools, teachers have historically objected to student use of spoken Spanish; thus, many students are fearful of using Spanish words in formal writing. Nevertheless, code switching between L1 oral forms and L2 written forms can be readily found in many different cultures, for example, in the writings of many Yiddish speaking immigrants like Harry Golden.

4. *Oral Strategies in Literate Discourse.* Writing analyzed in this chapter contained phonological, lexical, and syntactical features of utterances characteristic of speech. A number of the Snoopy Sno Cone Machine writings contained *uh*'s, *umm*'s, and *so*'s—like the Unknown Son's *hmm*—usually

functioning as a way of putting the discourse on hold while the "speaker" decided what to say next—acceptable in informal speech, but kids have not yet learned that this does not get transposed to writing. We find writing gets translated into a narrative structure even though what is called for is an expository rhetorical structure (e.g., Billie Jo's story), sometimes because narrative is a more familiar genre and easier to produce. Unusually long sentences—comprised of simple conjoined or collocated clauses or just items listed in a series—appeared in different forms in adult and children's writings (see Richard Burton's rugby text and Marilyn's writing about all of her relatives who would enjoy the Sno Cone Machine).

Some punctuation is inadvertently incorrect or purposely altered to represent speech patterns—not typical syntax of writing. It appears some writers manipulate punctuation to represent speech for a listener-audience, whereas others may manipulate punctuation in ways to represent speech for a reader-audience. (See the rugby text, which appears to be punctuated for an oral reading and audience of listeners. See the department store advertising text for unusual use of punctuation of single words and phrases, which may be intended to evoke sensual sounding speech for an audience of readers.)

5. *Voice.* The writings examined in this chapter often convey a distinct personality, tone, or mood and contain cadence, pitch, stress selections, and unique pausing. While I say this, it is often difficult to pinpoint what exactly is creating "the voice" that is being heard. Martin Luther King, Jr.'s "I Have a Dream" speech was printed, that is, became writing, and contains voice merging—Biblical speech overlaid upon King's voice—to create a new voice. Another point to be noted is: The voice the writer uses is often instantiated and becomes or shapes the voice of the reader. But there may not be consistency across readers. When someone orally read to me several of the texts in this chapter, I heard a different voice than I had mentally heard when reading the texts myself. Finally, the voices used in conversation, I believe, set the stage for writing, reading, and cohesive texts. Voices need to be tried out through oral discourse in classrooms.

This chapter demonstrates the moving ways in which speech in writing can reflect the social identities of adults and children. The chapter demonstrates that some speech can be extremely useful in written language. Little, at this time, is known about what facilitates effective speech in writing or how writers naturally achieve this ability and develop formal, written academic English. These examples provide means for investigating how conversational speech in writing may reflect powerful aspects of the bilingual and bicultural individual's social and cultural background. Teachers need to support those expressions that help the student convey a message. Students also need to rework talk-based initial drafts to make them suitable for written communication and should be allowed to keep those conversational dimensions in texts that suit not only the author's personality and personae, but also the message, purposes, and audience in the author's mind.

The experience of writing this essay has led me to examine a number of terms that have been used in the literature to convey "speech in writing": voice, personae, personality, voice merging, speechlike strategies, talklike text, conversationallike speech. These terms are being used to describe a social identity in writing and the projection of that identity, through linguistic strategies. These terms, however, remain undefined or defined in different vague ways. Theoreticians will need to examine these concepts and distinguish what they mean for the study of writing—and oral language.

The work reported here is a follow-up to previous publications that examine orality and literacy (Horowitz, 1984, 1991; Horowitz & Samuels, 1987) and has been influenced by my exposure to socio-psycholinguistic perspectives in language learning and text processing at The University of Minnesota. The study of speech in writing provides more than an understanding of the bicultural writer. It allows us to describe linguistic pattern shifts within given cultures (Farr & Janda, 1985; Finnegan, 1992, 1993; Labrie, 1983; Rubin, Goodrum, & Hall, 1990). These shifts are becoming more and more prevalent as cultures change. The trend in many social contexts is for a conversational speechlike style of text (see Lakoff's, 1982, discussion of this; see also Bateson, 1987; Biber, 1988; Poplack, 1982). The samples of discourse included here— African-American, Jewish, and Hispanic-American—reflect oral-based cultures and literate culture practices, oral traditions, and their expressions in written communication, and are an avenue for understanding the beauty of bilingual and bicultural communities and the needs of learners in these communities.

ACKNOWLEDGMENTS

This chapter has been prepared in honor of my advisor, teacher, colleague, and friend, Gene L. Piché, Professor Emeritus of The University of Minnesota. Professor Piché was an inspiration, a source of faith and intellectual guidance from 1965 when I entered his office and speech-communications class as a sophomore. He planted the seeds, set the foundation, and influenced the work that I have pursued long before I fully understood what the possibilities might be and how it might all fit. As the years progress, I am more and more grateful.

I thank Charles Thurston for his assistance in faithfully tracking down sources in our university library. I also wish to thank Tonya Kelsey, Cheryl Dancak, and Judith Knight for their help in preparing the manuscript.

REFERENCES

Asking questions/Finding answers. (1989, August). Project SER Education Program, Session 2, San Antonio, TX.

Balz, D. (1990, November 10). Scholars question portions of King's academic papers. (Claybourne Carson discovers possible plagiarism of Martin Luther King Jr.'s doctoral dissertation). *The Washington Post,* p. A1.

Bateson, M. C. (1987, November 15). Ghosts to believe in: Recalling Bateson and Mead. *The New York Times Book Review,* p. 49.

Bereiter, C., & Scardamalia, M. (1981). From conversation to composition: The role of instruction in a developmental process. In R. Glaser (Ed.), *Advances in instructional psychology* (Vol. 2, pp. 1–64). Hillsdale, NJ: Lawrence Erlbaum Associates.

Biber, D. (1988). *Variation across speech and writing.* Cambridge, England and New York: Cambridge University Press.

Biber, D. (1991). Oral and literate characteristics of selected primary school reading materials. In R. Horowitz (Guest Ed.), *Text. Studies of orality and literacy: Critical issues for the practice of schooling* [Special issue], *11*(1), 73–96.

Bizzel, P. (1986, October). What happens when basic writers come to college? *College Composition and Communication, 37*(3), 294–301.

Bloomfield, L. (1933). *Language.* New York: Holt.

Bruner, J. (1990). Autobiography and self. In J. Bruner, *Acts of meaning. The Jerusalem-Harvard Lectures* (pp. 99–138). London and Cambridge, MA: Harvard University Press.

Bruner, J., & Weisser, S. (1991). The invention of self: Autobiography and its forms. In D. R. Olson & N. Torrance (Eds.), *Literacy and orality* (pp. 129–148). Cambridge, England: Cambridge University Press.

Chafe, W. (1986). Writing in the perspective of speaking. In C. R. Cooper & S. Greenbaum (Eds.), *Studying writing: Linguistic approaches* (pp. 12–39). Beverly Hills, CA: Sage.

Chafe, W., & Danielewicz, J. (1987). Properties of spoken and written language. In R. Horowitz & S. J. Samuels (Eds.), *Comprehending oral and written language* (pp. 83–113). London and San Diego: Academic Press.

Danielewicz, J., & Chafe, W. (1985). How "normal" speaking leads to erroneous punctuation. In S. W. Freedman (Ed.), *The acquisition of written language* (pp. 213–225). Norwood, NJ: Ablex.

de Beaugrande, R. (1983). Linguistic and cognitive processes in developmental writing. *International Review of Applied Linguistics in Language Teaching, 21*(2), 125–144.

Edelsky, C. (1986). *Writing in a bilingual program. Habia una vez.* Norwood, NJ: Ablex.

Einhorn, L. (1978). Oral and written style. *Southern Speech Communication Journal, 43,* 302–311.

Erftmier, T., & Dyson, A. H. (1986). "Oh, ppbbt!": Differences between the oral and written persuasive strategies of school aged children. *Discourse Processes, 9*(1), 91–114.

Farr, M., & Janda, M. A. (1985). Basic writing students: Investigating oral and written language. *Research in the Teaching of English, 19,* 62–83.

Finnegan, R. (1992). *Oral traditions and the verbal arts.* London and New York: Routledge.

Finnegan, R. (1993). *Literacy and orality.* Cambridge, MA: Blackwell.

Fishman, J. A. (1965). *Yiddish in America. Socio-linguistic description and analysis.* Bloomington: Indiana University Press.

Fishman, J. A. (1990). Four American examples: Navajo, Spanish and Yiddish (Secular and Ultra-Orthodox). In *Reversing language shift. Theoretical and empirical foundations of assistance to threatened languages* (pp. 187–229). Clevedon Avon, England: Multilingual Matters.

Flores, B. M. (1992, November). *Challenging the assumption that oral language must precede literacy.* Paper presented at the National Council of Teachers of English Conference, Louisville, KY.

Gibson, W. (1966). *Tough, sweet, & stuffy. An essay on modern American prose styles.* London and Bloomington: Indiana University Press.

Goffman, E. (1959). *The presentation of self in everyday life.* Garden City, NY: Doubleday Anchor.

Goldenberg, C. (1993). The home-school connection in bilingual education. In M. B. Arias & U. Casanova (Eds.), *Bilingual education: Politics, practice and research. Ninety-second yearbook of the National Society for the Study of Education* (pp. 225–250). Chicago: University of Chicago Press.

Greene, M. (1993, January/February). The passions of pluralism. Multiculturalism and the expanding community. *Educational Researcher, 22*(1), 13–18.

Grosjean, F. (1982). *Life with two languages. An introduction to bilingualism.* Cambridge, MA: Harvard University Press.

Halliday, M. A. K. (1987). Properties of spoken and written language. In R. Horowitz & S. J. Samuels (Eds.), *Comprehending oral and written language* (pp. 55–82). London and San Diego: Academic Press.

Hornberger, N. H. (1989, Fall). Continua of biliteracy. *Review of Educational Research, 59*(3), 271–296.

Horowitz, I. L. (1993, February 10). Martin Luther King and redefining plagiarism [Letter to the editor]. *The Chronicle of Higher Education,* p. B2.

Horowitz, R. (1984, Spring). Orality and literacy in bilingual-bicultural contexts. *National Association of Bilingual Education (NABE) Journal, 8*(3), 11–26.

Horowitz, R. (1990). Discourse structure in oral and written language: Critical contrasts for literacy and schooling. In J. H. A. L. de Jong & D. K. Stevenson (Eds.), *Individualizing the assessment of language abilities* (pp. 108–126). Clevedon Avon, England: Multilingual Matters.

Horowitz, R. (1991). Orality and literacy and the design of schooling for the twenty-first century: Some introductory remarks. In *Text. Studies of orality and literacy: Critical issues for the practice of schooling, 11*(1), 1–16.

Horowitz, R. (1992, June). *Differences in conceptual representation and construction of discourse structure and arguments in oral and written persuasion produced by second graders.* Paper presented at the Second Society for Text and Discourse Conference, San Diego.

Horowitz, R., & Samuels, S. J. (Eds.). (1987). *Comprehending oral and written language.* London and San Diego: Academic Press.

Kaplan, R. B. (1987). Cultural thought patterns revisited. In U. Connor & R. B. Kaplan (Eds.), *Writing across languages: Analysis of L2 text* (pp. 9–21). Reading, MA: Addison-Wesley.

Katriel, T. (1990). "Griping" as a verbal ritual in some Israeli discourse. In D. Carbaugh (Ed.), *Cultural communication and intercultural contact* (pp. 99–113). Hillsdale, NJ: Lawrence Erlbaum Associates.

Labrie, V. (1983, April). *Interaction of oral and literate cultures in a bilingual environment.* Paper presented at the American Educational Research Association Conference, Montreal, Quebec.

Lakoff, R. T. (1982). Some of my favorite writers are literate: The mingling of oral and literate strategies in written communication. In D. Tannen (Ed.), *Spoken and written language. Exploring orality and literacy* (pp. 239–260) Norwood, NJ: Ablex.

Magner, D. K. (1993a, June 2). Excerpts from the AHA statement on plagiarism. *The Chronicle of Higher Education,* p. A14.

Magner, D. K. (1993b, May 12). Historian charged with plagiarism. Disputes critics' definition of term. *The Chronicle of Higher Education,* pp. A16, A18–A20.

Magner, D. K. (1993c, June 2). History association to probe accusations of plagiarism against Stephen Oates. *The Chronicle of Higher Education*, pp. A12–A14.

Metzker, I. (Ed.). (1971). *A bintel brief. Sixty years of letters from the Lower East Side to The Jewish Daily Forward.* New York: Schocken Books.

Miller, K. D. (1992). *Voice of deliverance: The language of Martin Luther King, Jr. and its sources.* Toronto and New York: Free Press.

Miller, K. D. (1993, January 20). Redefining plagiarism: Martin Luther King's use of an oral tradition. *The Chronicle of Higher Education*, p. A60.

Olson, D. R. (1991). Children's understanding of interpretation and the autonomy of written texts. In R. Horowitz (Guest Ed.), *Text. Studies of orality and literacy: Critical issues for the practice of schooling.* [Special issue]. *11*(1), 3–23.

Olson, D. R. (1993). How writing represents speech. *Language & Communication, 13*(1), 1–17.

Olson, D. R. (1994). *The world on paper.* Cambridge and New York: Cambridge University Press.

Ong, W. J. (1982). *Orality and literacy. The technologizing of the word.* London: Methuen.

Padilla, A. M. (1993, March 30). *Growing up in two cultures.* Lecture presented in the series, New Directions in Hispanic and Cross-Cultural Research: Themes, Perspectives, and Methodologies. Delivered at The University of Texas at San Antonio.

Pellegrini, A. D., Galda, L., & Rubin, D. (1984). Persuasion as a social-cognitive activity: The effects of age and channel of communication on children's production of persuasive messages. *Language & Communication, 4*(4), 285–293.

Phaneuf, W. (1993, April 3). Biculturalism reshapes region. *Union-News.*

Phelon, C. (1993, April 1). Biculturalism has profound effect on U.S. society. *Union-News,* p. 34.

Poplack, S. (1982). "Sometimes I'll start a sentence in Spanish y termino en espanol": Toward a typology of code-switching. In J. Amastae & L. Elias-Olivares (Eds.), *Spanish in the United States: Sociolinguistic aspects* (pp. 230–263). Cambridge, England: Cambridge University Press.

Robinson, W. P. (1972). *Language & social behavior.* London and Baltimore: Penguin Books.

Rodriguez, R. (1982). *Hunger of memory. The education of Richard Rodriguez.* Toronto and New York: Bantam Books.

Rose, M. (1989). *Lives on the boundary. A moving account of the struggles and achievements of America's educational underclass.* New York: Penguin Books.

Rubin, D. L., Goodrum, R., & Hall, B. (1990). Orality, oral-based culture, and the academic writing of ESL learners. *Issues in Applied Linguistics, 1*(1), 59–79.

Scardamalia, M., Bereiter, C., & Goelman, H. (1982). The role of production factors in writing ability. In M. Nystrand (Ed.), *What writers know: The language process and structure of written discourse* (pp. 173–210). New York: Academic Press.

Shuman, A. (1986). *Storytelling rights: The uses of oral and written texts by urban adolescents.* Cambridge and New York: Cambridge University Press.

Shuy, R. W. (1985). A comparison of oral and written language functions. In K. Jankowski (Ed.), *Scientific and humanistic dimensions of language* (pp. 471–480). Philadelphia: John Benjamins.

Staton, J., & Shuy, R. W. (1988). Talking our way into writing and reading: Dialogue journal practice. In B. A. Rafoth & D. L. Rubin (Eds.), *The social construction of written communication* (pp. 195–217). Norwood, NJ: Ablex.

Staton, J., Shuy, R., Payton, J. K., & Reed, L. (1988). *Dialogue journal communication.* Norwood, NJ: Ablex.

Tannen, D. (1981a). Indirectness in discourse: Ethnicity as conversational style. *Discourse Processes, 4,* 221–238.

Tannen, D. (1981b). New York Jewish conversational style. *International Journal of the Sociology of Language, 30,* 133–149.

Tannen, D. (1981c). The machine-gun question: An example of conversational style. *Journal of Pragmatics, 5,* 5.

Tannen, D. (1982). Oral and literate strategies in spoken and written narratives. *Language, 58,* 1–21.

Tannen, D. (1983). *Conversational styles.* Norwood, NJ: Ablex.

Tannen, D. (1988). The commingling of orality and literacy in giving a paper at a scholarly conference. *American Speech, 63*(1), 34–43.

Tannen, D. (1989). *Talking voices: Repetition, dialogue, and imagery in conversational discourse.* Cambridge, England and New York: Cambridge University Press.

Temple, J. M., Wu, H. F., & Snow, C. E. (1991). Papa pig just left for pigtown: Children's oral and written picture descriptions under varying instructions. *Discourse Processes, 14*(4), 469–495.

Waldman, P. (1990, November 9). To their dismay, King scholars find a troubling pattern: Civil rights leader was lax in attributing some parts of his academic papers. *The Wall Street Journal,* p. A1.

Wertsch, J. V. (1991). *Voices of the mind: A sociocultural approach to mediated action.* Cambridge, MA: Harvard University Press.

Williams, J. M. (1990). *Style. Toward clarity and grace.* Chicago: University of Chicago Press.

Zellermayer, M. (1988). An analysis of oral and literate texts: Two types of reader–writer relationships in Hebrew and English. In B. A. Rafoth & D. Rubin (Eds.), *The social construction of written communication* (pp. 287–303). Norwood, NJ: Ablex.

Zinsser, W. (1980). *On writing well* (2nd ed.). New York: Harper & Row.

CHAPTER FOUR

Examining Syntactic Variation Across Three English-Speaking Nationalities Through a Multifeature/Multidimensional Approach

Ulla Connor
Indiana University-Purdue University at Indianapolis

During the past couple of decades, textual features of student writing have been studied extensively by linguists and writing experts in attempts to understand writing quality and explain maturational levels in writing. Although studies examining text features across sentence boundaries—discourse analyses—have become more popular in the past decade (see reviews in Connor, 1987a, 1987b, 1990a, 1990b; Witte & Cherry, 1987), research on syntactic features of student texts has had an overall greater impact on the field of composition studies.

Studies of syntax in student texts proliferated after Hunt's (1965) research, which examined mean numbers of words per clause, mean numbers of words per sentence, mean numbers of words per T-unit, mean numbers of clauses per T-units, and so forth. A T-unit was defined by Hunt as any independent clause with all of its subordinate clauses and embeddings. Hunt's T-unit length for Grades 4, 8, and 12 came to be used as a norm of syntactic development in writing (Mellon, 1969; O'Hare, 1973; Stotsky, 1975). Furthermore, Hunt and others associated age with syntactic complexity as measured by T-unit length and other related quantitative measures.

It is only recently that researchers have pointed to the narrowness of Hunt's (1965) definition of T-unit and the related research. Among others, Witte, Daly, and Cherry (1986) questioned the positive linear relationship of writing quality and syntactic complexity found in Hunt's work. They showed, using empirical evidence, the flawed nature of the assumption about the positive linear relationship. Further, Williams (1986) criticized the narrowness of Hunt's research because it relies merely on word, clause, and sentence counts and does not consider the complexity of syntactic structures. As an example, Williams gave the case of nominalization, the formation of a noun from a cognate verb. A sample sentence from Williams' work is: "When we discussed why he failed it influenced what we decided" (p. 179). The same sentence with the verb nominalized reads: "Our discussion of his failure influenced our decision." The proportion of clauses to T-units is smaller in the nominalized sample sentence, because clauses are reduced to noun phrases. At the same time, the word-per-clause ratio increases. In other words, the syntactic complexity or the maturity of texts, as determined by the T-unit analysis, decreases with increased nominalization. Williams' assertion clearly points to the weakness in Hunt's theory because nominalized style is considered more mature by readers, especially by English teachers, as Williams' own experiments show.

Most writing experts today agree with the opinions of Witte et al. (1986), Williams (1986), and others who have questioned the narrowness of previous syntactic analyses of student writing. This chapter describes a research study that was designed to examine the usefulness of a new, comprehensive syntactic system for describing and evaluating student writing. This new system, originally developed by Biber (1984), is sensitive to the semantic level of sentence structures; thus it extends beyond the mere counting of words and T-unit lengths of sentences. The system consists of a multidimensional, computerized analysis whose value in explaining variation in style in a variety of text types has been determined in numerous previous studies. With the exception of one unpublished English-as-a-second-language (ESL) study (Grabe & Biber, 1987), the present study is the first attempt to apply the system to student writing (as opposed to the polished writings of expert and professional authors).

In this chapter, I first explain this syntactic analysis system, the theory behind it, and how it works. Second, I discuss the results of a study in which the system was used to compare persuasive essays written by students from three different cultures—American, British, and New Zealand. Implications of this research for future investigations as well as for the teaching and evaluating of writing are then explored.

THE SYNTACTIC ANALYSIS: DESCRIPTION
OF VARIABLES AND TEXTUAL DIMENSIONS

When one compares and contrasts text passages, it is not usually any single feature alone that suggests a certain style of writing. Instead, various features occur in systematic patterns to create style and tone. Sociolinguists—like Biber—work to identify co-occurring features in texts.

The syntactic analysis system used in the present study is based on the sociolinguistic principle of co-occurring features. This multifeature/multidimensional approach designed by Biber (1984, 1985, 1986, 1987, 1988) was designed to study variation of textual features among texts. This approach uses computer programs for frequency counts of linguistic features and multivariate statistical techniques to analyze co-occurrence patterns among linguistic features in texts.

Based on Biber's dissertation research and explained in detail in his recent book (Biber, 1988), the approach assumes that there is no single parameter of linguistic variation that distinguishes among different types of texts. Instead, Biber's approach seeks to systematically describe the linguistic characteristics of different types of texts in English and explain variation in text types using a key notion of his framework, "textual dimension." According to Biber, "dimensions are bundles of linguistic features that co-occur in texts because they work together to mark some common underlying function" (p. 55). Scientific texts when compared to conversations, for example, differ in the dimension of formality versus informality. Accordingly, frequency counts within dimensions show that when a text has many passives, it also has many nominalizations, as in the scientific text. Contrastingly, when a text has few passives, as in the conversational text, it also has few nominalizations. Thus, dimensions encompass features that consistently occur together and those that consistently complement one another.

The identification of dimensions in Biber's research is unique in that frequency counts of particular features in texts were first used to identify the groups of features that co-occur in texts, and only afterwards were these groupings interpreted in functional terms as dimensions. Most previous research had started with speculative, functional terms, thus bypassing the empirical first step, which is a bottom-up inductive distinguishing of dimensional chunks.

To examine variation in speech and writing in English texts, Biber (1988) analyzed 67 different linguistic features in 481 texts.[1] These analyses iden-

---

[1]Biber (1988) included a discussion of each linguistic feature. It gives the algorithm for the feature's automatic identification, a description of the functions associated with the features, and a list of previous studies that discuss the feature in functional terms or as a marker of situational differences among genres (pp. 221–245). A sample entry describing a linguistic feature of "nominalizations," feature #14, is given next:

14. **nominalizations**
All words ending in -*tion#*, -*ment#*, -*ness#*, or -*ity#* (plus plural forms).
Nominalizations have been used in many register studies. Chafe (1982, 1985) focused on their use to expand idea units and integrate information into fewer words. Biber (1986) found that they tend to co-occur with passive constructions and prepositions and thus interpreted their functions as conveying highly abstract (as opposed to situated) information. Janda (1985) showed that nominalizations are used during note taking to reduce full sentences to more compact and efficient series of noun phrases. Other references: Carroll (1960), DeVito (1967), Marckworth and Baker (1974), Grabe (1984). (p. 227)

tified the following initial list of functional dimensions: informal/formal, restricted/elaborated, contextualized/decontextualized, involved/detached, integrated/fragmented, abstract/concrete, and colloquial/literary. After the initial functional interpretation of the dimensions, Biber used factor analysis to identify a grouping of linguistic features that co-occur with a high frequency along each dimension.

Although Biber's research began as an investigation of speech and writing, the final analysis presents an overall description of the relations among texts in English. Biber (1988) stated that as fundamental parameters of linguistic variation among English texts, "the dimensions can be used to specify the relations among many different types of texts, for example, texts from different historical periods, texts from different social dialects, or texts from student writers of differing abilities" (p. 200).

THE STUDY

The Participants and Purpose of the Study

The present study is part of a large-scale project funded by the Exxon Education Foundation to develop an analytic system to describe and evaluate persuasive student writing cross-culturally (Connor, 1990b; Connor & Lauer, 1985, 1988). The data set in the project was unique; the compositions were randomly selected from among the compositions of the International Association for Evaluation of Educational Achievement (IEA; Purves & Takala, 1982). Fifty compositions were chosen randomly out of thousands of compositions written by U.S. high school students 16 years of age. Fifty compositions were also randomly chosen from among essays written by high school students of the same age in England and New Zealand, respectively. The composition task itself was a persuasive essay topic used in schools requiring students to describe a problem and offer solutions to it. (See Appendix.) Students had been given 50 minutes to write an essay.

All the subjects in the sample wrote their compositions in English, their first language. This enabled an examination of cross-cultural variation without the interference of differing languages. Much previous contrastive rhetoric research, in examining the potential transfer of first-language (L1) writing patterns when students write in their second language (L2; see Connor & Kaplan, 1987, for a review), thereby obscured cross-cultural variation per se. In other words, studying L2 writing may not reveal pure and true L1 cultural styles. Instead, L2 instruction impedes—we ESL teachers hope—a direct transfer of L1 writing patterns and styles.

The goal of the overall project was to identify valid and reliable measures of writing quality in persuasive compositions (Connor & Lauer, 1985, 1988). See Table 4.1 for all the features. In looking at English-speaking students'

TABLE 4.1

Concepts and Measures for Analyzing Persuasive Student Writing

Concept	Measure
1. Syntactic features	Computerized analysis of syntactic features; two underlying factors: *Interactive vs. Edited Text* and *Abstract vs. Situated Content*
2. Coherence	Scale including nine different variables related to topic development in texts based on topical structure analysis, a linguistically grounded theory
3. Persuasiveness	
a. Superstructure	Frequency of four different argument slots (Connor, 1987a; Connor & Lauer, 1985, 1988)
b. Levels of reasoning	Scale measuring Toulmin's categories claim, data, and warrant (Connor & Lauer, 1988)
c. Persuasive appeals	Scale measuring three appeals: rational affective, and credibility (Connor & Lauer, 1988)
d. Persuasive adaptiveness (Connor & Takala, 1987)	Scale measuring levels of audience awareness and persuasive adaptiveness (Connor & Takala, 1987)

Note. From Ulla Connor, "Linguistic/Rhetorical Measures for International Persuasive Student Writing," *Research in the Teaching of English*, February 1990. Copyright © 1990 by the National Council of Teachers of English. Reprinted by permission.

writing in three countries, the study attempted to discover national preferences in writing styles. The research resembles in its methods the research by psychologists such as Hofstede (1980), which identifies cross-cultural differences in value dimensions (e.g., tolerance for ambiguity, individualism, and power distance). The psychological research on values and cultural norms points to significant differences among Western countries, including the United States, New Zealand, and England—the nationalities in the present study.

Analysis of Syntactic Features in the Essays

Several previous studies by Biber using a multifeature/multidimensional approach to identify textual dimensions in speech and writing in English texts have identified three primary dimensions of linguistic variation among texts in English. To reflect their underlying functions, Biber labeled these dimensions as *Dimension 1: Interactive Versus Edited Text, Dimension 2: Abstract Versus Situated Content*, and *Dimension 3: Reported Versus Immediate Style*. As mentioned earlier, the interpretation of these dimensions is discussed in detail in Biber (1986, 1987); a full model of variation is presented in Biber (1988).

In the present study, I decided to limit the analyses to textual features under Factors 1 and 2, corresponding with Dimensions 1 and 2. Factor 3 identifies a co-occurrence relation among features such as past tense, third-person pronouns, perfect aspect, present tense, and adjectives, which distinguish primarily between narrative and non-narrative texts. This dimension was discarded in the present study at the personal recommendation of Biber, who maintains that the dimension would be useful if I were examining the amount of reported speech in students' story writing, for example. However, according to Biber, the dimension was unlikely to distinguish writing quality or reflect cross-cultural differences in persuasive student writing; rather, this study focused on Factors 1 and 2 as plausible indicators of writing quality or cross-cultural differences in student writing.

Dimension 1 includes features related to personal involvement and interaction versus features reflecting careful editing and high precision in lexical choice. Features that mark a high degree of interaction are (a) *that* relative clauses (both in subject and object positions, e.g., "the dog that bit me," and "the dog that I saw"), (b) subordinate cause clauses (i.e., clauses beginning with causative adverbial subordinator *because*), (c) subordinate conditional clauses (i.e., clauses beginning with conditional adverbial subordinators *if, unless*), (d) first-person pronouns (i.e., *I, me, we, us, my, our, myself, ourselves*), (e) second-person pronouns (i.e., *you, your, yourself, yourselves*), (f) contractions (i.e., all contractions of pronouns, all contractions of auxiliary forms), (g) pronoun *it*, and (h) type/token ratio (i.e., the number of different lexical items in a text, as a percentage. A negative weight was given to this feature in the analysis because, following Biber (1988), it is expected that a high degree of personal involvement and interaction is characterized by a relatively small number of different lexical items).

The features on Dimension 2, however, share a function marking a highly abstract content and a formal style. The label *Abstract Versus Situated Content* was used for this dimension. The features included in this dimension are (a) nominalizations (i.e., all words ending in *-tion, -ment, -ness, -ity*, plus plural forms), (b) prepositions (the list of prepositions was taken from Quirk, Greenbaum, Leech, & Svartvik, 1985, pp. 665–667, and includes 41 prepositional phrases, among them *against, among, except, throughout, via*), (c) passives (both agentless and by-passives), and (d) specific conjuncts (i.e., *alternatively, altogether, consequently, conversely, e.g., else, furthermore, hence, however, i.e., instead, likewise, moreover, namely, nevertheless, nonetheless, notwithstanding, otherwise, rather, similarly, therefore, thus, via, in comparison/contrast/particular/addition/conclusion/consequence/sum/ summary/any event/any case/other words, for example/instance, by + contrast/comparison, as a + result/consequence, on the contrary/other hand*). A summary of the 12 features from these two factors is given in Table 4.2.

Factors were used to compare student writing across cultures by computing *factor scores*, a single score that represents an entire factor computed for a set of essays from each of the three countries—England, the United States, and New Zealand. Factor scores were computed by summing the frequencies of

TABLE 4.2
Summary of the Factorial Structure of Linguistic Features

Factor 1	Factor 2
that clauses	nominalizations
subordinate cause clause	prepositions
subordinate conditional clause	specific conjuncts
first-person pronouns	agentless passives
second-person pronouns	
contractions	
pronoun *it*	
type/token ration (negative loading)	

the salient features on each factor, for each essay. For example, the factor score for Factor 2 was computed by adding together the number of nominalizations, prepositions, specific conjuncts, and agentless passives. A feature with a negative weight, type/token ratio, was subtracted from the sum.

Results

Table 4.3 shows the mean factor scores of essays from the three countries with respect to the two textual dimensions.

The mean scores on Factor 1 are −27.94, 4.74, and −23.49 for British, American, and New Zealand essays, respectively. The dramatically higher, positive mean of the American essays was associated with a large number of features such as *that* clauses, first- and second-person pronouns, contractions, and subordinate clauses, indicating an interactive, colloquial style. The British and New Zealand essays, on the other hand, had lower mean scores along this dimension, associated with greater lexical variety (shown by a higher type/token ratio), indicating a carefully produced, noninteractive style. The difference between the American essays on one hand and the British and New Zealand essays on the other was statistically significant at the .01 significance level using the Scheffé test. New Zealand and British scores, however, did not differ significantly from each other.

To better determine the exact nature of this difference, we can compare the frequencies of particular features. Table 4.4 presents mean frequencies of all the features.

TABLE 4.3
Means and Standard Deviations for Factors 1 and 2 by Country

	England		*United States*		*New Zealand*	
	M	*SD*	*M*	*SD*	*M*	*SD*
Factor 1	−27.94	18.86	4.74	45.55	−23.49	25.35
Factor 2	14.44	3.42	12.39	4.43	14.55	3.71

This table shows consistent differences between American essays and the essays written by students from England and New Zealand with respect to every feature along Factor 1. With respect to the frequencies of the seven features with positive loadings, American means were consistently higher than the corresponding British and New Zealand means. This difference seems to reflect a greater use of informal, colloquial, and interactional features in American essays. Type/token ratio is the feature with a negative weight on Factor 1, representing the degree of lexical specificity used in texts. The American mean was substantially lower than the British and New Zealand means, reflecting less variety in lexical choice.

Moving on, the overall means and standard deviations with respect to Factor 2 are shown likewise in Table 4.4. The mean score for the American essays along this dimension was significantly lower (12.39) than the means for the British and New Zealand essays (14.44 and 14.55, respectively), at the .05 significance level using the Scheffé test. As Table 4.4 indicates, the American essays had consistently lower frequencies on each of the four features (nominalization, prepositions, conjuncts, and passives). The significantly higher frequencies for the British and New Zealand essays suggest a more abstract and formal style.

Discussion of Results in Light of Holistic Ratings

The systematic differences found in the use of syntactic textual features are important in comparing the overall ratings of the essays from the three countries. The compositions were rated for overall impression by three independent raters, who were not connected with the IEA study. The scale range was 1–5, 1 being the lowest and 5 the highest. The raters were third-year PhD students in the Purdue University, Lafayette, Indiana, U.S.A., Rhetoric and Composition Program who had several years' experience in teaching and evaluating writing. The raters were shown the task description and were asked to work quickly at a single session supervised by the researcher. The agreement among the raters was high; the Cronbach alpha coefficient was .83. Table 4.5 shows the means and standard deviations for the holistic scores for the essays by country.

There was a significant difference in the holistic ratings among students from the three countries ($F_{2,146} = 12.31$, $p < .01$). The Scheffé post hoc test showed that American students were rated significantly lower than the other two groups, whereas there was no significant difference between the English and New Zealand students. Corresponding to these differences in holistic scores, the present study identified systematic differences in the use of lexical and syntactic features.

Both Factor 1 and Factor 2 had relatively strong correlations with the holistic rating. For Factor 1 and holistic ratings, r = −.37, accounting for

TABLE 4.4
Means and Standard Deviations for Syntactic Features by Country

	England		United States		New Zealand	
	M	*SD*	*M*	*SD*	*M*	*SD*
Factor 1						
that clause	2.78	2.17	4.14	5.63	2.22	2.03
subordinate cause clause	1.96	2.27	2.26	2.75	2.00	2.43
subordinate conditional clause	3.70	2.75	4.64	4.75	3.18	2.75
first-person pronoun	16.44	11.13	20.32	18.14	17.10	14.64
second-person pronoun	3.72	5.08	8.06	11.95	6.39	7.93
contraction	4.84	5.16	8.58	8.18	6.20	5.39
pronoun *it*	7.62	5.36	8.14	7.86	6.20	4.31
type/token ratio	69.00	4.77	51.40	27.98	66.76	11.24
Factor 2						
nominalization	5.78	5.37	4.44	5.96	5.73	5.51
prepositions	42.98	9.86	39.48	14.01	45.67	9.84
conjuncts	.94	1.66	.26	1.14	.98	1.21
passives	8.04	6.14	5.40	5.04	5.82	4.30

13.7% of the shared variance. In the case of Factor 2, r = .31, accounting for 9.6% of the variance. These correlations indicate that raters tended to rate compositions more highly if they were less involved and more carefully edited (with respect to Factor 1) and if they are more abstract and formal (with respect to Factor 2).

Interestingly, the differences found here are very similar to those found by Biber (1987) in a general comparison of nine British and American written genres: American genres consistently use more colloquial and interactive features than do British genres, and American genres consistently use a more nominalized style than do British genres. It was suggested in that study that both of these differences reflect a greater awareness of and concern about the forms of "good" writing in British English.

Returning to the essay differences found in the present study, I can suggest a similar correlation: The British and New Zealand essays tend to have a more frequent use of the linguistic features associated with "literary" writing.

TABLE 4.5
Means and Standard Deviations for Holistic Scores by Country
(Range 1–5)

	M	*SD*
England	2.29	0.81
United States	1.75	0.69
New Zealand	2.48	0.82

On Factor 1, literary writing is associated with careful lexical choice and an avoidance of colloquial and interactive features. Attitudes associated with Factor 2, however, are not as clear-cut. Although there is a general avoidance of passive and nominalized style in professional writing, teacher-raters tend to be positively influenced by a more frequent use of these features (Williams, 1986); it is apparently for this reason that we find more of these features in the British and New Zealand essays.

Conclusion

The present study suggests that the multifeature/multidimensional approach to syntactic analysis designed by Biber has promise for specifying relations among textual features in student essays. Biber's analytic system allowed for multifeature/multidimensional analyses of cross-cultural differences in the present sample. Systematic differences in the use of lexical and syntactic features were found in the writing of students in English by English, U.S., and New Zealand high school students.

In addition to identifying differences among student-writers stemming from students' backgrounds, the multitexture/multidimensional approach to syntactic analysis also helped explain writing quality as determined by im-pressionistic, holistic ratings. At this time, holistic ratings are the main in-strument for large-scale assessment of student writing quality. Yet, little is known about what text features influence holistic ratings of writing (Charney, 1984). Therefore, Biber's comprehensive text-analytic system seems ideal for analyzing compositions in large data sets such as the IEA and many national and statewide assessments. In the present study, the Biber analysis system was able to identify cross-cultural differences in writing styles.

These findings suggest interesting speculations for U.S. educational prac-tice. The U.S. students in the sample did not score as well as their English and New Zealand counterparts. There may be many reasons to explain the difference. Perhaps U.S. students truly do not write as well, or perhaps they do not take essay tests in class seriously. After all, the IEA test, from which the data were sampled, was not a "high-stakes" test ordered by school systems.

Based on many recent performance studies of U.S. students' literacy skills, one is tempted to conclude that U.S. students lag behind because they are not given enough opportunities to write at school. The situation is very different in Britain, for example, where students write essays for all subjects (Hamilton-Wieler, 1987). British and New Zealand students are exposed to writing for many different tasks and purposes. U.S. students in this sample favored more informal, orallike style as opposed to formal, literate style. The teacher-raters in the study did not reward colloquial style, perhaps expecting students at 16 years of age to be able to demonstrate a more formal written argumentative style in a test situation.

In future research it would be useful to compare students' writing for a variety of tasks, for example, narrative and informative writing, in addition to persuasive writing. Examinations of students' syntactic variation as measured by Biber's dimensions would reveal important insights concerning students' repertoires of styles and level of formality.

I am not suggesting in text-analytic research of student writing that we should rely solely on the linguistic categories in Biber's system. It is important that we continue studying cohesion, cohesive chains, and coherence patterns and other measures that have been found to relate to writing quality, all of which are teachable concepts. I do think, however, that Biber's analysis could provide teachers with a quick look at the students' style of writing. As far as I know, Biber's analysis has been used only in research so far, and not for instructional purposes. In my opinion, however, it would be a superior teaching tool compared to many commercial text-analysis programs for editing (e.g., *Grammatik, Writer's Workbench*). Unlike the commercial programs just mentioned Biber's system does not merely provide simple counts, but it helps interpret how well the text works because of these text features.

ACKNOWLEDGMENT

I wish to thank Douglas Biber for his generous assistance in the analyses as well as commentary on previous versions of this chapter.

REFERENCES

Biber, D. (1984). *A model of textual relations within the written and spoken modes.* Unpublished doctoral dissertation, Department of Linguistics, University of Southern California, Los Angeles.

Biber, D. (1985). Investigating macroscopic textual variation through multi-feature/multi-dimensional analyses. *Linguistics, 23,* 337–360.

Biber, D. (1986). Spoken and written textual dimensions in English: Resolving the contradictory findings. *Language, 62,* 384–414.

Biber, D. (1987). A textual comparison of British and American writing. *American Speech, 62,* 99–119.

Biber, D. (1988). *Variation across speech and writing.* New York: Cambridge University Press.

Carroll, J. B. (1960). Vectors of prose style. In T. Sebeok (Ed.), *Style in language* (pp. 283–292). Cambridge, MA: MIT Press.

Chafe, W. L. (1982). Integration and involvement in speaking, writing, and oral literature. In D. Tannen (Ed.), *Spoken and written language: Exploring orality and literacy* (pp. 35–54). Norwood, NJ: Ablex.

Chafe, W. L. (1985). Linguistic differences produced by differences between speaking and writing. In D. R. Olson, N. Torrance, & A. Hildyard (Eds.), *Literature, language, and learning: The nature and consequences of reading and writing* (pp. 105–123). Cambridge, England: Cambridge University Press.

Charney, D. (1984). The validity of using holistic scoring to evaluate writing: A critical overview. *Research in the Teaching of English, 18,* 65–81.

Connor, U. (1987a). Argumentative patterns in student essays: Cross-cultural differences. In U. Connor & R. B. Kaplan (Eds.), *Writing across languages: Analysis of L2 text* (pp. 57–72). Reading, MA: Addison-Wesley.

Connor, U. (1987b). Research frontiers in writing analysis. *TESOL Quarterly, 21,* 677–695.

Connor, U. (1990a). Discourse analysis and writing/reading instruction. In W. Grabe (Ed.), *Annual Review of Applied Linguistics* (Vol. 11, pp. 164–180). New York: Cambridge University Press.

Connor, U. (1990b). Linguistic/rhetorical measures for international persuasive student writing. *Research in the Teaching of English, 24,* 67–87.

Connor, U., & Kaplan, R. B. (Eds.). (1987). *Writing across languages: Analysis of L2 text.* Reading, MA: Addison-Wesley.

Connor, U., & Lauer, J. (1985). Understanding persuasive essay writing: Linguistic/rhetorical approach. *Text, 5,* 309–326.

Connor, U., & Lauer, J. (1988). Crosscultural variation in persuasive student writing. In A. C. Purves (Ed.), *Contrastive rhetoric* (pp. 138–159). Beverly Hills, CA: Sage.

DeVito, J. A. (1967). Levels of abstraction in spoken and written language. *Journal of Communication, 17,* 354–61.

Grabe, W. P. (1984). *Towards defining expository prose within a theory of text construction.* Unpublished doctoral dissertation, Department of Linguistics, University of Southern California, Los Angeles.

Grabe, W. P., & Biber, D. (1987). *Freshman student writing and the contrastive rhetoric hypothesis.* Paper presented at the Second Language Research Forum, University of Southern California, Los Angeles.

Hamilton-Wieler, S. (1987). *Context-based study of writing of eighteen-year-olds with special attention to biology, English, history, history of art, physical geography, and sociology.* Unpublished doctoral dissertation, Department of English Mother Tongue, University of London, London.

Hofstede, G. (1980). *Cultures' consequences: International differences in work-related values.* Beverly Hills, CA: Sage.

Hunt, K. W. (1965). *Grammatical structures written at three grade levels* (NCTE Research Report No. 3). Urbana, IL: National Council of Teachers of English.

Janda, R. D. (1985). Note-taking as a simplified register. *Discourse Processes, 8,* 437–454.

Marckworth, M. L., & Baker, W. J. (1974). A discriminant function analysis of co-variation of a number of syntactic devices in five prose genres. *American Journal of Computational Linguistics,* Microfiche 11.

Mellon, J. C. (1969). *Transformational sentence-combining: A method for enhancing the development of syntactic fluency in English composition* (NCTE Research Report No. 10). Urbana, IL: National Council of Teachers of English.

O'Hare, F. (1973). *Sentence combining: Improving student writing without formal grammar instruction* (NCTE Research Report No. 15). Urbana, IL: National Council of Teachers of English.

Purves, A. C., & Takala, S. (Eds.). (1982). *An international perspective on the evaluation of written composition.* London: Pergamon.

Quirk, R., Greenbaum, S., Leech, G., & Svartvik, J. (1985). *A comprehensive grammar of the English language.* London: Longman.

Stotsky, S. L. (1975). Sentence-combining as a curricular activity: Its effect on written language development and reading comprehension. *Research in the Teaching of English, 9,* 30–71.

Williams, J. M. (1986). Non-linguistic linguistics and the teaching of style. In D. A. McQuade (Ed.), *Linguistics, stylistics, and the teaching of composition* (pp. 174–191). Carbondale: Southern Illinois University Press.

Witte, S. P., & Cherry, R. D. (1987). Writing processes and written products in composition research. In C. R. Cooper & S. Greenbaum (Eds.), *Studying writing: Linguistic approaches* (pp. 112–154). Beverly Hills, CA: Sage.

Witte, S. P., Daly, J. A., & Cherry, R. D. (1986). Syntactic complexity and writing quality. In D. A. McQuade (Ed.), *Linguistics, stylistics, and the teaching of writing* (pp. 150–164). Carbondale: Southern Illinois University Press.

APPENDIX

Assignment

There are several things people can like or dislike in their life or the world around them. They might have noticed that young people find work or that people smoke in public places, or have noticed problems in their community, such as that certain places are unsafe, that certain opportunities are missing, or that particular groups should get to understand each other better.

In this writing task, you have to explain what you think is an important problem in your community or in the life of people your age. You can use one of the examples described previously or choose a problem of your own.

You have to imagine that you have to write to people who can solve this problem but are not familiar with it.

Therefore, you should explain the problem clearly in order to convince your audience that the problem is an important one. After that, describe your plan for improving the situation in sufficient detail so that they know what you want done. Be sure to give details, facts, and examples to support your description and suggestion.

Your composition should be two or three pages long. Before you give your composition in, reread it in order to see: (a) how clearly you have described the problem and your solution, and (b) how convincing you have been in presenting your arguments.

Your composition will be graded according to the aforementioned criteria.

If you want to change or correct something you may do it on your original; you do not have to recopy the whole composition.

CHAPTER FIVE

Social Dimensions of Second-Language Writing Instruction: Peer Response Groups as Cultural Context

Gayle L. Nelson and Joan G. Carson
with Ned Danison and Linda Gajdusek[1]

Writing is a socially constructed act as well as a cognitive one, and the social dimension of writing is often reflected in pedagogical practices designed to develop writing skills. Furthermore, these pedagogical practices are likely to reflect the values of the culture in which the writing instruction is being done. For example, in the United States, a highly individualistic culture, pedagogical practices are geared to developing and maintaining individualism and individuated skills. Chinese culture, on the other hand, is highly collectivist and pedagogical practices tend to reflect the importance of the group (Carson, 1992). What happens, then, when Chinese students accustomed to being socialized to value the group find themselves in classrooms where activities highlight the importance of the individual? This dissonance between the group and the individual is one that seems to present itself to Chinese students when peer response groups are used in writing instruction in U.S. classrooms.

As a result of cultural differences, writing groups may be problematic for students from the People's Republic of China (PRC) and Taiwan because writing groups, as used in composition classes in the United States, function differently than groups in collectivist cultures (e.g., PRC and Taiwan). As Carson and Nelson (1994) pointed out, students are grouped in both the United States and Chinese classrooms; however, there the similarity ends. People in collectivist cultures believe that the collective or group is the smallest unit of

---

[1]Ned Danison, graduate research assistant, was the third interviewer in this study; Linda Gajdusek was the classroom teacher.

survival (unlike people in individualist cultures who believe that the individual is the smallest unit of survival). The primary goal of the group in collectivist cultures is to maintain the relationships that constitute the group, to maintain cohesion and group harmony among the group members (Bond, 1986; Hofstede, 1984, 1991; Triandis, 1988, 1989; Triandis, Brislin, & Hui, 1988). Because societal institutions reflect and maintain cultural values, it is not surprising that schools in the PRC and Taiwan are structured to reflect the central role of the group in those cultures; the group exists to serve the collective good. For example in the PRC, students are organized into class collectives, usually consisting of 15 to 20 students, and these collectives form the basis for students' academic and social life. Students seldom interact with students who are not members of their collective (Hu & Grove, 1991).

Given that groups serve a collectivist function in their home country's educational settings, it is not unreasonable to assume that Chinese students would function well in collaborative learning situations such as writing groups in which the social nature of learning is recognized and social interaction is valued. However, what makes writing-group interaction potentially problematic for English-as-a-second-language (ESL) writers from the PRC and Taiwan is the fact that North American writing groups function in a way that is antithetical to the values of collectivist cultures. That is, writing groups, as they are frequently implemented in composition classrooms in the United States, more often function for the benefit of the individual writer than for the benefit of the group. Writing groups are usually structured to focus group attention on individual writing, rather than on a single project that has been negotiated and enacted by and for the group. In fact, in many academic settings, composition teachers understand their goal to be preparing students to write as individuals, not as collaborators. This individualist ethic, according to Clark and Doheny-Farina (1990), is one that treats community as an arena for seeking private good.

The kinds of behaviors that Chinese students would normally exhibit with group members in their cultures are different from what may be desired in writing groups. For example, when interacting with members of their groups, collectivists will generally work toward maintaining group harmony and mutual face saving to maintain a state of cohesion. Zander (1983) described this behavior as "gracious, courteous, and gentle . . . eschew[ing] behaviors that might ruffle the composure of those assembled" (p. 7). Such harmony-maintenance strategies, however, may not work toward the development of students' individual writing products. It may be difficult for a Chinese student to respond to other students' written texts in any manner other than being positive. The motivation behind their responses is likely to come from a need for a positive group climate rather than from a need to help an individual writer with his or her writing. The Chinese student may say what the writer wants to hear rather than what might be helpful.

The present study was designed to investigate the following two research questions:

1. What characterizes the interaction styles of Chinese students in peer response groups?
2. What do Chinese students perceive to be the primary goal of peer response groups?

METHOD

Because we were interested in group interaction as it occurred naturally, we conducted a microethnographic study of three peer response groups in an ESL advanced composition class. Microethnographics typically focus on detailed description of a particular phenomenon, and involve systematic data collection through videotaping, audiotaping, observations, and interviews. Furthermore, language is understood as central to the social phenomenon being studied and "each event is seen as part of a dynamic interaction wherein roles and meanings are continuously negotiated" (Trueba & Wright, 1980/1981, p. 37) As with other studies of this type, this one focuses on a small sample and therefore has limited generalizability. Its primary purpose is to provide a better understanding of how Chinese students interact with their non-Chinese peers in peer response groups.

Participants

Eleven students in an advanced ESL writing class at a large metropolitan university in the United States participated in the study. Students' placement at this level was determined by a combination of listening, grammar, vocabulary, reading, and writing scores from a university-developed placement exam. Scores for students in this class correspond roughly to TOEFL (Test of English as a Foreign Language) scores ranging from 460 to 530. Decisions on group placement were based on gender and nationality. Two of the groups were composed of four students; one consisted of three students. Group A included women from the PRC (Clara) and Laos (Aeenoy) and men from Bangladesh (Hussein) and Mexico (Carlos); Group B consisted of women from Taiwan (Daisy) and Argentina (Alma) and a man from Iran (Ahmad); Group C consisted of women from Taiwan (Lin) and Thailand (Yaowanee) and men from Haiti (Jean) and Thailand (Sasin).

The three key informants were Chinese students. Clara, the informant from the PRC, was 19 years old, had been in the United States 3 years, and graduated from a U.S. high school. Daisy was 20 years old, and like Clara, had been in the United States for 3 years and graduated from a U.S. high school. Of the three informants, Lin was the only graduate student. She was 23 years old, had graduated from a university in Taiwan, and had been in the United States for 4 months.

Writing Class

These students were taking a 10-week writing course that met 2 days a week, with each class lasting 2 hours and 15 minutes. The overall course objective was for students to produce clear and effective expository essays. The instructor used a process approach to teach writing (Leki, 1989), incorporating peer response in which students responded to their peers' written texts (Mittan, 1989). Before the peer response groups were initiated, students were instructed in helpful peer response group behaviors through a series of role plays in which three ESL instructors (actors) visited the class and played the roles of student-writers. During the role plays, the ESL students talked to the actors playing the roles of the writers about their writing. The first actor was argumentative, the second meek and quiet, and the third negotiated with the group to clarify her understanding of their comments. After each role play, the class discussed the effects of each writer's reaction and the behaviors that contributed to effective peer response groups.

Procedure

Ethnographic methodology calls for multiple perspectives in data collection and analysis in order to reach a fuller appreciation of the phenomena under investigation (Yin, 1984). Our data included (a) videotapes of the peer response group sessions, (b) audiotaped interviews with the Chinese students, and (c) transcriptions of audiotapes. In addition, student journals, researchers' field notes, and all drafts of compositions were collected.

Because this study is concerned with the participants' views of their social realities (i.e., it is phenomenological in nature), we employed key informant interviews as our primary data collection procedure. The three interviewers (two faculty and one graduate research assistant) attended the first meeting of the class and explained the study to the students, stating that they were investigating cultural differences in group interactions and would like to videotape their response group interactions. They also met with the three Chinese students and asked them for additional participation, which included (a) meeting with one of the interviewers soon after each of the six videotaped writing-group sessions to discuss the videotape, and (b) being interviewed on audiotape about the interactions that occurred in the group. To decrease students' anxiety about being videotaped, we followed Erickson and Wilson's (1982) suggestions to clearly explain the study's purpose and confidentiality procedures and also to allow participants to become familiar with the videotape equipment before using it in the class. Interviewers also observed and videotaped the class on the day when the instructor was training the students in desirable writing-group interactions.

Six sessions of each of the three groups were videotaped. One videotape had no sound due to difficulties with the microphone and had to be eliminated from the study, making a total of 17 writing-group videotapes. One interviewer was paired with one Chinese student. Within 5 days after each session, an interviewer and a Chinese student met to view the videotape of the session and to discuss the group's interactions. Using an adaptation of Erickson and Schultz's (1982) method of stimulated recall, the interviewer used a remote control to stop the videotape after each exchange initiated by the informant, after each exchange directed at the informant, and at other times when the interviewer had questions about what the informants were thinking or feeling in response to their peers' interactions (particularly if the informant had not spoken for a while). In later sessions, the informants used the remote control to stop the videotape when they had something to say. As much as possible, the interviewers avoided responding to the subjects' utterances with evaluative comments.

In general, three broad categories of questions were used: (a) those inquiring about the subjects' affective states (e.g., What were you feeling when Y said that?), (b) those inquiring about the subjects' cognitive states (What were you thinking here?), and (c) those inquiring about the subjects' pragmatic intent (Why did you do that?). These questions, along with others, were developed by the researchers during the planning stages of the study. After the first videotaping session, the interviewers met to view the videotapes to ensure that they were consistent in the types of questions they asked. During this viewing, it became apparent that the three types of questions listed previously produced richer responses than did other questions. This realization resulted in a focus on the three questions. In addition, at the end of the viewing sessions, subjects were asked about additional topics such as the group's purpose and functioning (e.g., How do you think your group is working?), about the subject in relationship to the others (e.g., What do you think your position is in the group?), and about the others in relation to subject (e.g., How do you feel about the other members of your group?). The three interviewers continued to meet after each interview session to view the videotapes. In these review sessions, the interviewers indicated to one another where each would have stopped the tape and what questions would be asked. The audiotaped interviews were also transcribed within a week of the interviews so the interviewers were able to use the transcripts to compare questions asked in the interviews. This procedure served as another check on the equivalence of the interview procedures.

The transcripts from the 15 interviews (2 interviews were lost due to malfunctioning tape recorders) were then examined recursively by the two senior researchers. While examining the data, the researchers noted certain emerging patterns or themes. These themes or coding categories are listed in Table 5.1. The data were analyzed again using these themes as coding categories and the data were organized according to these categories. The unit of analysis, then, was the stretch of discourse (a sentence, a turn, or several turns) identified as "about" a specific theme or topic (Brown & Yule,

TABLE 5.1
Primary Coding Categories With Corresponding Examples From
Transcripts of Interviews

I. Initiating Comments

Ex.　I:　Okay, you were the first one to start talking there. Can you tell me a little about that?
　　　S:　Well, that was really, really, I think she should change it . . . so I feel like this—if nobody's talking I should like start. [Daisy (2), 159–162]

II. Not Initiating Comments

Ex.　I:　But you don't say anything this time.
　　　S:　No, because it didn't work the last time I say it. [Clara (4), 902–903]

III. Responding to Peer Comments: Agree

Ex.　I:　Do you usually agree with Yaowanee's comments?
　　　S:　Well, most of the time I agree with her because. . . . [Lin (5), 138–139]

IV. Responding to Peer Comments: Disagree

　　　I:　Okay, do you agree with what they're saying?
　　　S:　No, because he say like the paragraph is too long . . . and I have to separate it. [Clara (3), 684–687]

V. Effectiveness of Comments

Ex.　I:　Do you think Yaowanee understands what you are saying?
　　　S:　I don't think so. (Lin (5), 414–415)

VI. Feelings in Group

A.　Toward self
Ex.　S:　I feel better about them and now I think I'm relaxed and sometimes I joke, sometimes. [Clara (4), 85–86]
B.　Toward others
Ex.　S:　Yeah, I don't want to hurt him. [Lin (2), 88]

VII. Comparison to Groups in PRC/Taiwan

Ex.　I:　If this group were in Taiwan, would it work?
　　　S:　It would seem kind of strange. . . . it's just we feel so embarrassed to change our papers. [Daisy (2), 396–408]

Note.　This chapter is an analysis of categories I–IV only.

1983), the topic being the coding categories that had emerged from the preliminary analysis. This inductive analysis ultimately yielded a description of the key informants' (Chinese students') perceptions of their construction of peer response group interactions. It is important to emphasize here that the transcripts that were transcribed, coded, and analyzed were of the interview sessions, not the peer response group sessions.

ANALYSIS AND DISCUSSION

In Group A, the two men, Hussein and Carlos, often engaged in interactions that excluded the two women, Clara and Aeenoy. Clara commented on feeling excluded by the men, and also on her close relationship to Aeenoy, resulting (according to Clara), from their both being female and Asian. Group B appeared to be the least cohesive of the groups; the group's interactions were characterized by long silences and restlessness. Alma, a woman from Argentina, talked the most and seemed to dominate the group, in part, because neither Ahmad or Daisy talked much. Ahmad appeared to withdraw from the group early in the quarter and participated only marginally. Daisy, the informant from Taiwan, participated in the group's interactions, but she seemed uncomfortable and resistant. Group C was perhaps the most cohesive and the students appeared to truly enjoy their interactions. The relationship between Lin, the second informant from Taiwan, and Yaowanee was close but it did not exclude Sasin or Jean.

The Chinese students were relatively active participants in the peer response groups, but the nature of that participation was constrained by the students' expressed sense of their goals for the group. Their primary goal was social—to maintain group harmony—and this goal affected the nature and types of interaction they allowed themselves in group discussions. When asked to describe her group, Lin mentioned first its social dimensions and last her sense of its pedagogical effectiveness. "I think we are very cooperative, and we are polite, and sometimes it's helpful" [Lin (6), 521].[2]

Initiating Comments

In their interactions with members of their peer response groups, the Chinese students generally preferred to respond to other group members rather than to initiate comments on their own, and initiating comments were minimal compared to response comments. When they did choose to initiate, however,

---

[2]The coding conventions are as follows: I = interviewer; S = student\key informant [informant's name (interview session), transcript line number(s)].

they tended to focus on two specific issues: facilitating group interactions and criticizing peers' essays.

Facilitating Group Interaction. The informants reported initiating conversations as a way of serving a facilitative social function. This concern for maintaining positive group relations tended to result in three types of initiating comments. First, informants indicated that they sometimes felt the need to begin the group discussion:

I   Okay, you were the first one to start talking there. Can you tell me a little bit about that?

S   Oh, well, that was really, . . . I think she, he should change it cause, so I feel like this—if nobody's talking, I should like start. [Daisy (2), 159–160]

Second, the Chinese participants expressed concerns about running out of time, and keeping the group on track:

I   Did you agree with her there? Do you remember?

S   Well, I think we, in fact, I don't agree we should spend so much time on discussing a word, so in the group, every time I tell a writer something, I just want to tell things that my problem is, so I seldom discuss a topic for very long time. . . . [Lin (5), 59–63]

The third facilitative social function served to stop arguments among other members of the group:

I   Couldn't they explain [about Jean's paper] for themselves?

S   Well, no, because I want to end the argument. [Lin (4), 171–172]

However, the Chinese students weren't always comfortable with the role of initiator. Clara clearly saw one contribution as an imposition on the group:

I   So, when you say "I have something more to say" and then you laugh. Why did you laugh?

S   Because I thought we [were] supposed to finish and it's just because [of] me, and then we had to stay a few minutes more. . . . It's like ask them to stay for a few minutes more and I laugh because it's—I don't know how to say it—it's my fault. [Clara (6), 724–729]

Criticizing Peers' Essays. More often, however, initiated comments focused on criticizing the essays—the primary function of peer response groups as understood by the Chinese students. When they did criticize a peer's essay, the informants tended to focus on major writing problems in a specific essay such as thesis statement, or else on general comments about introduction and conclusion, with no specific references.

For all three informants, the usual procedure in offering criticism was to begin first with a few positive statements:

> S   . . . first I want to give him the encouragement, and then I think this won't embarrass him, and then I will give him my opinion. Yeah, I think that is the best way. [Lin (2), 47–49]

Critical comments were expressed in a variety of ways, most of which were intended to make the criticism seem less harsh. The strategy most often reported by the informants was to reject a claim to authority. They felt that their comments were "only my opinion," a perspective that not only protected the writer's feelings, but also did not obligate the writer to make any changes:

> I   . . . you said "it's only my opinion."
> S   Yeah, that means you don't have to listen to that. [Lin (2), 125–127]

> I   So, do you feel that your point was a good point and was right?
> S   I think it was right, but . . . like everybody can have different opinions . . . it's okay. [Daisy (5), 202–204]

In the following exchange, Lin expressed clearly the balance she tried to maintain between the need to not hurt the writer's feelings or force the writer to change his work ("he has his own opinion"), and her need to say what she thinks about the essays:

> I   Why did you say "I have some questions" rather than just "You don't have to tell us the story"?
> S   Well, because he has his own opinion, yeah, so I don't want to change his mind, but I want to express myself. So I just tell him that's my question and can he explain it to me. But he did, and so I don't [say anymore]. Yeah,— What I want to say to him is I don't think you can change the story, but I don't want to say it to him because it hurts. [Lin (2), 63–69]

The informants' reluctance to offer criticism seemed to be based on their understanding of what it meant to be a peer reader, as opposed to a teacher or a critic:

> S   Yes, I gave up, and I think if next time I feel the same problem about his essay, I just give up.
> I   Because—

S   I think even a teacher cannot change [the writer] so fast. And it's really a process. It's improving a little bit every time. And if you want to improve like a big step, it's hard. And I'm not a teacher. I don't know how to teach, so I give up. [Clara (4), 1015–1022]

S   . . . when I wrote my essay, because— I think a lot and then I realize that I'm not a critic. I'm just a reader. If I read something, I cannot say, "Oh, the writer is wrong." . . . [Being a critical reader], I don't think, is a good idea. Because I think every time when I read something, he give me the information. But we don't have the right to judge it—especially for this essay—because we have different ideas. [Lin (3), 473–479]

In addition to rejecting a claim of authority to soften their criticism, informants also tended to speak indirectly, particularly through the use of questions as opposed to direct statements. However, these questions did not always have the desired effect of helping the writer recognize a problem in his or her writing. In one exchange Carlos interpreted Clara's criticism of his conclusion differently than Clara had intended:

I   Now why did you ask that question?

S   Because I didn't understand why he put the sentence in the conclusion.

I   Okay, so you understood the sentence but you didn't know why the sentence was in the conclusion?

S   Yeah, because there's no connection between the sentence to the conclusion or the paragraph.

I   Oh, okay, and when he explained to you what the sentence meant, did that satisfy you?

S   Hmmm, not a lot. [Clara (3), 823–840]

Another type of indirection that the Chinese students used to soften the criticism was to underspecify the writer's problem. This strategy, however, resulted in comments that were more often wishful than directive—comments that could have unforeseen consequences:

S   I think she know my meaning, my suggestion is, like, put more about personality. But I didn't ask her, like, where you can put this . . . I thought she might go home and do it. [Daisy (2), 106–110]

S   Carlos still has only one source about the movie and I think he doesn't know about it. . . . I think Carlos thought two examples from the movie [were two sources].

I   Oh, so he thinks that's like two sources.

S   Yeah, and I don't know how to explain to him. And then he says he will add another source from his own experience, and I say, "yeah, it will be good" and I think I don't have to explain to you about the two sources.

I   So, in other words, when you said that and when you say "that will be good" then he'll know that's what two sources are.

S   Yeah, I hope so. [Clara (6), 577–591]

S   We suggest to her last time that maybe she can omit some personal experience. Yeah, we didn't mention which one she should omit—because we think she knows that. But then she omit the wrong one! [Lin (2), 378–380]

When indirect comments about peers' essays were not understood as intended, the Chinese students tended not to have clarification strategies available to them. In the following exchange, Lin tried to tell Sasin politely what the problem was with his essay, and she was not quite sure how she could make her point after he failed to understand the criticism implied in her questions:

I   Now, you're trying to tell him. You said you still have some questions. And, well, what was the problem?

S   Well, I think because he give us the wrong information about the story. I don't agree with him. Yeah. So I just use the polite way to tell him, but he tried to explain it to me. I know the story, he need not to explain it for me. So I'm not . . . I don't know what should I do now. [Lin (2), 53–58]

In general, the Chinese students tended to initiate comments only rarely, voicing infrequent concerns about the dynamics of the group and making a few negative comments about their peers' essays. When the informants did criticize the essays, they tended to soften the comments by using various strategies intended to protect the writers' feelings and to avoid positioning themselves in the role of critic. However, these strategies often resulted in their comments being misunderstood by the writers, and as a result, tended to result in inadequate and ineffective feedback.

Not Initiating Comments

More often though, the Chinese students chose to remain silent rather than to initiate talk, although their reasons for remaining silent varied. At times, they chose not to talk about the content of their peers' drafts, and at other times, not to talk because of possible social consequences.

Content Issues. Sometimes they did not talk about the essays because they did not have anything to say:

I   So, what are you going to tell Jean here? That you think he should change it a little, or that . . .

S   Well, I didn't tell him. In fact, this time I just read his essay, and I didn't think about it, I just read it. So, I cannot give him any good suggestions. [Lin (6), 285–288]

Other times, they refrained from speaking because another person in the group had already said what they wanted to say:

I   Okay, so you didn't say, "Wait a minute, I didn't have my turn?"

S   No, because they already said what I want to say. [Clara, (5), 307–308]

Often the Chinese students were confused about the topic under discussion and/or could not find the item in their copies of their peers' papers. In these cases, they were generally reluctant to ask for the clarification that would allow them to participate in the discussion, and sat silently while either their peers talked or the discussion turned to another topic:

S   I didn't understand him.

I   Yeah, I'm having a hard time understanding him, too.

S   It confuses me.

I   Yeah, okay, but you just keep listening. You didn't say—

S   Yeah, it's better that he talk [until I hear] something I know, something clear.

I   Okay, so you're waiting till something appears. [Clara (4), 622–628]

I   So, did you ever say to her, "I don't understand your paper?"

S   Not really. Maybe I'm just don't get her idea. Maybe the teacher will. . . . [Daisy (2), 139–141]

Social Issues. The general reluctance to speak up when they were confused is matched by a reluctance to talk because of their concerns about the social consequences of their speaking. The Chinese students reported three general areas of concern about the social dimension of the peer response group: concern for feelings about themselves (particularly the need for self-protection); concern for the feelings of their peers (particularly the need to not hurt or embarrass the writer); and concern for a positive group climate.

In terms of feelings about themselves, the informants reported that they sometimes said nothing because they believed that their comments would be ineffectual:

S   If someone is defensive or reluctant to listen to me, I won't express myself. I just listen to him, and then I won't tell him anything. [Lin (2), 495–496]

Another Chinese student said nothing out of fear of retaliation:

I But you were thinking about it. Why didn't you say anything?

S Why? Well, I think if nobody raise this question, that means they all think the conclusion is okay. And then if I tell him, Oh, your conclusion too short, you should extend your idea, and then I think that's not good! Yeah, maybe they will say the same words to my conclusion. That's terrible! [Lin (2), 490–496]

These writers were equally concerned, though, for the writer's feelings. The Chinese informants did not want to embarrass the writer, and they sometimes felt that silence was the most polite response:

S The reason why I keep my questions [to myself] sometimes is . . . because some of them are quite tricky, . . . so I write it down. I don't want to embarrass the writer or arouse an argument. [Lin (5), 225–229]

I Okay, if a student's writing is bad, how do you react—with politeness or honesty?

S Politeness. [Daisy (2), 318–320]

S . . . But I think I am not a critic, so I don't need to tell him about this. But I really want!

I Oh, you really wanted to? Now why didn't you?

S I have no right to say he's wrong, to tell him he's wrong.

I It's politeness, right?

S It's not polite [to criticize]. [Lin (3), 207–218]

In addition, the Chinese students were reluctant to impose the burden of revision on the writers, possibly because of the potential implication that the writer had not tried hard:

S I didn't want to say you need to rewrite.

I Yeah, why?

S It's so hard for somebody to hear that, because I think Carlos tried his best to do this .. it's a hard job. . . . [Clara (4), 856–862]

One informant mentioned the dilemma inherent in encouraging the writer—the fear that an implied criticism of the previous essay would be hurtful:

S I think Yaowanee needed encouragement, but I don't know how to encourage her. Because if I say, "Oh, you really did a better job," that means I don't appreciate her last essays. I think that's hurt! [Lin (3), 308–311]

Concerns about not embarrassing or hurting their peers are reflected in the Chinese students' concerns for group harmony. In general, in spite of the few instances already mentioned, all three of these writers tended to defer to their peers to initiate a topic, and to begin and end the peer group sessions; none was the peer- or self-acknowledged leader of their respective groups. There seemed to be a collective sense among the informants that comments they initiated about peers' essays were intrusive and disruptive (or just plain wrong), and they preferred not to speak at all.

Responses to Peers' Comments

Chinese participants' contributions to group interaction came predominantly in the form of responses to peers' comments rather than in the form of initiation. In their responses, the Chinese students both agreed and disagreed with their peers, again showing the same concerns for group harmony by subordinating honesty to politeness.

Comments: Agreeing With Peers. The informants tended to listen to and seriously consider the comments their peers made about their (the informants') drafts. In general, the Chinese gave their peers a great deal of authority as illustrated by the interaction below:

I Do you usually agree with Yaowanee's comments [about your paper]?

S Well, most of the time I agree with her because, well, in fact, every time when they raise their comments, I listen to them and I will think about it. I seldom disagree. If one of them thinks it is a problem, I think maybe it is a problem because I am very careless . . . [Lin (5), 138–143]

As Lin's comments suggest, if peers mentioned problems in the informants' drafts, the informants tended to view whatever was mentioned as problems—as *their* problems as writers. This contrasts with the tendency already noted for the Chinese students to not initiate comments about their peers' drafts because they blamed themselves as readers for being confused. Clara reported not wanting to argue with Hussein about his essay because:

S I think it confuses me . . . because it's my problem.

I Okay, so you think Hussein's probably a good writer, but you're not a good reader.

S That's right.

I Okay.

S Because for me, the essay's too hard to read. [Clara (4), 263–269]

In other words, problems with informants' drafts were interpreted as writer problems, whereas problems with peers' drafts were interpreted as reader problems.

Responses in which the Chinese students agreed with peer comments were typically minimal verbal and nonverbal responses (e.g., nodding the head or smiling):

I   So you're just paying attention

S   That's right and I think because they're talking about the word and I agree with Hussein, so I don't have to do something special—like I just look. [Clara (5), 241–243]

In fact, the informants rarely voiced agreement with a peer who was discussing a group member's draft, even when they did agree with a particular point. One reason for this, as Clara reported, is that:

S   I just don't want to interrupt him, you know. And if he says something like I want to argue with, I would say, "yeah" at that time. But if I agree, I just keep it to myself. [Clara (3), 137–139]

In addition to not wanting to be intrusive, the informants were focused on attending to and seeking consensus in the group. It was important to the Chinese writers to both solicit agreement from other group members, and to agree with others' comments—even when they were not sure what those comments were:

I   What are you thinking? I mean, are you agreeing?

S   Yeah.

I   With what Sasin is saying?

S   Mmmm, well, I didn't notice what they are talking about.

I   You didn't know?

S   Yeah, so when Jean asked me I just, "Oh yeah." I just agreed with him. [Lin (3), 119–124]

The informants appeared to be pleased when they agreed with someone; agreement and consensus were clearly valued behaviors:

S   It feels really good, when I think I agree with somebody and that makes me happy too, and that's the same like if somebody agrees with me. [Clara (5), 138]

As noted earlier, the informants viewed criticizing essays as the primary function of peer response groups. Even though they viewed the group as serving a critical—and thus, a divisive—function, their behavior worked toward the maintenance of the group as a cohesive unit. Agreeing with peer comments facilitated positive social relationships, but even when they disagreed, the Chinese students worked hard to minimize potential conflict.

Comments: Disagreeing With Peers. All the informants reported that if they did not agree with a peer's comments, they would state their disagreement:

S   If I agree with somebody, I will say yes or I don't say anything. If I don't agree with somebody, I will argue with him. [Clara (5), 286–287]

Arguments, as Clara reported, are "good for the group" [Clara (1), 513]. However, in actuality, the informants did not frequently disagree with their peers, and when they did, they found ways to soften their criticism:

S   . . . I don't want Hussein to feel like— You say, "You're totally wrong and I'm correct." I don't want to say it that way.

I   So, how do you say it so that he doesn't feel that?

S   I think this way. You know, talk soft. [Clara (3), 175–178]

Furthermore, they tended to drop a point quickly if no one else agreed with them:

I   Did you raise the point again or did you let it drop?

S   Well, I persisted a little bit, but since they don't agree with me, so just think maybe I should give up.

I   Do you still think you're right?

S   Yeah. [Lin (6), 126–130]

Most often the Chinese writers attempted to provide an illusion of agreement, by simply writing down comments they disagreed with as if they agreed, or by treating a critical comment as a misunderstanding and creating an opportunity for explanation instead of argument. They also hedged their responses so that their peers would not be offended:

S   . . . Sometimes I say "Yeah." It means I understand what you said. [Lin (2), 373–374]

I   How do you respond to him?

S   I say, I understand what he means, but I didn't say I don't agree with you.

I   Okay, you didn't want to say you don't agree with him?

S   No.

I   Because—

S   Because it's really hard for me to say that I don't agree with someone.

I   Is it? Why?

S   It's really hard for me to . . . I think, I think if I said something like "I don't agree with you," it's like I'm really mad at him or her or really angry. [Clara (3), 740–753]

Although the Chinese students were quite proficient in finding creative solutions to potential conflict-inducing criticisms, they were far more likely not to verbalize their disagreement with comments their peers had made:

I   Okay, now you're saying, "yeah that's right."

S   Yes, right.

I   Why did you agree with Carlos there? Did you think that he needed support at that point?

S   Hmmmm, no. But Carlos say like . . . [the essay needs] more information about George's parents. I didn't agree with that.

I   Okay, when he said something that you didn't agree with, you didn't say anything.

S   Right.

I   But when he said something you did agree with, you did say something. [Clara (1), 727–736]

This exchange with Clara was typical of Chinese students' tendencies to avoid disagreeing with their peers. Their reasons for choosing not to disagree sometimes focused on pragmatic concerns. As they did when they chose not to initiate comments, at times the informants questioned their competence as readers of their peers' writing and, as a result, chose not to disagree with others' responses. In the following exchange, Lin reported her belief that she had interpreted her essay incorrectly (i.e., had a reader problem), rather than indicating that she recognized the possibility of two opposing views to the written text (or a writer problem):

S   Well, I feel a little bit embarrassed (laugh).

I   Oh really?

S   Yeah

I   Because you think that they're right or they're wrong or what? What do you think?

S   What do I think? Well, I don't think they are wrong. I think maybe the problem is in myself, yeah. So I accept their idea. [Lin (1), 271–277]

The informants also claimed lack of expertise as a reason for not agreeing with peers' comments. When Clara did not like the example that the writer had given to illustrate a point, she did not say anything because "I cannot think of another one [example] so I just gave up" [Clara (6), 201]. Another time, Clara had checked a word meaning in the dictionary but Hussein's argument made her question her information. She stopped arguing because "I'm not sure about this . . . and I didn't have the dictionary" [Clara (5), 107–111]. Lin mentioned her lack of English proficiency as a reason for not agreeing with a peer:

S   I think I cannot insist on my own opinion. I should be in the middle point. I am the reader, not the criticizer. . . .

I   Why are you not the critic?

S   Well, because I'm not the expert in English. Maybe if he write in Chinese, maybe I can give him my opinion, I can teach him how to write a good Chinese article. But now I am also a student. I'm just his classmate, his friend, so I just think, oh, I don't need to do that. I don't need to criticize. [Lin (3), 157–168]

Another pragmatic concern had to do with the fact that arguments took/wasted time:

I   [Carlos] doesn't agree. So, do you argue with him?

S   No, it's really too hard time to . . . Because he's— I know if I argue with him and he wouldn't change his idea and I would not change mine. It just wastes time. [Clara (1), 628–634]

Nevertheless, the usual reason the informants gave for not arguing with their peers centered around the need to maintain positive social relationships:

S   Sometimes I agree with him, but most of the time I don't think so.

I   Do you say that you disagree with him?

S   Yeah, I don't want to hurt him. [Lin (2), 86–88]

I   Later, do you tell her that you disagree?

S   I don't . . . well, it's hard to say like in front of her face, yeah—to say you are wrong; you need to change this, to change that. [Daisy (2), 39–48]

In addition to being aware of their peers' feelings, the informants were concerned about presenting themselves to the group in a favorable light. Sometimes they avoided arguments so as to not be seen as defensive or aggressive, perhaps being unwilling to set up conditions for conflict:

S   I didn't say anything to him.

I   Why not?

S   Because I don't want to be defensive. [Lin (2), 443–445]

I   Okay [you didn't argue] because you don't know each other very well yet?

S   Right. And this was the first time and I didn't want to be so aggressive. [Clara (1), 746–748]

Lin expressed clearly how her concerns for her and Sasin's feelings led her to remain silent about what she perceived as a problem with Sasin's draft:

I   Because you said that in the beginning he didn't have a thesis.

S   Well, I didn't tell him, but I write it on my response form, because I think if I tell him [that] it's not a thesis, it's a topic, I don't think [the] other students will agree with me, so I just give him a suggestion that you should think about your topic because it's not really a thesis statement.

I   Okay. I'm going to say this again, just to make sure I've got it. You didn't say that he didn't have a thesis because you were afraid the others would disagree with you, so instead you just wrote it on the form, okay? Why were you nervous about the others disagreeing with you?

S   Well (laugh) because I think it will arouse a big argument about it. . . .

I   Why is an argument bad?

S   Well, I think if I tell him that's only a topic, it's not a thesis statement . . . I think it will be embarrassing for Sasin. . . .

I   . . . when the group gets into an argument, how does that make you feel?

S   Argument? (laugh); well, I just try to end this argument . . . if they will argue, if it's very serious or even fight, I will hide myself (laugh).

I   You'll hide yourself.

S   Yeah, I think it's very terrible. [Lin (5), 171–200]

CONCLUSION

In peer response groups, students share their drafts with each other "as the drafts are developing in order to get guidance and feedback on their writing" (Leki, 1993, p. 22). It is assumed or hoped that the guidance or feedback will result in improved compositions. But what happens if, during peer response group interactions, few suggestions are made? What happens if the students are more interested in maintaining positive group relations than in helping each other with their writing?

The results of this study support the argument that the kinds of behaviors that Chinese students would normally exhibit in groups are different from the behaviors that are frequently desired in writing groups. Although the students in this study perceived the goal of the writing group as criticizing each other's drafts, they were reluctant to do so, recognizing, it seems, that making negative comments on a peer's draft leads to division, not cohesion, in a group. It would trivialize the complexity of the students' interactions to sum them up in a sentence or two; however, it seems clear that, for the most part, the Chinese students were more concerned with the groups' social dimension than with providing their peers with suggestions to improve their essays. It would be interesting to find out if and/or how these issues relate to Chinese students' written texts. For example, in writing argumentative essays, do Chinese students tend to take a middle rather than an extreme position? This question calls for further research.

REFERENCES

Bond, M. (1986). *The psychology of the Chinese people.* Oxford, England: Oxford University Press.

Brown, G., & Yule, G. (1983). *Discourse analysis.* Cambridge, England: Cambridge University Press.

Carson, J. (1992). Becoming biliterate: First language influences. *Journal of Second Language Writing, 1,* 37–60.

Carson, J., & Nelson, G. (1994). Writing groups: Cross-cultural issues. *Journal of Second Language Writing, 3,* 17–30.

Clark, G., & Doheny-Farina, S. (1990). Public discourse and personal experience: A case study in theory-building. *Written Communication, 7,* 456–481.

Erickson, F., & Schultz, J. (1982). *The counselor as gatekeeper: Social interaction in interviews.* New York: Academic Press.

Erickson, F., & Wilson, J. (1982). *Sights and sounds of life in schools: A resource guide to film and videotape for research and education.* East Lansing: Michigan State University, Institute for Research on Teaching of the College of Education.

Hofstede, G. (1984). *Culture's consequences: International differences in work-related values.* Beverly Hills, CA: Sage.

Hofstede, G. (1991). *Cultures and organizations: Software of the mind.* New York: McGraw-Hill.

Hu, W., & Grove, C. (1991). *Encountering the Chinese.* Yarmouth, ME: Intercultural Press.

Leki, I. (1989). *Academic writing: Techniques and tasks.* New York: St. Martin's Press.

Leki, I. (1993). Reciprocal themes in reading and writing. In J. Carson & I. Leki (Eds.), *Reading in the composition classroom: Second language perspectives* (pp. 9–33). Boston: Heinle & Heinle.

Mittan, R. (1989). The peer review process: Harnessing students' communicative power. In D. M. Johnson & D. M. Roen (Eds.), *Richness in writing: Empowering ESL students* (pp. 207–219). New York: Longman.

Triandis, H. C. (1988). Collectivism vs. individualism: A reconceptualization of a basic concept in cross-cultural social psychology. In G. K. Verma & C. Bagley (Eds.), *Personality, cognition, and values: Cross-cultural perspectives on childhood and adolescence* (pp. 60–95). London: Macmillan.

Triandis, H. C. (1989). The self and social behavior in differing cultural contexts. *Psychological Review, 96*, 506–520.

Triandis, H. C., Brislin, R., & Hui, C. H. (1988). Cross-cultural training across the individualism-collectivism divide. *International Journal of Intercultural Relations, 12*, 269–289.

Trueba, H., & Wright, P. (1980/1981). On ethnographic studies and multicultural education. *NABE Journal, 5*(2), 29–56.

Yin, R. K. (1984). *Case study research: Design and methods.* Beverly Hills, CA: Sage.

Zander, A. (1983). The value of belonging to a group in Japan. *Small Group Behavior, 14*, 3–14.

PART TWO

COMPOSING
GENDER IDENTITY

CHAPTER SIX

Gender and Language Variation in Written Communication

Duane H. Roen
Chere Peguesse
Valentina Abordonado

"When the lamb takes place of the lion as the emblem of nations, both women and men will be as children of one spirit, perpetual learners of the word and doers thereof, not hearers only".

—Margaret Fuller, 1843/1979, p. 1420)

BACKGROUND

Terminology

Before turning to a discussion of politeness strategies in written discourse, we offer a brief note on terminology. The distinction between the terms *gender* and *sex* has been noted recently (Deaux & Major, 1990; Poynton, 1985; Roen & Johnson, 1992; Schor, 1992). However, Rhode (1990) reminded us of the interdependence of social and biological factors. In a fashion similar to West and Zimmerman (1991), Scott (1988) explained that gender is "a social category imposed on a sexed body" (p. 32).

Although agreeing on the distinction, Coates and Cameron (1988) preferred the term *sex* to describe the social catagory because *gender* has a technical meaning for linguistics. In this study, we use both terms: *sex* to denote biological differences, and *gender*, as McConnell-Ginet (1985) did, to refer to the "complex of social, cultural, and psychological phenomena attached to sex" (p. 76). Chodorow (1989), Thorne and Henley (1975), and Hymes (1974) agreed with McConnell-Ginet's observation that the term *gen-*

113

der "suggests an arbitrariness of conventionality in the sociocultural construction of the (nonsexual) significance of sex and sexuality" (p. 77).

As a part of our work in feminist theory, we wish to discover whether certain patterns of language use or evaluations of those patterns has become conventionally associated with males or females in this culture. Our purpose is to revalue the "feminine" voice as a powerful way of knowing (Belenky, Clinchy, Goldberger, & Tarule, 1986; Chodorow, 1989; Showalter, 1978, 1985).

Gender and Politeness

The theoretical framework basic to our research is Brown and Levinson's (1978) sociolinguistic theory of politeness. This theory is useful for the analysis of politeness strategies in persuasive discourse as they are used to redress face-threatening acts (FTAs).[1] Since the initial articulation of this paradigm in 1978, it has been the key to a wide range of empirical studies. It has also been cited more than 200 times in the sociolinguistic literature as an important construct of cross-cultural communication studies. In Brown and Levinson's terms, people use language to address face concerns. Positive face is a person's need to be approved of by others or to have one's goals thought well of by others. For example, one of the students in our study wrote, "In reply to your anti-smoking letter, I am deeply moved and very dearly appreciate your overwhelming concern" (Paper No. 35). This conveys approval and an attempt to establish social solidarity with the school nurse to whom students wrote. In the context of persuasive writing, it also functions as a redress to an FTA.

Johnson (1992) explained that in peer reviews, FTAs are of two types. Although our study focuses on persuasive letters, the definitions still apply. First, the entire act of writing the letter is considered a face-threatening act because what often appears is negative criticism or strong disagreement. The entire act of letter writing, then, is hereafter referred to as a *global FTA*. Within the letter, writers use specific strategies such as questions, suggestions, and individual criticisms to persuade. These are referred to as *specific FTA*s. Brown and Levinson (1978) maintained that there are certain social principles that guide human communication. To select strategies, we assess the seriousness of an FTA by taking into consideration interpersonal factors such as social distance (D), power (P), and perceived (rank) degree of imposition (R), and a complex host of other audience factors such as affect.

In our study of gender and politeness, two recent analyses of sex differences in spoken compliments are most applicable here. In a study of New

---

[1]As endnoted in Johnson (1992), Kasper (1990) observed that a theory approaching politeness strategies as only redressing FTAs is a rather negative and paranoid view of human communication.

Zealand English, Holmes (1988) found that women gave significantly more compliments than did men. In addition, both men and women complimented women more than they did men. Herbert (1990) had similar results in a larger New York study. Both scholars suggested that compliments generally serve different functions for men and women; that is, compliments predominately work for women as offers of solidarity, whereas they function more often for men as actual assertions of praise.

Gender and Oral Language

The most well-known study of gender differences in language is Robin Lakoff's early work, *Language and Woman's Place* (1975). Although it has been widely criticized for its lack of empirical evidence, Coates (1986) noted that "it is the work that for many people marks the beginning to twentieth-century linguistic interest in sex differences" (p. 18). Although subsequent empirical research has not supported all of Lakoff's early claims, the body of research does suggest that mens' language use tends to be task-oriented, proactive, and dominant, and womens' tends to be social-emotional, reactive, and supportive (Aries, 1987; Gilligan, 1982).

Modeled on Gumperz and Cook-Gumperz's (1982) work on interethnic misunderstanding, Maltz and Borker (1982) claimed that differences arise out of different sociolinguistic subcultures. They found, along with Coates (1988b) and Tannen (1990a, 1990b) that the "most significant difference between male and female communicative competence is that men's conversational style is based on competitiveness, while women's is based on co-operativeness" (Coates, 1988b, p. 70).

Gender and Writing

Although much of the work in gender and language has focused on speech (Henley & Kramarae, 1991; Holmes, 1991; Preisler, 1986; Thorne, Kramarae, & Henley, 1983), scholars have also observed variations in written discourse. Early studies suggested that female students prefer connected modes of discourse whereas male students favor writing tasks emphasizing autonomy. For instance, Emig (1971) found that female twelfth graders preferred expressive writing assignments whereas male age-mates favored informative writing tasks. Britton, Burgess, Martin, McLeod, and Rosen (1975) also found that women liked to write for an audience of trusted adults whereas men preferred an audience of teacher evaluators. Keroes (1990) provided recent evidence suggesting that women are more likely to select topics focusing on interpersonal relationships whereas men tend to choose topics emphasizing more autonomous themes.

In addition to gender differences in student writing, research spanning several decades has revealed that gender stereotypes may influence the way teachers respond to student writing. For example, secondary teachers tend to evaluate female writing more favorably than male writing (Baker, 1954; Donelson, 1963; Martin, 1970, 1972; National Assessment of Educational Progress, 1980; Roen, 1992; Stalnaker, 1941; Woodward & Phillips, 1967). Roulis (1990) also found that university-level instructors rate female writers higher on socio-intellectual, aesthetic, and cooperative factors. Of course, some of these results may indicate that particular groups of women do, indeed, write more effectively than men do.

Gender and Persuasive Discourse

In an attempt to articulate differences in women's and men's argumentative styles, Farrell (1979) defined a female mode of rhetoric that he said is less inclined toward closure and less likely to rely on antithesis to structure reasoning. He also characterized this mode as low-key, integrative, supportive, and open-ended. Finally, he noted that female rhetoric is less concerned with maintaining boundaries because of its generative-process orientation and respect for audience. However, Farrell betrayed an underlying patriarchal view in a conclusion that privileges male modes of rhetoric in the writing classroom.

Gearhart (1979) rejected what she termed "the insidious violence" of the belief in rhetoric as persuasion. As an alternative to this conquest/conversion model of rhetoric, she proposed a dialogic model of communication concerned with listening and receiving in a collective rather than a competitive mode. She suggested the metaphor of the womb or matrix to describe an ideal communication environment where an idea can be nurtured and where growth and change can take place.

Similarly, Taylor (1978) lamented the negative criticism that women endure for expressing themselves in language considered too personal to maintain a keen argumentative edge. She suggested that such writing would no longer be considered a liability if writing teachers were more flexible about acceptable argumentative styles.

Flynn (1988) proposed that these stylistic differences may be attributable to women's affiliative rather than competitive interests. Flynn suggested that women may rely on identification and collaboration to resolve conflict. Lunsford and Ede (1990) also endorsed collaboration as a "feminine" mode of composing.

Lynch and Strauss-Noll (1987) found that both male and female first-year college students produced argumentative essays that were judged to be "forceful" or "mild." Perhaps these findings can be explained by what Coates (1986) called "psychological androgyny." Coates observed that American women college students tend to score high on both masculine and feminine psychological dimensions because androgynous behavior offers numerous rewards in contemporary society. In spite of these mixed and inconclusive findings on argumentative styles of writing, recent scholarship has continued to criticize agonistic modes of argumentation in favor of a feminist writing pedagogy (Cooper, 1989; Flynn, 1988; Gearhart, 1979; Lamb, 1991). Teich (1987, 1992), for instance, advocated Rogerian principles of communication and communication for teaching writing.

Explanations for Gender Differences

Much of the current scholarship on gender and language has attempted to explain gender differences. Nancy Chodorow (1978) hypothesized that, as a result of being parented primarily by a woman, men and women develop different gender identities. Through their early relationship with their mother, women develop a sense of self that is continuous with others. Men, on the other hand, develop a sense of self based on denial of this relationship. Thus, the female gender identity is based on a basic sense of connectedness, whereas the male gender identity is grounded in the belief in a separate self.

Building on Chodorow's (1978) work, Gilligan (1982) proposed that women's epistemologies are grounded in an ethic of care and responsibility rather than an ethic of autonomy and justice. Belenky, Clinchy, Goldberger, and Tarule (1986) grouped women's perspectives on knowing into five major epistemological stances: silence, received knowledge, subjective knowledge, procedural knowledge, and constructed knowledge.

Three theories of gender differences have emerged from recent studies. The first theory posits that linguistic differences might be the result of subcultural differences (Maltz & Borker, 1982; Tannen, 1982). This theory is particularly useful for describing variations within same-sex groups. However, Poynton (1985) considered this theory inadequate for describing variations in mixed-sex groups that she claimed are more accurately characterized as differences in power (see also West, 1984; West & Zimmerman, 1977). As Poynton observed, "men are culturally legitimated as powerful and women are not. . . . Hence, relations between women and men are culturally defined as between powerful and powerless and this shows up linguistically in a variety of ways" (pp. 84–85). Miller (1976) extended Poynton's claim with the contention that women are repositories of qualities of affiliativeness, relatedness, empathy, and nurturance that are devalued and distorted in male-dominant culture and by men. Therefore, she recommended that women reclaim and revalorize these qualities.

The third theory of interest to current scholars is the psychological gender role or gender schema theory. This theory posits that an individual's gender orientation rather than his or her biological sex is the most important factor influencing written production (Bem, 1974, 1981). Rubin and Greene (1992) found tentative support for this hypothesis, suggesting the need for further research in this area.

METHOD

Participants

The participants were 71 eleventh-grade English students enrolled in three sections in a predominately middle-class, White suburban high school in the upper Midwest. Of these 71 students, 32 (45.1%) were girls, and 39 (54.9%) were boys. They were the same participants described by Piché and Roen (1987) in an earlier study of cognition and writing.

Procedures and Instruments

In some cases, we used some of the same scores derived by Piché and Roen (1987). Based on previous studies of male and female discourse practices in speech, we added a number of our own scores, such as politeness strategies (Brown & Levinson, 1978), polite questions (Goody, 1978; Keenan, Schieffelin, & Pratt, 1978), hedging, ways of knowing (Belenky et al., 1986), personal involvement, and the use of intensifiers. Unlike Piché and Roen, our primary lens for analysis was the gender of the writer.

Writing Task. As described by Piché and Roen (1987) in more detail than space allows here, the 71 students wrote persuasive letters in response to a letter written by a school nurse who argued that a particular fictitious high school should not establish a smoking lounge for students because doing so would constitute condoning or even encouraging an unhealthy activity.

Quality of Writing. Three trained independent judges first assigned each paper a holistic score (1–5) for overall quality. In a second reading, the same three judges each assigned scores (1–7) for six analytic features: coherence, organization, sentence structure, logic, grammaticality, and vocabulary. Spearman-Brown split-half reliability coefficients (Specht & Bubolz, 1986) indicated high levels of interrater reliability on the holistic scores (.958), as well as for the analytic scores: coherence (.847), organization (.829), sentence structure (.771), logic (.835), grammaticality (.743), and vocabulary (.796).

TABLE 6.1
Example Politeness Strategies

P1:	Validate nurse's point and then drive home own point ("I agree that smoking is dangerous to your health, but I also do believe that a student should have the right to smoke if he wants to."—Paper No. 20).
P2:	Express understanding ("Your anti-smoking campaign may help a lot of students and we do not feel you should stop this action."—Paper No. 13).
P3:	Seek nurse's understanding ("Wouldn't it be better to have the smoking area than to have people smoking in the bathrooms?"—Paper No. 11).
P4:	Express consensus or agreement (". . . personal health and smoking laws are very serious things."—Paper No. 10).
P5:	Seek consensus, agreement, or support ("I hope you understand me and go along with me."—Paper No. 25).
P6:	Express appreciation or thanks ("Thank you again for your letter"—Paper No. 23).
P7:	Reference to future resolution, consensus, or understanding ("If you have any suggestions of what we can do, please tell us."—Paper No. 44).
P8:	Express support ("I would like you to know that I support your efforts."—Paper No. 5).
P9:	Express understanding but disagree ("We are sorry you have such strong objections to our proposal, but . . ."—Paper No. 15; or "I understand that smoking can be harmful to your health but . . ."—Paper No. 24).

Politeness Units. We have defined "politeness unit" as a phrase or group of phrases that contain certain polite discourse strategies. A common strategy was to precede a disagreement with an agreement (AGREE + DISAGREE). For example, one student in the study wrote: "I know a person's health is very important, but please remember and consider that everyone is different, whether you approve of it or not" (Paper No. 19). This student tries to create a point of identification while at the same time disagreeing with the nurse. Another polite discourse strategy was to acknowledge the legitimacy/validity of the addressee's points, arguments, or concerns. One student wrote: "We are glad that there are people like you that will give their opinion on such matters" (Paper No. 23).

As suggested to us by Donna Johnson,[2] we used the coding system outlined in Table 6.1 to rate other rhetorical strategies of politeness units.

These politeness units were occasionally two or more phrases or sentences long, with several politeness strategies strung together. Subtle distinctions separated some of the aforementioned strategies. For example, the categories P1 and P9 were similar, and called for close reading. The statement "We are truly sorry for our disagreement and hope that in the future we can please you on other issues" (Paper No. 15) shows sympathy to the nurse, but covertly disagrees. This was categorized as P9, expresses understanding but disagrees. A P1 statement, on the other hand, involves more subtlety: "Having an opinion like yours is fine, but other students have their opinions too, and should be treated equally" (Paper No. 12). This statement attempts to validate the nurse's

---

[2]We wish to thank Donna Johnson for her comments on an earlier version of this chapter.

point, but drives home the point that everyone's opinion is equally valid. As our analysis progressed, we noticed a high amount of distinctly impolite elements. Some attempts definitely failed to be effective as polite: "Your concern is reasonable, but ancient" (Paper No. 60).

Hedges. We analyzed the students' use of hedges in their persuasive letters to the school nurse. Specifically, we identified hedges that appeared in negative criticisms, complaints, requests, promises, offers, suggestions, insults, assertions, and agreement. Listed in Table 6.2 are examples of hedges in each of these categories.

Questions. Using a scheme suggested by Goody (1978) and Keenan et al. (1978), we examined eight kinds of questions: implying the ignorance of the writer, transferring initiative to the addressee, expressing interest in the addressee, masking a command or assertion, making a joking challenge, making a greeting, seeking agreement, and asking for pure information. Of these eight kinds of questions, we only found instances of four types:

1. PI: Asking for pure information ("How about us non-smokers? Where would we go?"—Paper No. 30).
2. D1: (Deference) Implying ignorance of speaker ("Isn't it against the law?"—Paper No. 30).
3. D4: (Deference) Masking a command or assertion, questioning authority ("Wouldn't it be better to have the smoking area than to have people smoking in the bathrooms?"—Paper No. 11).

TABLE 6.2
Example Hedges

HNC:	Hedge on a negative criticism ("I do not think you gave it enough thought."—Paper No. 65).
HC:	Hedge on a complaint [We did not find any instances of this hedge in the data].
HR:	Hedge on a request ("Please remember and consider that everyone is different."—Paper No. 19).
HP:	Hedge on a promise ("We really don't know what to say to you on this matter except that we will not comment until the school comes up with some kind of debate."—Paper No. 23).
HO:	Hedge on an offer [We did not find any instances of this hedge in the data].
HS:	Hedge on a suggestion ("Just give the students a chance to stand up and defend their rights."—Paper No. 12).
HINS:	Hedge on an insult ("I feel you should keep your stupid nose out of other people's business."—Paper No. 17).
HAP:	Hedge on an assertion of a proposition ("I believe, along with other members of the student council, that smoking or not smoking should be left up to the individual."—Paper No. 24).
HSA:	Hedge on a statement of agreement. ("I can understand your strong objection to smoking."—Paper No. 22).

4. R3: (Rhetorical) Seeking agreement or consensus ("After all, are students not people? Don't people not have rights to make their own choices?"—Paper No. 24).

By posing the first question, the student is apparently seeking the reader's agreement. The second question masks an assertion about student rights.

Intensifiers. As Roen and Johnson (1992) and Wolfson (1989b) noted, the literature on politeness theory also suggests that women intensify their compliments more than men do in English in the United States. In their study of peer reviews, Roen and Johnson expected the use of intensifiers to be generally less because of the "greater formality of the academic setting, the seriousness of the topic, the written modality, and the situational equality of the participants" (p. 41). They found, however, that women did use significantly more compliment intensifiers (such as "very interesting" and "really enjoyed") than did men in peer reviews.

Personal Involvement. Like Roen and Johnson (1992), we used Chafe and Danielwicz's (1987) methodology to examine personal involvement. We assessed the degree of explicit reference to oneself as measured by the use of first-person pronouns *I, me, we, us,* and *our,* as well as the degree of explicit reference to the addressee as measured by the use of second-person pronouns *you* and *yourself.* We assessed personal focus on the self or the addressee in the third-person reference by coding the use of the possessive pronouns *my* and *your,* as in "your paper." We summed occurrences of first-, second-, and third-person reference to yield an overall indicator of personal involvement.

Ways of Knowing. We scored each persuasive letter holistically, using a coding scheme based on the epistemological stances described by Belenky et al. (1986): silence, received knowledge, subjective knowledge, procedural knowledge-separate, procedural knowledge-connected, and constructed knowledge.

RESULTS AND DISCUSSION

Assessments of Writing Quality

We used a multivariate analysis of variance (MANOVA) procedure to examine whether the 39 male and 32 female students' persuasive letters differed on seven measures of writing quality: overall quality, coherence, organization, sentence structure, logic, grammaticality, and vocabulary. We first calculated a Hotelling's T^2 for all seven variables because we had found relatively strong correlations among the measures of quality, ranging from a low of r = .7998 to a high of .9464, with p values of .000 for all of the correlations. The observed value of Hotelling's T^2 did not quite reach significance (F = 1.864, p = .091), although, as Table 6.3 indicates, univarate tests revealed that females' and males' letters differed on six of the seven measures. What the multivariate and univaritate tests indicate, when considered together, is that the seven measures of quality may not be independent of one another.

As Table 6.4 reports, a t test indicated that girls wrote letters that were significantly and substantially longer than those written by boys. Length, incidentally, correlated significantly with overall quality (r = .5834, p = .000).

That girls in this study outscored boys on these measures of persuasive writing comes as little surprise. Among those who have previously reported women's superior performance on a variety of writing tasks is Stalnaker (1941), who examined gender differences in essays that secondary students wrote for the College Entrance Examination Board in 1940. In a sample of 3,879 boys and 2,178 girls, with mean scores of 485 and 527, respectively, the difference of 42 points was, in Stalnaker's words, "large and significant" (p. 533). This is consistent with Maccoby and Jacklin's (1974) observation that girls, from about age 10 to college age, in general, outperform boys in

TABLE 6.3
Quality Measures of Boys' and Girls' Persuasive Letters

Variable	n	M	SD	F	f
OVERALL QUALITY					
Boys	39	9.385	4.037	−3.15	.002
Girls	32	12.344	3.815		
COHERENCE					
Boys	39	10.282	3.220	−1.64	.106
Girls	32	11.781	4.470		
ORGANIZATION					
Boys	39	9.821	3.493	−2.40	.018
Girls	32	11.906	3.771		
SENTENCE STRUCTURE					
Boys	39	10.667	3.190	−3.22	.002
Girls	32	13.063	3.026		
LOGIC					
Boys	39	10.128	3.427	−2.91	.005
Girls	32	12.594	3.688		
GRAMMATICALITY					
Boys	39	11.539	2.634	−2.73	.008
Girls	32	13.438	3.232		
VOCABULARY					
Boys	39	11.385	2.612	−2.90	.005
Girls	32	13.281	2.899		

Note. df = 1,69.

TABLE 6.4
Length of Boys' and Girls' Persuasive Letters

Variable	n	M	SD	t	df	p
LENGTH (WORDS)						
Boys	39	132.5641	42.609	−3.46	69	.001
Girls	32	169.4375	47.053			

verbal skills. It is also congruent with Kaestle's (1991) comment that "on most measures of rudimentary and middle-level literacy in the past century, women have outperformed men" (p. 124). Results from the National Assessment of Educational Progress (NAEP; Applebee, Langer, & Mullis, 1986, 1990; NAEP, 1980) indicate that adolescent girls normally outperform boys on a variety of writing tasks. In 1969, 1974, and 1979 (NAEP, 1980) girls wrote better papers than boys did in narration, explanation, and, as in our current study, persuasion.

Regarding the average length of the letters, the results are consonant with other studies that have found greater fluency (or verbosity) among women (Labrant, 1933). This finding corresponds to common stereotypes about women's and men's language use (Poynton, 1985; Spender, 1980).

In general, our results are consistent with Goodwin and Goodwin's (1987) observation, in a study of oral argument, that "girls are not only just as skilled in argument as boys but have types of arguments that are both more extended and more complex in their participation structure than those among boys" (p. 200).

Politeness

We next examined the extent to which the male and female participants used politeness strategies (Brown & Levinson, 1978) in addressing the school nurse: validating nurse's point and then driving own point home, expressing understanding, seeking understanding, expressing consensus or agreement, seeking consensus or agreement, expressing appreciation or thanks, referring to future resolution, expressing support, and expressing understanding but disagreeing. We again calculated a Hotelling's T^2 statistic, which yielded a nonsignificant level of significance ($F = .927$, $p = .508$). Further, as Table 6.5 indicates, only two of the univariate analyses yielded significant differences (seeking understanding, expressing appreciation or thanks), even though girls had higher scores on seven of the nine measures of politeness.

We also examined the frequencies of boys' and girls' uses of opening and closing politeness strategies. A chi-squared analysis indicated no significant gender difference in the presence or absence of opening politeness strategies. However, girls were significantly more likely to use closing politeness strategies (χ_2 [$df = 1$] = 4.469, $p = .0345$). A chi-squared analysis of

TABLE 6.5
Politeness Strategies in Boys' and Girls' Persuasive Letters

Variable	n	M	SD	F	p
SEEKING UNDERSTANDING					
Boys	39	.1282	.409	4.658	.034
Girls	32	.3750	.554		
EXPRESSING APPRECIATION OR THANKS					
Boys	39	.2051	.570	4.524	.037
Girls	32	.5625	.840		

Note. df = 1,69.

the use of framing strategies (the presence of both an opening and closing politeness strategy) yielded no significant differences; both girls and boys tended not to use them.

Questions

We further examined the use of questions as politeness strategies as Goody (1978) and Keenan et al. (1978) did. Specifically, we looked at eight kinds of questions: implying the ignorance of the writer, transferring initiative to the addressee, expressing interest in the addressee, masking a command or assertion, a joking challenge, a greeting, seeking agreement, and asking for pure information. In our first attempt to calculate a MANOVA, we discovered that we could not test four of the question types (transfering initiative to the addressee, joking challenge, greeting, asking for pure information) because they were variables that were linearly dependent on others. In the subsequent MANOVA, in which we eliminated those four question types (which left implying the ignorance of the writer, expressing interest in the addressee, masking a command or assertion, and seeking agreement), the Hotelling's T^2 did not reach of level of significance ($F = .880$, $p = .481$). None of the univariate tests yielded significant results.

The results related to politeness units do not offer much support for the commonly made observation that women tend to use them more often than men do, for we did not find a consistency of significant differences in such language usage. If we consider the women's politeness units in light of their significantly higher scores on language measures (coherence, sentence structure, grammaticality, and vocabulary), though, we might argue, as Deuchar (1988) did, that women use a variety of forms (e.g., politeness strategies, standard or even prestigious language) to attend to both the positive face of the addressee and their own positive face. Women may do so, Deuchar argued, because they possess less social power than do men.

Hedges

We next examined girls' and boys' uses of hedges in their persuasive letters to the school nurse. In particular, we looked at hedging of negative criticism, complaints, requests, promises, offers, suggestions, insults, assertions, and agreement. In our first attempt at calculaing a MANOVA, we discovered that one of the types of hedges, hedging an offer, was linearly dependent on others. We removed that type of hedge from the subsequent MANOVA. In that subsequent test, Hotelling's T^2 did reach significance ($F = 2.225$, $p = .037$). We then ran univariate tests on the eight types of hedges. Of these, only hedging on assertions yielded significant results. (See Table 6.6.) We next combined several logically related kinds of hedges, as described by Brown and Levinson (1978): hedging threats to other's positive face, hedging threats to other's negative face, hedging threats to own positive face, and hedging threats to own negative face. To do this, we summed several logically related hedges into the following categories suggested by Brown and Levinson: (a) hedging threats to other's positive face: hedges on negative criticism + hedges on complaints + hedges on suggestions + hedges on insults + hedges on assertions of propositions; (b) hedging threats to other's negative face: hedges on requests + hedges on suggestions; (c) hedging threats to own positive face: hedges on suggestions + hedges on assertions of propositions; and (d) hedging threats to own negative face: hedges on promises + hedges on offers. In this case, a MANOVA yielded a significant level for Hotelling's T^2 ($F = 2.663$, $p = .040$). In the subsequent univariate analyses, as Table 6.6 indicates, two of these four analyses yielded significant results—hedging threats to other's and own positive face.

TABLE 6.6
Hedging Strategies in Boys' and Girls' Persuasive Letters

Variable	n	M	SD	F	p
HEDGING ASSERTIONS					
Boys	39	1.3333	1.737	−2.72	.008
Girls	32	2.4063	1.542		
HEDGING THREATS TO OTHER'S POSITIVE FACE					
Boys	39	1.8462	2.046	−2.35	.021
Girls	32	2.9063	1.673		
HEDGING THREATS TO OWN POSITIVE FACE					
Boys	39	1.9231	2.057	−2.08	.041
Girls	32	2.9063	1.890		

Note. $df = 1,69$.

These results, especially the last two dealing with positive face, support the observations of many scholars (Deuchar, 1988; Johnson & Roen, 1992; Roen & Johnson, 1992) whose research suggests that women do attend to positive face more than men do. There are are several possible reasons for this attention: women lack social power (Deuchar, 1988; Hekman, 1990; Poynton, 1989); they desire to facilitate verbal interaction (Coates, 1988a; Gilligan, 1982; Tannen, 1986); they live part of their lives in subcultures that differ from men's (Maltz & Borker, 1982; Tannen, 1990b).

Personal Involvement and Intensifiers

To examine personal involvement in the politeness strategies, we counted the number of first- and second-person pronouns that appeared within the politeness units described previously (except in questions). We also looked at the intensifiers that writers used. T-tests yielded no significant difference on any of these measures.

These results contradict those of earlier studies (Herbert, 1990; Johnson, 1989, 1992; Johnson & Roen, 1992; Roen & Johnson, 1992; Rubin & Greene, 1992; Wolfson, 1989a) that have found gender differences in personal involvement and intensifiers. It may be that in politeness strategies other than compliments personal involvement and intensifiers serve a less important interpersonal function (Halliday, 1978, 1985; Halliday & Hasan, 1985).

Epistemological Stance (Ways of Knowing)

We used Belenky, Clinchy, Goldberger, and Tarule's (1986) categories for ways of knowing to score each of the persuasive letters. A chi-squared analysis revealed that the distribution of scores for boys and girls was about the same ($\chi^2 = 3.128$, $df = 4$, $p = .537$). (See Table 6.7.)

Although our results do not directly substantiate this assertion, we have come to believe that one of the benefits of engaging students in writing, particularly persuasive writing, is that the activity encourages movement along the continuum from silence to constructed knowledge. Annas (1987) partially concurred by arguing that writing at least moves us beyond silence. One may be troubled that 47 of the 69 participants in the study wrote letters that were scored as subjectivist, but as Belenky noted (Ashton-Jones & Thomas, 1990), these students, like many of their age-mates probably have not been "asked to compare their view of things with external realities" (p. 287). Further, as Flynn (1991) noted, ". . . the movement toward mature writing or mature intellectual development is not simply a matter of moving from self toward other, from writer toward reader, but of integrating the self with the other, integrating writer and reader" (p. 175), which is no mean feat. She went on to suggest that writing teachers, "may have to coax students out of their habitual silence" (p. 175).

TABLE 6.7
Distribution of Ways-of-Knowing Scores for Boys and Girls

Ways of Knowing	Boys	Girls
Silence	0	0
Received	1	0
Subjective	27	20
Separate	2	2
Connected	9	9
Constructed	0	1
Totals	39	32

CONCLUSION

This study contributes to the growing body of research on gender and language in written discourse by examining specific politeness strategies that men and women use to persuade others. As Roen and Johnson (1992) noted, there are social consequences, both positive and negative, for using linguistic strategies associated with male and female language.

Whatever theory we might use to explain the kinds of gender differences that we found, Chodorow (1989) reminded us that gender differences must be represented as points on a continuum rather than as absolute dichotomies. Moreover, Chodorow insisted that these differences should be conceptualized as both psychologically and socially situated; these differences grow out of experience, learning, and self-definition in the family and in the culture. She also pointed out that these differences do not necessarily imply distinctness and separateness; rather, they represent a particular way of being connected to others. Finally, she noted that these differences are processual; they are created and situated rather than permanent.

ACKNOWLEDGMENTS

Duane thanks Gene L. Piché for many years of guidance and friendship. The three of us are grateful to him for the inspiration for this study. Maureen Roen helped us with the Margaret Fuller epigraph. Finally, we wish to express our appreciation to Donna M. Johnson, a colleague of the highest caliber.

REFERENCES

Annas, P. J. (1987). Silences: Feminist language research and the teaching of writing. In C. L. Caywood & G. R. Overing (Eds.), *Teaching writing: Pedagogy, gender, and equity* (pp. 3–17). Albany: State University of New York Press.

Applebee, A. N., Langer, J. A., & Mullis, I. V. S. (1986). *The writing report card: Writing achievement in American schools.* Princeton, NJ: National Assessment of Educational Progress/Educational Testing Service.

Applebee, A. N., Langer, J. A., & Mullis, I. V. S. (1990). *The writing report card, 1981–1988.* Princeton, NJ: National Assessment of Educational Progress/Educational Testing Service.

Aries, E. (1987). Gender and communication. In P. Shaver & C. Hendrick (Eds.), *Sex and gender* (pp. 149–176). Newbury Park, CA: Sage.

Ashton-Jones, E., & Thomas, D. K. (1990). Composition, collaboration, and women's ways of knowing: A conversation with Mary Belenky. *Journal of Advanced Composition, 10,* 275–292.

Baker, W. D. (1954). In investigation of characteristics of poor writers. *College Composition and Communication, 5,* 23–27.

Belenky, M., Clinchy, B., Goldberger, N., & Tarule, J. (1986). *Women's ways of knowing: The development of self, voice, and mind.* New York: Basic Books.

Bem, S. (1974). The measurement of psychological androgyny. *Journal of Consulting and Clinical Psychology, 42,* 155–162.

Bem, S. (1981). Gender schema theory: A cognitive account of sex typing. *Psychological Review, 88,* 354–364.

Britton, J., Burgess, T., Martin, N., McLeod, A., & Rosen, H. (1975). *The development of writing abilities (11–18).* London: Macmillan Education LTD.

Brown, P., & Levinson, S. (1978). Universals in language usage: Politeness phenomena. In E. N. Goody (Ed.), *Questions and politeness: Strategies in social interaction* (pp. 56–289). New York: Cambridge University Press.

Chafe, W., & Danielwicz, J. (1987). *Properties of spoken and written language* (Tech. Rep. No. 5.). Berkeley: University of California, Berkeley, and Pittsburgh, PA: Carnegie Mellon University.

Chodorow, N. J. (1978). *The reproduction of mothering: Psycholanalysis and the sociology of gender.* Berkeley: University of California Press.

Chodorow, N. J. (1989). *Feminism and psychoanalytic theory.* New Haven, CT: Yale University Press.

Coates, J. (1986). *Women, men, and language.* London: Longman.

Coates, J. (1988a). Gossip revisited: Language in all-female groups. In J. Coates & D. Cameron (Eds.), *Women in their speech communities* (pp. 94–122). New York: Longman.

Coates, J. (1988b). Introduction: Language and sex in connected speech. In J. Coates & D. Cameron (Eds.), *Women in their speech communities* (pp. 63–73). New York: Longman.

Coates, J., & Cameron, D. (Eds.). (1988). *Women in their speech communities.* New York: Longman.

Cooper, M. M. (1989). Women's way of writing. In M. M. Cooper & M. Holzman (Eds.), *Writing as social action* (pp. 141–156). Portsmouth, NH: Boynton/Cook.

Deaux, K., & Major, B. (1990). A social-psychological model of gender. In D. L. Rhode (Ed.), *Theoretical perspectives on sexual difference* (pp. 89–99, 275–278). New Haven, CT: Yale University Press.

Deuchar, M. (1988). A pragmatic account of women's use of standard speech. In J. Coates & D. Cameron (Eds.), *Women in their speech communities* (pp. 27–32). New York: Longman.

Donelson, K. L. (1963). *Variables distinguishing between effective and ineffective writers at the tenth grade level* (Vinton). *Dissertation Abstracts International, 24,* 2734A. (University Microfilms No. 63-07998)

Emig, J. (1971). *The composing processes of twelfth graders.* Urbana, IL: National Council of Teachers of English.

Farrell, T. J. (1979). The female and male modes of rhetoric. *College English, 40,* 909–921.

Flynn, E. (1988). Composing as a woman. *College Composition and Communication, 39,* 423–435.

Flynn, E. (1991). Politicizing the composing process and women's ways of interacting: A response to "A conversation with Mary Belenky." *Journal of Advanced Composition, 11,* 173–178.

Fuller, M. (1979). The great lawsuit: MAN versus MEN. WOMAN versus WOMEN. In R. Gottesman, L. B. Holland, D. Kalstone, F. Murphy, H. Parker, & W. H. Pritchard (Eds.), *The Norton anthology of American literature* (Vol. 1, pp. 1384–1425). New York: Norton. (Reprinted from *Boston Dial*, July 1843, 4, 1–47)

Gearhart, S. M. (1979). The womanization of rhetoric. *Women's Studies International Quarterly, 2*, 195–201.

Gilligan, C. (1982). *In a different voice: Psychological theory and women's development.* Cambridge, MA: Harvard University Press.

Goodwin, M. H., & Goodwin, C. (1987). Children's arguing. In S. U. Philips, S. Steele, & C. Tanz (Eds.), *Language, gender, and sex in comparative perspective* (pp. 200–248). New York: Cambridge University Press.

Goody, E. N. (1978). Towards a theory of questions. In E. N. Goody (Ed.), *Questions and politeness: Strategies in social interaction* (pp. 17–43). New York: Cambridge University Press.

Gumperz, J. J., & Cook-Gumperz, J. (1982). Interethnic communication in committee negotiations. In J. J. Gumperz (Ed.), *Language and social identity* (pp. 145–162). Cambridge, England: Cambridge University Press.

Halliday, M. A. K. (1978). *Language as social semiotic: The social interpretation of language and meaning.* London: Edward Arnold.

Halliday, M. A. K. (1985). *An introduction of functional grammar.* London: Edward Arnold.

Halliday, M. A. K., & Hasan, R. (1985). *Language, context, and text: Aspects of language in a social semiotic perspective.* Victoria, Australia: Deakin University Press.

Hekman, S. J. (1990). *Gender and knowledge: Elements of a postmodern feminism.* Boston: Northeastern University Press.

Henley, N. M., & Kramarae, C. (1991). Gender, power, and miscommunication. In N. Coupland, H. Giles, & J. M. Wiemann (Eds.), *"Miscommunication" and problematic talk* (pp. 18–43). Newbury Park, CA: Sage.

Herbert, R. K. (1990). Sex-based differences in compliment behavior. *Language in Society, 19*, 201–224.

Holmes, J. (1988). Paying compliments: A sex-preferential politeness strategy. *Journal of Pragmatics, 12*, 445–465.

Holmes, J. (1991). Language and gender. *Language Teaching, 24*, 207–220.

Hymes, D. (1974). *Foundations in sociolinguistics.* Philadelphia: University of Pennsylvania Press.

Johnson, D. M. (1989). Politeness strategies in L2 written discourse. *Journal of Intensive English, 3*, 71–90.

Johnson, D. M. (1992). Compliments and politeness in peer-review texts. *Applied Linguistics, 13*(1), 51–71.

Johnson, D. M., & Roen, D. H. (1992). Complimenting and involvement in peer reviews: Gender variation. *Language in Society, 21*, 27–57.

Kaestle, C. F. (1991). *Literacy in the United States: Readers and reading since 1880.* New Haven, CT: Yale University Press.

Kasper, G. (1990). Linguistic politeness: Current research issues. *Journal of Pragmatics, 14*, 193–218.

Keenan, E. O., Schieffelin, B. B., & Pratt, M. (1978). Questions of immediate concern. In E. N. Goody (Ed.), *Questions and politeness: Strategies in social interaction* (pp. 44–55). New York: Cambridge University Press.

Keroes, J. (1990). But what do they say? Gender and the content of student writing. *Discourse Processes, 13*, 243–257.

Labrant, L. (1933). A study of certain language developments of children in grades 4–12 inclusive. *Genetic Psychology Monographs, 14*, 387–491.

Lakoff, R. (1975). *Language and woman's place.* New York: Harper & Row.

Lamb, C. E. (1991). Beyond argument in feminist composition. *College English, 42*, 11–24.

Lunsford, A., & Ede, L. (1990). Rhetoric in a new key: Women and collaboration. *Rhetoric Review, 8*, 234–241.

Lynch, C., & Strauss-Noll, M. (1987). Mauve washers: Sex differences in freshman writing. *English Journal, 76*, 90–94.

Maccoby, E., & Jacklin, C. (1974). *The psychology of sex differences.* Stanford, CA: Stanford University Press.

Maltz, D. N., & Borker, R. A. (1982). A cultural approach to male–female miscommunication. In J. J. Gumperz (Ed.), *Language and social identity* (pp. 196–216). Cambridge, England: Cambridge University Press.

Martin, W. D. (1970). *Applying and exploring the Diederich method for measuring growth in writing ability in a high school* (Vinton). *Dissertation Abstracts International, 31*, 2616A. (University Microfilms No. 70-23921)

Martin, W. D. (1972). The sex factor in grading composition. *Research in the Teaching of English, 6*, 36–47.

McConnell-Ginet, S. (1985). Language and gender. In F. J. Newmeyer (Ed.), *Linguistics: The Cambridge survey: Vol. 4. Language: The socio-cultural context* (pp. 75–99). Cambridge, England: Cambridge University Press.

Miller, J. B. (1976). *Toward a new psychology of women.* Boston: Beacon Press.

National Assessment of Educational Progress. (1980). *Writing achievement, 1969–79: Results from the third National Writing Assessment: Vol. 1. 17-year-olds.* Denver: Education Commission of the States.

Piché, G. L., & Roen, D. H. (1987). Social cognition and writing: Interpersonal cognitive complexity and abstractness and the quality of students' persuasive writing. *Written Communication, 4*, 68–89.

Poynton, C. (1985). *Language and gender: Making the difference.* Oxford, England: Oxford University Press.

Poynton, C. (1989). *Language and gender: Making the difference.* New York: Oxford University Press.

Preisler, B. (1986). *Linguistic sex roles in conversation: Social variation in the expression of tentativeness in English.* Berlin: Mouton de Gruyter.

Rhode, D. L. (1990). Theoretical perspectives on sexual difference. In D. L. Rhode (Ed.), *Theoretical perspectives on sexual difference* (pp. 1–9). New Haven, CT: Yale University Press.

Roen, D. H. (1992). Gender and teacher response to student writing. In N. M. McCracken & B. C. Appleby (Eds.), *Gender issues in the teaching of English* (pp. 126–141). Portsmouth, NH: Heinemann/Boynton-Cook.

Roen, D. H., & Johnson, D. M. (1992). Perceiving the effectiveness of written discourse through gender lenses: The contribution of complimenting. *Written Communication, 9*, 435–464.

Roulis, E. (1990). *The relative effect of gender-linked language effect and a sex role stereotype effect on readers' responses to male and female argumentative-persuasive writing.* Unpublished doctoral dissertation, University of Minnesota, Minneapolis.

Rubin, D. L., & Greene, K. (1992). Gender-typical style in written language. *Research in the Teaching of English, 26*, 7–40.

Schor, N. (1992). Feminist and gender studies. In J. Gibaldi (Ed.), *Introduction to scholarship in modern languages and literatures* (pp. 262–287). New York: Modern Language Association.

Scott, J. (1988). *Gender and the politics of history.* New York: Columbia University Press.

Showalter, E. (1978). *A literature of their own: British women novelists from Brontë to Lessing.* London: Virago.

Showalter, E. (1985). *The new feminist criticism: Essays on women, literature, and theory.* New York: Pantheon.

Specht, D. A., & Bubolz, T. A. (1986). Reliability. In *SPSSX user's guide* (pp. 856–874). Chicago: SPSS Inc.

Spender, D. (1980). Talking in class. In D. Spender & E. Sarah (Eds.), *Learning to lose: Sexism and education* (pp. 148–154). London: Women's Press.

Stalnaker, J. M. (1941). Sex differences in the ability to write. *School and Society, 54*, 532–535.

Tannen, D. (1982). Ethnic style in male–female conversation. In J. J. Gumperz (Ed.), *Language and social identity* (pp. 217–231). Cambridge, England: Cambridge University Press.

Tannen, D. (1986). *That's not what I meant: How conversational style makes or breaks relationships.* New York: Ballantine.

Tannen, D. (1990a). Gender differences in topical coherence: Creating involvement in best friends' talk. *Discourse Processes, 13*, 73–90.

Tannen, D. (1990b). *You just don't understand: Women and men in conversation.* New York: Morrow.

Taylor, S. O. (1978). Women in a double bind: Hazards of the argumentative edge. *College Composition and Communication, 29*, 385–389.

Teich, N. (1987). Rogerian problem-solving and the rhetoric of argumentation. *Journal of Advanced Composition, 7*, 52–61.

Teich, N. (Ed.). (1992). *Rogerian perspectives: Collaborative rhetoric for oral and written communication.* Norwood, NJ: Ablex.

Thorne, B., & Henley, N. (1975). Difference and dominance: An overview of language, gender, and society. In B. Thorne & N. Henley (Eds.), *Language and sex: Difference and dominance* (pp. 5–42). Rowley, MA: Newbury House.

Thorne, B., Kramarae, C., & Henley, N. (1983). Language, gender and society: Opening a second decade of research. In B. Thorne, C. Kramarae, & N. Henley (Eds.), *Language, gender and society* (pp. 7–24). Cambridge, MA: Newbury House/Harper & Row.

West, C. (1984). When the doctor is a lady. *Symbolic Interaction, 7*, 87–106.

West, C., & Zimmerman, D. (1977). Women's place in everyday talk: Reflections on parent–child interaction. *Social Problems, 24*, 521–529.

West, C., & Zimmerman, D. H. (1991). Doing gender. In J. Lorber & S. A. Farrell (Eds.), *The social construction of gender* (pp. 13–37). Newbury Park, CA: Sage.

Wolfson, N. (1989a). *Perspectives: Sociolinguistics and TESOL.* New York: Harper & Row/Newbury House.

Wolfson, N. (1989b). The social dynamics of native and nonative variation in complimenting behavior. In M. Eisenstein (Ed.), *The dynamic interlanguage: Empirical studies in second language variation* (pp. 219–236). New York: Plenum.

Woodward, J. C., & Phillips, A. G. (1967). Profile of the poor writer—The relationship of selected characteristics of poor writing in college. *Research in the Teaching of English, 1*, 41–53.

CHAPTER SEVEN

The Suppressed Voice Hypothesis in Women's Writing: Effects of Revision on Gender-Typical Style

Donald L. Rubin
The University of Georgia

Kathryn Greene
East Carolina University

> *I have observed what seem to me to be such womanly touches, in those moving fictions, that the assurance on the title-page is insufficient to satisfy me, even now. If they originated with no woman, I believe that no man ever before had the art of making himself, mentally, so like a woman . . .*
> —Charles Dickens (commenting on his first readings of George Eliot, quoted in Heller, 1992, p. 4)

Strong conceptual foundations undergird the supposition—like that expressed by Charles Dickens in the opening epigraph—that women and men write with distinct, gender-typical styles. Rubin and Greene (1992; see also Annas, 1987; chapters 6 and 8 of this volume) reviewed three bodies of literature that support the notion of gender-typical style in written language: (a) research on women's speech, (b) analyses of women's literature, and (c) theories of women's epistemologies. Extrapolating from work on gender differences in oral language, some analysts have postulated, for example, that women's writing is marked by especially frequent use of hedges (*sort of, almost*) that blunt the force of assertions (e.g., Lynch & Strauss-Noll, 1987; Taylor, 1978). Some examinations of literary language conclude that women's writing style—at least in fiction writing—is marked by grammatical parallelism and balance and also by some features of emotional expression (e.g., Hiatt, 1977). Inspired by theories of women's "ways of knowing," yet other scholars conclude that women's writing manifests a rhetorical style characterized by indirectness, narrative, and interpersonal connectiveness rather than confrontative argumentation (e.g., Cooper, 1989; Flynn, 1988).

133

These accounts of style in women's writing are conceptually compelling, but the empirical evidence upon which they draw bears closer scrutiny. Often the writing episodes used to explicate and illustrate the purported nature of women's writing are—quite naturally—anecdotal and deliberately selective (e.g., Lunsford & Ede, 1990). Moreover, a number of the anecdotal studies (e.g., Cooper, 1989), as well as some more social scientific investigations (e.g., Hunter et al., 1988), are flawed for yet another reason: They draw conclusions about gender-typical style without in fact comparing women's writing to men's. Indeed, a good deal of research on gender, such as the otherwise invaluable work of Gilligan (1982), suffers from failure to directly compare male responses with those of women (Crawford, 1989).

Those studies that employed more systematic methods to confirm gender differences in writing have collectively yielded mixed and often undramatic results. For example, two separate studies of male and female business writers (Smeltzer & Werbel, 1986; Sterkel, 1988) examined a wide range of text features, and neither detected any gender differences. Roen, Hansen, and Abordonado (chapter 6 of this volume) did find that women generally exceeded men in hedging their writing, particularly in hedging threats to face. But most expected differences did not arise in production of politeness units, nor even in expressions of women's epistemological stances.

On the other hand, Roulis (chapter 8 of this volume) infers from her findings that evaluators are in fact sensitive to some set of rhetorical features that must be distributed in gender-typical fashion. But her design does not identify exactly what those features may be. Mulac, Studley, and Blau (1990) did present one of the few compelling demonstrations of highly distinctive gender patterns in written language. In their study, impromptu writings were collected from 4th-, 8th-, and 12th-grade boys and girls. Each of the ages displayed a particular constellation of linguistic features that discriminated (with an impressive accuracy of about 85%) among boys and girls. For example, among high school seniors, uncertainty verbs, subordinating conjunctions, judgmental phrases, and sentence initial adverbs were all typical of male writing; whereas progressive verbs and fillers discriminated female from male. Moreover, these features of written language did also predict raters' impressions of the writers (again, see chapter 8 of this volume).

Unfortunately, it is difficult to impose conceptual coherence on the findings of Mulac and his colleagues (1990). Some of the linguistic features examined appear to be ad hoc choices, not clearly linked to gender in any theoretic way. This is the case, for example, for sentence initial adverbs. In addition, the list of features represents mixed and seemingly overlapping levels of linguistic analysis. We find oppositions ("It seems like a good idea, but it isn't") (Mulac et. al, 1990, p. 448) tabulated separately but alongside coordinating conjunctions (of which *but* is an instance). A final difficulty in interpreting these findings is the degree of inconsistency in the gender identity of particular linguistic features across the grade levels. For example, longer sentences are typical of boys in the fourth grade, but sentence length fails to discriminate among male and female writers in any of the other grades. Sentence initial adverbs are typical of 4th-grade girls, but in the 12th-grade they are typical of boys.

Rubin and Greene (1992) examined gender effects by taking into account not only biological gender, but also psychological gender role orientation (Bem, 1981). Characterizing women's writing were a prevalence of exclamation marks, "egocentric" formulae (e.g., *I guess, I think*), and certain hedges (auxiliaries of possibility, e.g., *could, might*). Women were also more likely than men to acknowledge some legitimacy to an opposing point of view (similar to two-sided argument).

These findings of Rubin and Greene (1992) must be interpreted in light of the full complement of results. First, it is important to recognize what was *not* found: Most candidate features were not found to be affected by the writer's biological or psychological gender. Even some features for which women showed greater affinity than men were not used by a *preponderance* of women. Only 24% of men writers acknowledged opposing points of view. In contrast, 52% of women writers did so. But it hardly seems reasonable to label a feature used by barely more than half the women a feature of "women's written language." Moreover, it is interesting to note that men in the Rubin and Greene study exhibited higher relative frequencies of certain features—first-person pronouns constitute one example—that had been conceptually linked to women's discourse. Finally, the amount of variance in language use that was attributable to gender was of much smaller magnitude than the amount of variance attributable to writing task (instrumental/persuasive vs. reflexive/expressive tasks). That is, writing task was a more powerful determinant of gender-typed style than was gender itself.

Several explanations may account for the disjunctures between grounded theory and empirical evidence for gender typing in written language. We must look to methodological inadequacies, first off. It may be that stylisticians are unable to adequately articulate and code subtle textual features that evoke women's (or men's) voice in writing. Rubin and Greene (1992), by way of illustration, expected that women would use more illustrator connectives (*such as, for example*) than men, because women's style has been portrayed as particularistic and experientially based. Contrary to that expectation, men produced a significantly higher frequency of illustrators. This finding properly signifies less than what it initially might seem to mean. It means only that men were more likely to *explicitly mark* illustrations. We do not know if women used numerous illustrations that they wove into their discourse in a more seamless way.

Besides rough-hewn methods of text analysis, two hypotheses in fact predict lack of differentiation between male and female writing. One potential explanation points to the highly conventionalized nature of written language. Unlike speech, writing is learned primarily through the uniform institution of schooling, and it is regulated by the standardization of publishers. Therefore, according to this view, written language (or at least mature writing) is perforce devoid of sociolinguistic patterning, devoid of social markers. Writing is gender-neutral because it is socially neutral. And that neutrality is regarded as a positive attribute for a communication system that functions as writing does. This position was expressed by Lakoff (1977), whose own work is the touchstone for most contemporary scholarship on gender and language.

The second possible explanation for scarce gender differences in writing rejects the view that style in writing is socially neutral. As proposed by a number of feminist scholars (e.g., Annas, 1987; Ritchie, 1990), this alternative view posits that the "conventions" of writing in fact impose male-oriented norms. These imposed norms, such as third-person voice or explicit syllogistic conclusions, are not gender-free. They require women to adopt male modes of thinking and valuing and languaging. They demand that women suppress their voices in writing in ways that men need not.

According to Spender (1980):

> Women writers can attempt to pre-empt . . . criticisms by careful reproduction of the male scale of values but to do so would be to accept external demands that play no role for the male writer. And it is possible that such demands take their toll, that they introduce a "translation" factor which distorts what it is that the writer wishes to say. (p. 202)

Cayton (1990) similarly concluded on the basis of her study of gender differences in writer's block:

> Trying to write academic prose seemed to give many [female college seniors] a sense that they were obliterating themselves from the project; nevertheless, when they wrote of their own experiences in a voice that they felt comfortable with, they expressed doubts that the problems they addressed were anything other than idiosyncratic, and they feared that no one would attend to their message. (p. 325)

Limited and indirect support for the suppressed voice hypothesis arises from studies that examined the interaction between gender and genre in writing. In general, gender differences were most apparent in less formal or less conventionalized genres, whereas male and female styles converged in more expository genres (e.g., Hiatt, 1977; Lentz, 1986). The Rubin and Greene (1992) study provides a clear illustration of this phenomenon. With respect to egocentric sequences (*I guess, I think*), men used about equal frequencies when writing first drafts of expressive messages to friends, compared to when they were writing revised drafts of persuasive messages to a university official. Women produced relatively more egocentric sequences. But they did so mainly when writing in an expressive mode to friends. When women were writing revised drafts to a distant audience, their production of this feature purportedly associated with women's language converged with men's. In this case, women tended to make an adaptation when moving from informal to formal writing that men did not.

If it is the case that women "obliterate" their voices when writing and that they do so by "translating" their writing into a particularly alien idiom, then the process of revision must take on a different cast for women than it does for men. Flower and her colleagues (Flower, Hayes, Carey, Shriver, & Stratman, 1986) presented an elaborate model of revision, wherein the writer detects and ultimately changes text features that are at variance with her goals. Usually we think of the goals that drive revision as relating to clear and rhetorically effective expression.

It is the thesis of this book, of course, that identity management goals likewise drive composing processes, including processes of revision. For women revising formal expository prose, accordingly, one set of revision goals may pertain to detecting and eliminating vestiges of female-typical language. Campbell (1992) quoted a Radcliffe student in the early 20th century who was learning to adopt exactly that goal:

> There were too many short sentences, the transitions were a little too obviously thought out, there was repetition of thought, above all there was too personal [an] element. I must write it over and make it flat, insipid, take out all individuality, and I can do this . . . as the section man likes it written. (p. 479)

To be sure, a great deal of revision occurs pretextually; no visual trace of it ever appears on the written page. In fact, pretextual revision is particularly common among high-ability writers (Witte, 1985). A number of observers note a sort of syndrome in which especially high-achieving women self-monitor, self-censor, or otherwise mute themselves in anticipation of convention or readers who might react negatively against authentic female-identified voice (e.g., Boice & Kelly, 1987; Cayton, 1990; Spender, 1980). Sperling and Freedman (1987) aptly stated that such writers need not be reminded, "a good girl writes like a good girl" (p. 357).

Pretextual revision notwithstanding, the suppressed voice hypothesis can be evaluated in part by comparing male and female production of gender-typical features, examining how those features vary across successive drafts. The suppressed voice hypothesis would predict that women produce a high frequency of features like hedges and audience acknowledgments in first drafts that they know will not be evaluated. The frequency of such gender-marked features should drop as a result of revision, particularly as women revise for a formal (and male?) reader. The between-draft decline, if any, should be much less pronounced in men's writing. Women's use of female-typical features in revised drafts of formal writing, according to this hypothesis, should conform closely to the male norm.

As a follow-up to Rubin and Greene (1992), this chapter reports just such a test of the suppressed voice hypothesis as it bears on women's and men's revision of formal instrumental writing.

METHODS

Participants

This study analyzes additional data collected during the course of the research previously reported in Rubin and Greene (1992). Sixteen college men and 27 women volunteered to participate in this study in order to fulfill a class assignment for a basic course in speech communication.

Procedures

Participants wrote messages to a university vice president regarding a fictional proposal to test university students for illicit drug use. At the first session they received a fact sheet regarding the proposal. They were encouraged to write first drafts that captured their most persuasive ideas without worrying at that point about mechanical correctness. They were also urged to fill at least two pages. At the second session, about a week later, initial drafts were returned. Participants were told to rewrite their papers, making sure their final drafts were presentable for the university official. They also completed the Wheeless and Dierks-Stewart (1981) revision of the Bem (1981) sex role inventory. At the end of the session, participants were debriefed about the purpose of the study.

Analysis of Linguistic Features

The language analysis in the present study follows that described by Rubin and Greene (1992), which was, in turn, primarily adapted from methods developed by Rubin and Nelson (1983) and Hiatt (1977). The analytic scheme, depicted in Table 7.1, codes 23 distinct features that are linked in previous research or theory to gender-typed verbal expression. Although 2 of these features (refusals and enumerations) are treated solely in a univariate fashion, the remaining 21 features are grouped into six a priori multivariate clusters: (a) nonessentials—dashes and parentheses; (b) markers of excitability—exclamation points and underlining; (c) markers of subjectivity—

TABLE 7.1
Coded Language Features

I. Nonessentials	
A. parentheses	A drug class won't help (they know it all anyway)
B. dash	It could take a year-maybe more
II. Excitability Markers	
A. exclamation point	That's absurd!
B. underlining	There are a lot of people who will just go somewhere else
III. Audience Acknowledgment	
A. second-person address	I am writing to tell you this whole idea just won't work
B. questions	Who will pay the cost of these tests?
IV. Connectives	
A. illative	So this isn't going to solve anything
B. adversative	You might catch some people who are abusing drugs but innocent people will suffer too.
C. causal	The number of students will drop because some people will not apply
D. illustrator	Other things can make it seem like you're taking drugs, like if you're on birth control pills
E. additive	Some people just experiment a little and they only use drugs once or twice
F. temporal	Suppose someone takes the class, then will they really stop their drug habit?
G. conditional	If you test people for drugs, then what about alcohol?
V. Hedges	
A. intensifiers	It is so typical of this university
B. deintensifiers	Only a small minority abuse drugs
C. proximals	Almost everyone would have to take a class
D. modal adjuncts	Maybe 5% use drugs
E. auxiliaries of possibility	It could hurt innocent people
F. perceptual verbs	It looks like students have no rights
VI. Subjective Reference	
A. egocentric sequence	I think it's just a bad idea
B. first-person reference	We're all adults
VII. Refusals	I don't know, but it seems like this is not the best way to go about it
VIII. Enumeration	Applications will drop by 10 or 15%

egocentric sequences and other self-reference; (d) connectives—illative, adversative, causal, illustrative, additive, temporal, and conditional; (e) hedges—intensifiers, deintensifiers, proximals, modal adjuncts, auxiliaries of possibility, and perceptual verbs; and (f) audience acknowledgments—second-person reference and questions. In addition, verbosity was indexed by means of total numbers of words, and sentence length was indexed as words per sentence.

Two coders working independently analyzed each of the 86 scripts in the sample. Reliabilities (Cronbach's alphas) across drafts one and two averaged .86 for enumerations, .77 for refusals, .90 for nonessentials, .95 for markers of excitability, .86 for first-person references, .83 for connectives, .78 for hedges, .94 for audience acknowledgments, .99 for total number of words, and .98 for total number of sentences.

Data Analysis

The measure of psychological gender role yields two scores for each participant: (a) expressive gender role orientation and (b) instrumental gender role orientation. The former corresponds to traditional female gender roles like nurturing and empathy, whereas the latter corresponds to traditional male gender role traits like competitiveness and acquisitiveness (Bem, 1974; Wheeless & Dierks-Stewart, 1981). For this sample, the mean expressive score for women was 55.52, and 52.44 for men. No significant difference between these means was indicated by t-test analysis. For instrumental scores, the mean for women was 48.86, and 56.13 for men. This constituted a statistically significant difference ($t_{(42\ df)} = 3.64$; $p < .001$).

The study was conceptualized as a mixed factorial design with participants nested in gender (at two levels) and crossed with the repeated measure, draft (at two levels). Instrumental and expressive gender role orientations were treated as separate covariates. For each of the six multivariate clusters, separate multivariate analyses of covariance (MANCOVAs) were run with univariate analyses of covariance (ANCOVAs) run as follow-ups to statistically significant MANCOVAs, as well as for those features (refusals, enumeration, verbosity, sentence length) that were not included in multivariate clusters. All analyses were run on relative frequencies; that is, the feature counts for each language variable were divided by total number of words, to adjust for differences in sheer output.

Of particular importance in this analysis would be any findings of interactions between gender and draft. Consider the following *hypothetical* set of findings. Suppose, for example, it were found that women writers, relative to men, produced more of some gender-typed feature like egocentric sequences (*I guess, I think*). Suppose, further, that this main effect for gender were modified by a statistically significant interaction between gender and draft. If it were found that women produced more of these features in their first drafts than in their revisions (whereas the rate of production held constant for men across drafts), then we would have strong evidence for the suppressed voice hypothesis in writing. That is, this pattern of statistical interaction would be showing us that women edited out their use of some gender-typed feature as they moved from a relatively spontaneous and unmonitored writing to a revised draft intended for consumption by a psychologically remote reader. Student-Neuman–Keuls analyses were to be used for post-hoc comparisons among cell means within significant interactions.

RESULTS

Nonessentials

The MANCOVA for the cluster of nonessentials revealed a statistically significant covariate effect for expressive gender role orientation (lambda$_{2,38}$ = .741; $p < .005$). No additional main or interaction effect achieved significance in this MANCOVA.

To follow up this multivariate result, separate ANCOVAs were run for each of the two components of the nonessential cluster: dashes and parentheses. The expressive covariate effect did not prove statistically significant for the analysis of dashes. For the analysis of relative frequency of parentheses, however, expressive gender role orientation did exert a strong covariate effect ($F_{1,39}$ = 12.97; $p < .001$; eta^2 = .231). The negative slope of the regression coefficient (b = −.007) indicates an inverse relation between expressive gender role orientation and use of parentheses.

Markers of Excitability

The MANCOVA for markers of excitability yielded no significant covariate, main, or interaction effect.

Audience Acknowledgments

The MANCOVA for audience acknowledgments similarly manifested no statistically significant effect.

Connectives

The MANCOVA for connectives indicated a statistically significant effect only for the repeated measure, draft (lambda$_{7,35}$ = .597; $p < .01$).

To follow up this multivariate effect, separate ANCOVAs were run for each of the six types of connectives. No draft effect emerged for illatives, illustrators, additives, or conditionals. The effect of draft on adversatives ($F_{1,41}$ = 14.36; $p < .001$; eta^2 = .259) was due to a higher relative frequency of adversatives in second drafts (M = .0073) compared to first drafts (M = .0053). The effect of draft on temporal connectives ($F_{1,41}$ = 6.58; $p < .05$; eta^2 = .147) similarly appears attributable to a higher frequency of this connective in second drafts (M = .0027) relative to first (M = .0019).

Hedges

The MANCOVA for hedges yielded no significant covariate effect. The main effect for gender of writer, however, was statistically significant (lambda$_{6,34}$ = .696; $p < .05$). Separate univariate ANCOVAs for each of the six types of hedge indicated no significant gender effect for intensifiers, deintensifiers, proximals, perceptual verbs, or modal adjuncts. The effect for auxiliaries of possibility ($F_{1,39}$ = 6.80; p < .05; eta^2 = .146) was due to relatively higher usage among women (M = .0039) than among men (M = .0022).

Draft also exerted a significant multivariate effect on use of hedges (lambda$_{6,36}$ = .584; p < .005). No interaction between draft and gender emerged, however. Univariate follow-up of the multivariate draft effect revealed that second drafts (M = .0103) contained relatively more intensifiers than did first drafts (M = .0087; $F_{1,41}$ = 4.41; p < .05; eta^2 = .097). Similarly, deintensifiers were also relatively more common in second drafts (M = .0048) than in first (M = .0029; $F_{1,41}$ = 12.63; p < .005; eta^2 = .23). Perceptual verbs also manifested a main effect for draft ($F_{1,41}$ = 6.70; p < .05; eta^2 = .139). Once again, Draft 2 (M = .0016) exceeded Draft 1 (M = .0008).

Markers of Subjectivity

The main effect for draft was the sole statistically significant effect in the MANCOVA of markers of subjectivity (lambda$_{2,40}$ = .771; p < .01). As follow-up procedures, univariate ANCOVA indicated a statistically significant main effect only for first-person references (other than egocentric sequences ($F_{1,41}$ = 6.22; p < .05; eta^2 = .128). Second drafts (M = .0185) exceeded first drafts (M = .0159) on this variable.

Refusals

The ANCOVA for refusals revealed no statistically significant covariate, main, or interaction effects.

Enumeration

The ANCOVA for enumerations revealed no statistically significant covariate, main, or interaction effects.

Verbosity

The ANCOVA for total number of words indicated a single statistically significant effect. Participants' second drafts were longer (M = 361.73) than their initial drafts (M = 343.84; $F_{1,41}$ = 3.99, p < .05, eta^2 = .088).

Sentence Length

The ANCOVA for words per sentence revealed no statistically significant covariate, main, or interaction effect.

DISCUSSION

The primary purpose of this study was to examine gender differences in between-draft revisions of certain linguistic features. In particular, the study was designed to test whether women tend to suppress female-typical features during the process of revision, in order to more closely approximate male-typical norms in their final writing products. The results of this study provide no support for that suppressed voice hypothesis. The types of revision observed here were equally distributed across male and female writers.

Not all revision effects are observable, however, and for that reason, the present study cannot offer definitive proof against a suppressed voice hypothesis. As Witte (1985) noted, a considerable amount of revision may take place in mental rehearsal, that is, pretextually. The first draft is not always the first *written* draft. Skilled writers often engage in especially extensive pretextual revision; that is why their first written drafts often need undergo less change than those of less mature writers. It is altogether possible that women suppress their gendered voices as they revise pretextually. Gender identity is transformed (distorted?) before the pen ever touches the paper, perhaps.

Still, if it were the case that women's language were largely suppressed pretextually, one would expect to find at least some residue "leaking" through onto the page in Draft 1. This study found no such residue. If there is a women's voice that is suppressed pretextually in writing, it would appear to be silenced quite completely.

All writers must suppress voice in the most literal sense when they write, and some leakage from oral voice to written style is quite normal. Learning to differentiate spoken language from written is an important developmental task we all must undertake, and only the most successful among us learn eventually to reintegrate a measure of orality back into our writing (Rubin, 1987). More commonly, failing to adequately suppress more familiar speech forms can result in writing dysfunction (Shaughnessy, 1977). Horowitz (chapter 3 of this volume) shows how culturally distinct oral voices can infuse writing style, sometimes to very positive effect. In the present study, however, there simply is no evidence of a distinct female voice either leaking or infusing nor being suppressed.

Although our findings do not substantiate any gender-linked trends in revision practices, some individuals certainly did display patterns that were consistent with the suppressed voice hypothesis. Compare parallel sections of two drafts for one female participant:

Draft 1:
I don't know how to stop the drug problem on university campuses. I realize that it is very easy to get if you know the right people. I've been to party's

where my friends have been strung out on pot, acid, & X. One was a kindergarten teacher, a 26 yr. old clean cut senior, one got kicked out of [name of school], & the others are just avg people. So it's not horrible people who are doing this stuff. Some do it very rarely so I don't see a big deal with then right now. Later they could be a problem . . . I guess that drug testing in t/univ & then the 5 hr. noncredit course would be a help in some ways but at least 90% of the student pop will be enrolled in this class.

Draft 2:
Another aspect is the cost of running such a program. 90% of the college students have tried drugs sometime. That means practically a whole new department the size of t/English one would have to be put in. That is definilly out of most universities budget plans. . . . It also not just college students who do drugs. I know a kindergarten teacher who was on Ex this weekend. In order to stop the problem it should be the whole of society who changes and not just a part.

If nothing else, these two drafts show the writer moving from a mainly narrative-centered ("I've been to party's"), tentative style ("I don't know how . . . ;" "Later it could be a problem;" "I guess . . .") to a more linear ("I know a kindergarten teacher . . ."), conclusionary one ("That means . . . ;" ". . . it should be the whole of society who changes . . ."). Most readers to whom we have shown these samples concur that the first draft is marked by female voice much more so than the revision.

And yet other female writers actually seemed to *increase* their use of female-typed style as they moved from original to revised drafts. Examine the way one writer alters her opening paragraph.

Draft 1:
The proposal by the Georgia State Legislature to test all students for drugs is wrong. The concern for students using drugs is commendable, but the idea that students would be mandatorily tested is to me a violation of my Constitutional Rights.

Draft 2:
I'm writing you in concern for the proposal submitted by the Georgia State Legislature that suggests all students here at the University be tested for drugs. The concern for students abusing drugs is commendable, but frankly I feel it is very unnecessary. As well as being unnecessary, it is probably in violation of our students' Constitutional Rights. I believe this propaganda is another underlying technique from the Legislature to stir up attention and needed support from the community.

This writer does not appear to be suppressing a female voice as she revises, but rather accentuating it. The second draft is more clearly framed in a first-person, subjective stance. It is more patently interpersonal ("I'm writing you . . ."), includes egocentric sequences (*I feel, I believe*), and female-typed hedges (*very, probably*). Curiously, this writer registered the strongest traditional *male* gender role orientation—as measured on the adapted Bem sex role inventory—in the entire sample of participants. That is, she scored highest on instrumental gender roles and lowest on expressive. Was she perhaps "unsuppressing" a female identity as she revised?

If simple and systematic gender effects were not clearly visible in these data, strong effects of revision were quite apparent for a number of the variables examined. Temporal connectives, intensifiers, deintensifiers, perceptual verbs, first-person reference, and verbosity have all been associated in various places in the literature with women's writing. In the present study, these gender-typed features were instead associated with redrafting rather than with gender.

It is important to note first off that the instructions to revise apparently did exert a potent impact on these writers. Effect sizes for the draft factor (indexed by values of 1-lambda for the MANCOVAs or by eta^2 for the ANCOVAs) were not insubstantial. Our failure to find an interaction between gender and draft in these data cannot be attributed to any general failure among the participants to revise.

Second (with respect to the effects of revision), it is worth observing that both men and women have apparently assimilated the notion that writing is improved by increasing tentativeness (perceptual verbs like *seems to be*, deintensifiers like *only* or *just*), by increasing narrativity (temporal conjunctions like *then*, first-person point of view), by increasing intensity (*really* or *very*), and by simply elaborating (longer messages). It is particularly interesting that these norms emerged from a deliberately persuasive writing task, as they seem more attuned with what Bleich (1988) might have regarded as flexible or mixed (as opposed to "official") "genders" of writing. That is, irrespective of writers' actual gender, and even in the face of a very traditional argumentative task, writers tended to revise by augmenting elements of female-typed voice.

Of course what may be female-typed style in the collective imagination is not necessarily female-typical in the world of empirical evidence (Edelsky, 1979). Findings in the present study tend to confirm Rubin and Greene's (1992) conclusion about gender-typical style in writing, and to contradict that of Mulac et al. (1990). That is, writers' gender exerted only a small impact on style as tabulated here. In this corpus of writing, it is true, women tended to use a greater relative frequency of auxiliaries of possibility (*might, could*). Contrary to expectations, however, expressive gender role orientation was negatively associated with use of parentheses. In previous studies (e.g., Hiatt, 1977), the use of parentheses was taken to be a constituent of a nonlinear, digressive style that is supposed to be typical of female discourse.

Writing/Revision and Doing Gender

To its detriment, the design of this study treats biological gender, along with psychological gender role orientation, as if they were independent variables. The design of the study implies that language behaviors result from gender. Yet the conceptualization of gender we would instead profess asserts that gender is not a given, not an independent factor. Rather, gender is constructed individually and culturally (Kessler & McKenna, 1979). And as Rubin (1988) noted, writing is a "human activity that constructs roles. Texts bring social contexts into existence" (p. 13). Surely, therefore, writing is one behavior through which people do the work of constructing gender identities for themselves, one behavior through which people impose definitions of gender on contexts.

This view of writing as part of the activity of "doing" gender draws upon feminist critiques of gender research in communication (e.g., Putnam, 1982; Rakow, 1986). These critiques point out that because gender is an outcome (more correctly, a set of outcomes) of communication, it cannot be understood just as an input to a communication model. Nor can gender be understood as some static entity, as if it were apart from and prior to dynamic and contextualized interaction (see Hecht, 1993).

Thus, in the study of revision, we must appreciate that some writers on some occasions choose to en-gender their style in order to project a clearer or stronger gender identity. Revision, in such cases, might take the form of strategically augmenting gender-typed stylistic markers. The revised opening paragraph we presented earlier (beginning, "I am writing to you . . .") seems en-gendered in just this way, though we can only speculate on the reason for it.

To understand writing (including revision) as a kind of gendering activity, we would need to become privy to how people negotiate their gender identities in interaction with other writers and readers and in interaction with other aspects of rhetorical context. No doubt this project would require rich and diverse data. We would want to collect several writing samples from authors as those writers moved across audiences and modes. We would want to know how those authors construed power relations in each of those writing events. We would try to determine how stylistic choices exercised between drafts, that is, revision processes, reflected choices about constructing social identity. And one would want to know how each process of writing strengthened, enervated, or redefined the writers' own sense of social identity.

The present study is considerably more modest in scope than the research outlined previously. Still, it may furnish some tentative notions about writing and doing gender. For example, the presentation of unclear case writers showed at least that patterns of suppressing or augmenting gender in writing are not deterministically constrained by biological gender. According to the gender construction position, the writers were assuming or appropriating—not merely reflecting—gender role identities as they composed. The writer who in her second draft withheld narrative detail about her experience at a party was casting herself, perhaps reinforcing herself, as a person who understands how to write in the "male rhetorical mode" (Farrell, 1979). In that male mode, details must serve as evidence linked explicitly to conclusions. This writer does not construct herself as not some womanly person who would use narrative alone as a form of proof.

Moreover, it is noteworthy that men as well as women—unlike the case cited previously—generally increased female-typed language when revising. Because skilled writing is often stereotyped as a female-typical faculty, it may be that skilled writers habitually seek to construct a more female identity in their formal writing.

Feminist authors such as Penelope (1990) and hooks (1981) consciously manipulate language as a means for breaking free from imposed gender roles. The process of reflecting upon and appropriating written language is, for them, one tool for doing gender. They construct gendered identities for themselves by deliberately violating the status quo of power and identity relations that standard edited English helps enforce. By the same token, feminist writing teachers (e.g., Annas, 1985; Cooper, 1989; Fiore & Elsasser, 1981) encourage their students to work hard at doing gender as they write. They want their students to use writing as an opportunity for exploring what it means to be a gendered person. In that way, learning to write and developing gender are part of the same process.

When writing is seen as a way of doing gender, gender-typical style in written language is necessarily seen in more complex light: not as determined by gender, but in interaction with it. Sometimes gendered voice is suppressed, sometimes augmented. Sometimes gendered voice is distributed differentially among men and women, sometimes it is shared.

REFERENCES

Annas, P. J. (1985). Style as politics: A feminist approach to the teaching of writing. *College English, 47,* 360–371.

Annas, P. J. (1987). Silences: Feminist language research and the teaching of writing. In C. Caywood & G. Overing (Eds.), *Teaching writing: Pedagogy, gender, and equity* (pp. 3–18). Albany: State University of New York Press.

Bem, S. (1974). The measurement of psychological androgyny. *Journal of Consulting and Clinical Psychology, 42,* 155–162.

Bem, S. (1981). Gender schema theory: A cognitive account of sex typing. *Psychological Review, 88,* 354–364.

Bleich, D. (1988). Genders of writing. *Journal of Advanced Composition, 8,* 10–25.

Boice, R., & Kelly, K. (1987). Writing viewed by disenfranchised groups. *Written Communication, 4,* 299–309.

Campbell, J. (1992). Controlling voices: The legacy of English A at Radcliffe College 1883–1917. *College Composition and Communication, 43,* 472–485.

Cayton, M. K. (1990). What happens when things go wrong: Women and writing blocks. *Journal of Advanced Composition, 10,* 321–337.

Cooper, M. M. (1989). Women's ways of writing. In M. M. Cooper & M. Holzman (Eds.), *Writing as social action* (pp. 141–156). Portsmouth, NH: Boynton/Cook.

Crawford, M. (1989). Agreeing to disagree: Feminist epistemologies and women's ways of knowing. In M. Crawford & M. Gentry (Eds.), *Gender and thought: Psychological perspectives* (pp. 128–145). New York: Springer-Verlag.

Edelsky, C. (1979). Question intonation and sex roles. *Language and Society, 8,* 15–32.

Farrell, T. (1979). The male and female modes of rhetoric. *College English, 40,* 909–921.

Fiore, K., & Elsasser, N. (1981). Through writing we transform our world: Third world women and literacy. *Humanities in Society, 20,* 395–418.

Flower, L., Hayes, J., Carey, L., Shriver, K., & Stratman, J. (1986). Detection, diagnosis, and the strategies of revision. *College Composition and Communication, 37,* 16–55.

Flynn, E. (1988). Composing as a woman. *College Composition and Communication, 39,* 423–435.

Gilligan, C. (1982). *In a different voice: Psychological theory and women's development.* Cambridge, MA: Harvard University Press.

Hecht, M. L. (1993). 2002—A research odyssey: Toward the development of a communication theory of identity. *Communication Monographs, 60,* 75–82.

Heller, D. (1992, January 5). Letter to the editor. *The New York Times Book Review,* p. 4.

Hiatt, M. (1977). *The way women write.* New York: Teachers College Press.

hooks, b. (1981). *Ain't I a woman: Black women and feminism.* Boston: South End Press.

Hunter, P., Pearce, N., Lee, S., Goldsmith, S., Feldman, P., & Weaver, H. (1988). Competing epistemologies and female basic writers. *Journal of Basic Writing, 7,* 73–81.

Kessler, S., & McKenna, W. (1979). *Gender: An ethnomethodological approach.* Chicago: University of Chicago Press.

Lakoff, R. (1977). Women's language. *Language and Style, 10,* 222–247.

Lentz, T. M. (1986). Communication difficulties in a large federal agency. *American Behavioral Scientist, 29,* 303–319.

Lunsford, A., & Ede, L. (1990). Rhetoric in a new key: Women and collaboration. *Rhetoric Review, 8,* 234–241.

Lynch, C., & Strauss-Noll, M. (1987). Mauve washers: Sex differences in freshman writing. *English Journal, 76,* 90–94.

Mulac, A., Studley, L. B., & Blau, S. (1990). The gender-linked language effect in primary and secondary students' impromptu essays. *Sex Roles, 23,* 439–469.

Penelope, J. (1990). *Speaking freely: Unlearning the lies of the fathers' tongues.* New York: Pergamon.

Putnam, L. (1982). In search of gender: A critique of gender and sex roles research. *Women's Studies in Communication, 5,* 1–9.

Rakow, L. F. (1986). Rethinking gender research in communication. *Journal of Communication, 36,* 11–26.

Ritchie, J. S. (1990). Confronting the "essential" problem: Reconnecting feminist theory and pedagogy. *Journal of Advanced Composition, 10,* 249–273.

Rubin, D. L. (1987). Divergence and convergence between oral and written communication. *Topics in Language Disorders, 7*(4), 1–18.

Rubin, D. L. (1988). Introduction: Four dimensions of social construction in written communication. In B. Rafoth & D. Rubin (Eds.), *The social construction of written communication* (pp. 1–33). Norwood, NJ: Ablex.

Rubin, D. L., & Greene, K. G. (1992). Gender-typical style in written language. *Research in the Teaching of English, 26*, 7–40.

Rubin, D. L., & Nelson, M. W. (1983). Multiple determinants of a stigmatized speech style: Women's language, powerless language, or everyone's language? *Language and Speech, 26*, 273–290.

Shaughnessy, M. P. (1977). *Errors and expectations.* New York: Oxford University Press.

Smeltzer, L., & Werbel, J. (1986). Gender differences in managerial communication: Fact or folklinguistics? *Journal of Business Communication, 23*, 41–50.

Spender, D. (1980). Women and writing. In *Man made language* (pp. 191–233). London: Routledge & Kegan Paul.

Sperling, M., & Freedman, S. (1987). A good girl writes like a good girl: Written responses to student writing. *Written Communication, 4*, 343–369.

Sterkel, K. (1988). The relationship between gender and writing style in business communication. *Journal of Business Communication, 25*, 17–38.

Taylor, S. O. (1978). Women in a double bind: Hazards of the argumentative edge. *College Composition and Communication, 29*, 385–389.

Wheeless, V. E., & Dierks-Stewart, K. (1981). The psychometric properties of the Bem sex role inventory. *Communication Quarterly, 29*, 173–186.

Witte, S. (1985). Revising, composing theory, and research design. In S. Freedman (Ed.), *The acquisition of written language: Response and revision* (pp. 250–284). Norwood, NJ: Ablex.

CHAPTER EIGHT

Gendered Voice in Composing, Gendered Voice in Evaluating: Gender and the Assessment of Writing Quality

Eleni Roulis
University of St. Thomas

During the last two decades feminists and other researchers have examined a number of emerging issues related to the broad topic of language and gender, including the study of sex role differences and their impact on male/female speech and communication styles and the influence of sex role differences on audiences' perceptions and evaluations of communicators (Coates, 1986; McConnell-Ginet, Borker, & Furman, 1980; Phillips, Steele, & Tanz, 1987; Smith, 1985; Thorne, Kramarae, & Henley, 1983). Interest in these issues has coalesced with shifting goals and emphases in sociolinguistics and the impetus of the women's movement to produce new lines of research inquiry on various aspects of the interactions of language, gender, and society (McConnell-Ginet et al., 1980; Smith, 1985; Thorne & Henley, 1975).

Sex Role Stereotyping

One line of research inquiry that has established consistent perceptions of gender-linked differences has been the study of sex role stereotypes; that is, consensual beliefs about the differing characteristics of men and women are both traditional and widely held. Research results in this area have confirmed the existence of clearly defined stereotypes for men and women as well as a high consensuality with respect to sex role perceptions. For example, women are generally perceived as less competent, less logical, and less objective than men, whereas men are perceived as lacking interpersonal sensitivity, warmth, and expressiveness compared to women (Ashmore & Tumia, 1980; Broverman, Vogel, Broverman, Clarkson, & Rosen-krantz, 1972; Hargreaves & Colley, 1987). The ubiquitous term sex role has not been defined with clarity; its usage differs across disciplines. That is, in anthropology sex role refers to social positions, in sociology to social relationships, and in psychology to behavior differences. In psychology, a predominant view is that sex role refers to a set of behaviors and characteristics that are typical of men and women that are shaped by common social assumptions and expectations about masculinity and femininity (Miller, 1986). More often these assumptions become stereotyped, as it is easy for people to use notions of the typical man and the typical woman in assigning attributes to individuals or in responding to them (Hargreaves & Colley, 1987). It seems clearer to say that intellectual, emotional, and personality traits are distributed in a range of possibilities in humanity without restrictions of sex, race, or nationality. Furthermore, to believe that men and women cannot develop certain mental or psychological attributes because of their sex can result in patterns that people observe and believe to be inevitable (Kramer, 1991).

Male/Female Language Use

Stemming from this increased interest in the effects of sex role stereotypes, another line of inquiry has involved the study of gender-linked differences in male/female language use. The first generation of studies on male and female language identified and described formal linguistic differences that were presumed to mark the language of men and women (Crosby & Nyquist, 1977; Dubois & Crouch, 1975; Edelsky, 1977; Key, 1975; Kramer, 1975; Lakoff, 1975, 1977). Although the first-decade work on language and gender did not substantiate the existence of consistent differences in the formal features of language, this subsequent work rejected assumptions about difference stemming from any "natural" or intrinsic male/female differences in favor of a view of male/female speech and patterns of interaction as mirroring the social inequalities evident in other areas of male/female relations (Smith, 1985).

More recently, researchers have enlarged their focus to encompass a broader and a more pragmatic analysis of gender-linked differences in a variety of social dimensions. By the 1970s the study of language turned increasingly toward the study of performance, of pragmatics, toward the study of language in the actual context of actual communicative situations and use (Searle, 1974). As part of that larger pragmatic turn in the study of language, the emerging field of sociolinguistics emphasized the study of language variation in conjunction with speakers' social identities based on social class, ethnicity, and ultimately, sex or gender (Hymes, 1974).

The feminist movement challenged traditional approaches to sex-differentiated language by investigating stereotypical assumptions about differences in men's and women's language use and by raising questions concerning the ways in which language constructs and maintains gender roles and status in society (Kramarae, 1981; McConnell-Ginet et al., 1980; Spender, 1980; Thorne et al., 1983). Recent feminist scholarship examining the relationship between language and gender has sought to investigate how linguistic socialization shapes not only linguistic and communicative competence, but how it influences social behaviors and attitudes toward language used by men and women (Kramer, 1975; McConnell-Ginet et al., 1980; Scott, 1980; Thorne et al., 1983). Questions have been directed to the interactive roles of gender, context, and participants that were more precisely related to issues of status and power raised by feminists (Smith, 1985; West & Zimmerman, 1985). In conjunction with this work, other researchers have found that perceived gender differences in language or in other behaviors are often the result of listeners' perceptions of differences. The perceptions, in turn, are often based on listeners' stereotypes or beliefs about gender differences rather than on the existence of actual differences (Berryman, Fink, & Wilcox, 1983; Liska, Mechling, & Stathas, 1981; O'Barr & Atkins, 1980; Rasmussen & Moely, 1986; Wiley & Eskilson, 1985; Wilson & Gallois, 1985).

Overall, a more sophisticated understanding of male and female communication styles in our society has emerged as a result of this broader focus. The result has been a richer description of male and female speakers' communication strategies in broader contexts of use (Maltz & Borker, 1982; Thorne et al., 1983). Although this more recent work on language and gender has not produced univocal findings, it has shifted attention from formal linguistic features to aspects of language-in-use including attention to differences in use of organizational codes (Goodwin, 1980; Lever, 1976), interruptions (Zimmerman & West, 1975), questions, false starts, topic raising (Fishman, 1983), and the signaling of a variety of aspects of deference, accommodation, and power (Kramarae, Schultz, & O'Barr, 1984; Tannen, 1990; Thorne et al., 1983).

Feminist Perspectives on Discourse Studies

Alongside and undoubtedly influenced by work in this second generation of research on language and gender, there has been a growing body of feminist literature that addresses the role of language in constituting identities and ideologies. The feminist concern has been to draw attention to women's actual use of language on its own terms and to depart from past inquiries that have defined women's language primarily as the "marked" version in contrast to the male "unmarked" version. More recently, feminists have advocated a reassessment of conversational models to include attention to the dimensions of cooperation/collaboration versus assertiveness/competition in the communication patterns of men and women (Caywood & Overing,

1987; Goodwin, 1980; McConnell-Ginet et al., 1980; Thorne et al., 1983). Collectively, feminist scholars have emphasized the need to redefine discourse in terms of a collaborative effort in order to move women into public discourse and to work toward changing the accepted norms for discourse that incorporate a competitive, adversarial, phallocentric model (Farrell, 1979; Gearhart, 1979; Meisenhelder, 1985).

Closely related to this work, other feminists have inquired into how it is that men and women demonstrate different ways of constructing knowledge as a result of their differing patterns of social, psychological, moral, and intellectual development. Chodorow's (1978) male/female identity theory and her later study on the culture of gender (1989) both suggest male/female differences in relational capacities and in modes of interaction with others. Influenced by Chodorow's sociology of gender, Gilligan (1982, 1988, 1990) has written about differences in the ways men and women respond to moral conflict, an area that, she claims, demonstrates striking differences between the sexes and how they lend different meanings to connection, dependence, autonomy, peer pressure, loyalty, and violence. Her claim is that women view moral conflict in terms of conflicting responsibilities that are determined by context and participants whereas men equate morality with universal rights and rules. Gilligan's work, in its attention to the particularities of women's experience, offers a reinterpretation of Kohlberg's hierarchical theory of the stages of moral development modeled on the male experience. Her findings indicate that two moral voices can be distinguished and the justice perspective that is associated with male speakers and evaluated as normative needs to be reconsidered. Women's care perspective is an equally sophisticated and vital perspective complementing the more masculine concern for rights and justice.

In the course of her research Gilligan listened to the voices of adolescent girls for over 10 years. By following the girls through their school experience, Brown and Gilligan (1992) found that the passage out of girlhood to adolescence is one of silence, disconnection ". . . a giving up of voice, an abandonment of self, for the sake of becoming a good woman and having relationships" (p. 2). During this crucial developmental progress in girls' lives there is a loss of voice, a struggle to authorize or take seriously their own experience, and an impasse to deal and act in the face of conflict. In presenting this ongoing research on male and female voice, Gilligan emphasized the need to include women's thinking and girls' experiences that will generate "a new mapping of the moral domain, a new framework for theories of psychological development and new directions for the practice of psychotherapy and education" (Gilligan, Ward, Taylor, & Bardage, 1988, p. ii).

Drawing on Gilligan's work, Schweickart (1990) examined "the ethic of care" in conjunction with current theories of reading and writing in order to ultimately transform this research into classroom strategies that would not silence either male or female students. Specifically, she raised the issue of the role of gender and its relationship to theories of discourse communities, which she states are predominantly imbued with a sensibility of an "ethic of rights" that is associated with a rational, Western masculine way of looking at feeling and that perpetuates unequal distributions of power between readers, writers, and texts. For her, the crucial question becomes what difference would it make if women's distinctive subjectivities and social interests were incorporated in such theories. The feminine model of moral reasoning could make a difference in a theory of discourse, a theory that would emphasize a reciprocity of care.

Belenky, Clinchy, Goldberger, and Tarule (1986) also built on Gilligan's notion that the male experience has served as the model in defining processes and shifted the concern from moral development to male and female intellectual development. Building on Perry's *Forms of Intellectual and Ethical Development* (1970), they explored the experience and the problems women revealed as learners and knowers. They grouped women's perspectives on knowing in five epistemological categories: silence, received knowledge, subjective knowledge, procedural knowledge, constructed knowledge. They found that women were able to find their voice, and therefore, view themselves as creators of knowledge when they valued and connected both subjective (intuition, personal meanings, self-understanding) and objective strategies for knowing.

Male/Female Writing Differences

Associated with the study of gender-linked differences in communicative styles and in moral and intellectual development, feminists and other researchers have also been led to raise questions about the likelihood of differences in the writing of men and women. Consistent with the sociopragmatic turn in language studies, there has been a growth of interest in text or discourse analysis, in the analysis of features of naturally occurring written texts. With growing realization that speech and writing constitute systematically different means for the realization of meaning, the study of writing has taken on new significance. Much of this latter work, influenced by feminist critical theory (Belenky et al., 1986; Elshtain, 1982a, 1982b; Flynn, 1988; Gilligan, 1982; Lamb, 1991; Meisenhelder, 1985; Spender, 1989) posit differences in codes of interpersonal relationships including differences in moral and intellectual development.

In short, there is now a body of critical-interpretive work by feminists that argues on behalf of culturally mediated differences in development that likely lead to differences in the ways in which men and women write, which may in turn lead them to construct differing social and political realities, differences that have been described in terms of male pugilistic/phallocentric rhetorical stances versus female cooperative/nurturing rhetorical stances. In this context, feminist writers have claimed that "the male mode reflects an epistemology that perceives the world in terms of dichotomies, categories, roles, stasis, and causation, whereas the female expressive mode reflects an epistemology that perceives the world in terms of ambiguities, pluralities, processes and complex relationships" (Stanley & Wolfe, 1983, p. 126). Thus, a "woman's style" is perceived as grounded in the language of process and change that goes beyond the confines of masculine structures and is claimed to be more adequate to describe the new ways in which women conceptualize themselves in relation to each other and to the world (Annas, 1987; Stimpson, 1988).

Earlier studies of men's and women's written language reflect some of the first generation's preoccupation with the correlation of gender and a limited set of formal abstract linguistic features. Hiatt's (1977) investigation studied a large corpus of male and female texts for sentence length and complexity, number of similes, kinds of adjectives; Scates (1981) investigated male and female writing styles by analyzing word choice, syntax, figurative language; Keene (1985) examined freshman composition for differences in length of composition, choice of vocabulary, and types of punctuation; Peterson (1986) analyzed freshman argumentative texts for coordination, deductive connections, personal references, and abstract generalizations; Sterkel (1987) investigated differences by analyzing undergraduate students in business communications. In their most recent work on gender-typical style in written language Rubin and Greene (1992) subjected college students' spontaneous expressive writing and revised instrumental writing to lexical, syntactical, and text-level analyses for features previously linked to writer's gender. Their findings indicated that the writing of men and women is more similar than it is different and that both men and women adapted similarly and appropriately to the differing demands of the two types of discourse. Overall, this group of writing studies shows gender-based differences to be sex-preferential patterns rather than sex-specific patterns, as no set of characteristics, linguistic or otherwise, could be assigned to a single sex.

In contrast to these studies, another group of studies of differences in men's and women's writing has adopted a pragmatic orientation such as analyzing differences in topic choice, vocabulary, content development, and themes of assertiveness and connectedness. Thus, Waters (1975) analyzed freshman themes for subject matter, word choice, perspective, and tone; Flynn (1983) examined topic choice in drafts and revisions of freshman essays; Keroes (1986) examined essays for identifiable differences based on male concerns relating to autonomy and female concerns relating to connectedness; Lynch and Strauss-Knoll (1987) examined students' descriptive writing responses for differences in vocabulary. The results of these studies on differences in men's and women's written language are, at best, mixed. Male and female writing styles studied in the aforementioned groups seem to be more similar than different and the differences found are due more to modes of discourse than due to gender. Although it remains the case that there is little agreement regarding differences in the writing of men and women, the questions and claims upon which these studies have been founded are suggestive.

Readers' Perceptions of Male/Female Writing Differences

Although research studies examining differences in men's and women's written language have increased markedly during the last decade, there has been almost no attempt to assess the "psychological" or perceptual reality of such differences. In a series of studies, Anthony Mulac and associates have explored gender-linked differences in language use by examining differences in readers' perceptions of male and female speakers and writers (Mulac, Blau, & Bauqier, 1983; Mulac, Incontro, & James, 1985; Mulac & Lundell, 1981, 1982; Mulac & Rudd, 1977). The research of Mulac and associates on a gender-linked language effect (women perceived as nice, pleasant, beautiful; men perceived as strong, loud, active) has achieved results that appear to be analogous to more general research on sex role stereotyping (women perceived as tactful, charming, sensitive to the needs of others; men perceived as strong, dominant, independent). Additionally, Mulac's work, studying readers' responses rather than speaker/writers' performances, has shown that readers of transcripts of male and female speech reliably attribute different attributes or values to those transcripts even though those same readers are unable to independently identify speaker/writer sex.

Similarly, in a more recent work, Zahn (1989) built on Mulac's work by comparing the gender-linked language effect and sex role stereotyping effect by examining subjects' evaluative reactions to transcriptions of men and women speaking in naturally occurring conversations. Zahn's conclusions, although not statistically significant, suggested that both male and female speakers were responded to with considerable variability from conversation to conversation. His results indicated there was partial support for the gender-linked language effect and its impact on raters' evaluations but the findings did not demonstrate systematic rating differences based on sex role stereotyping.

In a subsequent study, Roulis (1990) replicated and extended Mulac's previous research on the relationship between a gender-linked language effect and a sex role stereotype effect on readers' perceptions of male and female writing. This study examined the responses of over 300 undergraduate composition students to argumentative-persuasive writing. Letters written to a university board of regents (six male and six female) in response to a gender-neutral writing task were presented to readers in three language/ stereotype conditions: (a) gender-linked language condition only, (b) gen- der-linked and stereotype condition, and (c) gender-linked language versus stereotype condition. In each condition, readers' responses were measured by the Speech Dialect Attitudinal Scale (SDAS) and a Rhetorical Stance Scale (RSS). The SDAS (consistent with previous studies) revealed a factor structure that included a Socio-Intellectual Status factor, an Aesthetic Quality factor, and a Dynamism factor. The RSS (developed especially for this study) was constructed to reflect claims of difference in the male and female rhetorical style, (i.e., the female mode incorporating more connection and interaction; the male mode incorporating more detachment and objectivity) revealed an underlying factor structure consisting of a Cooperative factor and a Com- petitive factor.

Roulis (1990) found that indeed there were differences in readers' re- sponses to male and female writing styles across all three language/stereo- type conditions. Multivariate analysis of variance (MANOVA) of the three SDAS dimensions demonstrated that female writers were rated higher on the Socio-Intellectual factor and the Aesthetic Quality factor, whereas both male and female writers were rated approximately the same on the Dyna- mism factor; results of the two RSS factors demonstrated that female writers were rated significantly higher than male writers on the Cooperative factor. These results provide further evidence for the psychological reality of dif- ferences in readers' perceptions and responses to male and female writing.

Additionally, results in the Roulis (1990) study demonstrated a difference between male and female readers' scores across the three language/stereo- type conditions; that is, there were rater sex main effects in four of the five attitudinal factors. Female readers scored male and female writers differently with significant differences for female readers in judgments of sex differences for the Aesthetic Quality factor and the Socio-Intellectual Status factor. Results indicated there were also rater sex main effects for both the Competitive and Cooperative factors on the RSS and that female readers again scored male and female writers higher on both the RSS factors. Finally, the results suggested that there were significant differences between male and female readers in terms of evaluation of male and female texts.

A handful of research studies have started examining the effects of gen- der-linked features of writing on raters' judgments and writing quality. Haswell and Tedesco (1991) examined raters' responses and evaluations of two separate essays, one written by a man and one written by a woman. Their results indicated that although the writer's gender had no influence on the success rate in guessing gender, gender did influence how essays were rated. Additionally, they concluded that there is a culturally determined way of looking at gender that students and teachers bring to the evaluation.

Burkhart and Sigelman (1990) examined the effects of gender on news article evaluation and found that students judge stories similarly regardless of whether the byline is male or female and that unsophisticated news readers tend to evaluate women higher on trustworthiness, writing style, and accuracy. Spear (1989) examined science teachers' attitudes toward differences between the written work of male and female students and what specific features science teachers associated with male and female written work.

Male/Female Classroom Interaction and Expectations

Provocative questions concerning the differing academic experiences men and women receive in elementary, secondary, and higher education have been prompted by feminist journals, government publications, and critics of educational policy (Kramarae & Treichler, 1990). Beginning in the 1980s there has been continuous development of research on the topic of gender and education, including complex and numerous issues of power, equity, and curriculum transformation for disenfranchised, invisible people (i.e., students not of the dominant race, class, or gender). Much of the research demonstrated that schools shortchange women, develop and reinforce sex segregations and stereotypes, and even support discriminations that exaggerate the negative aspects of sex roles in the wider society so that most women do not enjoy a fully equal educational opportunity (Delamont, 1990; Grossman & Grossman, 1994). The literature on gender equity and gender studies in the classroom illuminates issues of sex differentiation in the curriculum (Hall & Sandler, 1982; Riddell, 1992; Whaley & Dodge, 1993), cites examples of sex discrimination in classrooms (American Association of University Women, 1991), and explores gender differences in teachers' expectations, interactions, rewards, and preferences in the classroom (see collection in Gabriel & Smithson, 1990; Sadker & Sadker, 1980, 1986; Walker & Mehr, 1992; Weiss, 1988).

The concern with the influence of gender on learning is associated with the belief that men and women have differing learned roles, behaviors, and self-perceptions in society so that the strong social construction of the assumption of power and control is brought into the classroom (Annas & Maher, 1992; Finke, 1993; Wrigley, 1992). Consistent with these assumptions then are the specific notions of what education is, what are the proper roles of students and teachers, what is defined as excellence, and what are appropriate techniques for evaluation. Thus, the endeavor for the growing research on gender studies is to explore issues of gender, gender equity, and differences in the ways males and females write, think, speak, read, and participate in the classroom (Luke & Gore, 1992; Lewis & Simon, 1986).

Cumulative research evidence shows male students' efforts are more valued over female, male and female students receive qualitatively different evaluation and feedback, male students are challenged more, school authorities give tacit approval to sexual harassment, and school materials and classes often stereotype or ignore female students. Consequently, a dominant message throughout women's academic lives becomes that their achievement is dependent on compliance with formal rules, their accomplishments become attributed to luck, their failures are equated with intellectual disabilities, and their academic and career goals are not seriously entertained (Rich, 1979; Thorne, 1983). Whether overt or subtle, conscious or unconscious, differential treatment based on gender is far from innocuous and its cumulative effect can be damaging to the entire education process for both men and women, "the unnatural silences . . . the unnatural thwarting of what struggles to come into being . . . it is those circumstances which obstruct and crucially determine whether creative capacity will be used and developed or impaired and lost" (Olsen, 1978, p. 24).

Much of the feminist work that has been achieved in curriculum and pedagogy studies illustrates "how gender is socially constructed within institutional and ideological technologies of power that inform all aspects of school life . . . how the experiences of both teachers and student, along with the production of knowledge, meaning and values in school, can best be understood by recognizing and analyzing how specific pedagogical practices function within institutional sites to produce contradictory social forms and relations" (Giroux & Freire, 1988, p. xi). In viewing this ongoing struggle of political transformation within the classroom, feminist pedagogy is a practice that addresses the complexity of an ongoing pedagogical practice that is flexible and redefines itself by making the classroom context a place for women's knowledge and experience. "It is the reality of lived differences that critical pedagogy practice must claim as the agenda for discussion. In practice this often implies a struggle . . . a struggle that makes possible new knowledge that expands beyond individual experience and hence redefines our identities and the real possibilities that we see in the daily conditions of our lives" (Eichorn et al., 1992, p. 320).

Within a framework of radical educational theory, Weiler (1988) examined the interaction of race, gender, and social class and its effects on how teachers perceive themselves in the classroom, the way students respond to teachers, and how teachers respond to them. She further analyzed the contradictions that arise when teachers ignore students' voices and silence expression. In examining the role of gender in schooling, she found that schools transmit different cultures to boys and to girls that ultimately reproduce existing divisions of labor. Weiler emphasized pedagogy that celebrates the politics of difference and legitimizes the language and voice of the others in order to link the production of knowledge and the act of learning to forms rooted in the histories, experiences, and meanings of teachers and students.

Responding to Writing

The current research literature on response to writing (Anson, 1989; Freedman, 1987; Lawson, Ryan, & Winterowd, 1989; Prior, 1991) focuses primarily on ways in which oral and written response is attended to in the context of the composition classroom through a variety of activities including the teachers' written comments in margins, the structured peer groups, and conferences. However, response can be defined in a broader context that encompasses activities in a range of responses and reactions to writing: Formal, informal, written and oral, teacher to student, student to student, draft to draft, casual conversations, classroom lecture, student self-assessments, talking/writing, and think-aloud sessions can be considered responses to writing (Beach, 1989; Scardamalia & Bereiter, 1985). In particular, theories in composition process and general theories about intellectual skills suggest that greater positive results take place when all types of response play a central and positive role (Applebee & Langer, 1984). Additionally, the process of response affects not only the revision/draft process, but students' knowledge of themselves, attitudes toward their writing styles, and development of their subject matter. Consequently, a crucial question then is how can response support the teaching and learning of writing more equitably (see collection in Lawson et al., 1989).

Furthermore, taking into consideration the range and diversity of communication discourse styles within classrooms today, there is a fervent need to expand the understanding of the social, cognitive, and interpersonal nature of writing and the writing process and to challenge existing frameworks in order to redefine and make more inclusive the criteria for evaluation (Anson, 1989; Cooper & Odell, 1977; Farr & Daniels, 1986; Flynn, 1989). Revised notions of the canon, of language use, of alternative discourse forms demand a re-visioning of the process model and of cultural models, and of the teacher–student relationship during the process (Caywood & Overing, 1987). As Anson (1989) reminded us, ". . . from both the teacher's and the student's perspectives response to writing is often difficult and tense" (p. 2). Both teachers and students are faced with mixed tensions; teachers in their role of being both the guides/facilitators as well as gatekeepers of textual standards and students who are exposing their private creations for public scrutiny.

Freedman (1987) presented an especially detailed model of response to student writing. It is drawn from Vygotsky's theory on how collaboration and response can lead to significant developmental gains when the social nature of cognition is emphasized. That is, in order for response to be a central part of the teaching–learning interaction both participants play an active role. Through a process of collaboration, writers receive feedback and soon the learner becomes independent of the collaborator because he or she has become more self-critical and can self-monitor his or her own process. Thus, response then becomes what Freedman (1987) termed "collaborative problem-solving," which is similar to other teaching techniques such as scaffolding (Applebee & Langer, 1983), reciprocal teaching (Palinscar & Brown, 1984), and procedural facilitation (Bereiter & Scardamalia, 1982). Moreover, in applying Vygotsky's insights to response to student writing, it becomes clear that response should be collaborative, should help writers solve problems, and should lead to independent problem solving (Freedman, 1987). As teachers and agents of change in the writing field, it becomes apparent that to circumvent these tensions and complexities inherent in the response process involves careful inclusion of a variety of procedures and activities: specifically, to move beyond the accepted measures of socio-cognitive ability and to see "the full range of social cognition and social processes . . . to explore personal, social, historical contexts of human discourse in natural settings" (Prior, 1991, p. 305), and to explore the full range of human experience. Thus, the concern for gender equity in the writing classroom becomes a central issue in the teaching and in the assessment of writing. Revising aesthetic criteria and reevaluating forms of discourse mean taking seriously alternative forms of discourse used by both men and women (Daumer & Runzo, 1987). Equity in the writing classroom would then "create new standard[s] which accommodate and nurture differences . . . equity fosters the individual voice in the classroom, investing students with confidence in their own authority . . . equity unleashes the creative potential of heterogeneity" (Caywood & Overing, 1987, p. xi).

Recently, several studies investigated the varied ways in which teachers read and respond to student papers in general and also, specifically, to what extent gender influences teachers' comments to students' writing. In the Connors and Lundsford (1993) study, 50 raters examined the responses of 3,000 teacher-marked student essays that had been previously collected for a national study of patterns of formal error in college students' writing. Raters examined the papers to find examples of the top 20 error patterns in the student essays. They were specifically interested in global comments made by teachers, that is, comments in response to the content of the paper or to the rhetorical aspects of organization and structure, and what these comments reflected about the teacher–student relationships. The results were mixed in that 77% of all the papers contained global or rhetorical comments of some type and 75% of the papers bore some sort of grade, although many of the graded papers contained no other form of commentary. Additionally, the raters found that although teachers are genuinely interested in helping students with rhetorical issues in their writing, teachers do not communicate their rhetorical evaluations effectively in that the emphasis still seems to be on pointing out problems and giving standards by which to judge the finished piece.

Roen (1992) studied the extent to which gender influences teachers' responses to students' papers. Writing teachers (14 female and 14 male) were asked to read four persuasive letters written by high school juniors (2 boys and 2 girls) and to use criteria normally used for evaluation, to assign a grade, and to complete an evaluation scale. Each teacher read a complete set of papers containing either correctly identified writer gender or incorrectly identified writer gender. Overall, results on the holistic measure and most of the analytic measure showed that the gender of the teacher and the labeled gender of the writer made no significant difference in scores. However, there was a strong interaction between gender of the reader and real gender of the writer suggesting that gender-specific linguistic features had differential effects on male and female readers.

Barnes (1990) also examined the effect of gender influence in teachers' written responses to students' essays. Thirty-four college writing instructors were asked to comment on two students' essays, one by a man and one by a woman, that contained gender-based stereotypic linguistic and stylistic features. In order to examine whether the supposed gender of the writer influences the quality and quantity of the teachers' comments, one group of instructors received the two essays with the real writers' names whereas the second group received the same two essays with the names switched. Teachers' written comments were classified into two speech acts: directives and verdictives. Results demonstrated that regardless of whether the indicated writer was male or female, teachers' comments provided feedback more on form than on content. Furthermore, Barnes' results indicated the gender of the teacher plays a significant role in the pattern of the comments, in that generally, male teachers are intolerant of emotional writing especially when the writer is female and that female teachers are far more concerned about the form and mechanics of the essay. Her conclusions suggest that male and female teachers accord greater respect to what is identified as the male voice or rhetorical style, and that a typed woman's voice is not accepted.

STUDY

Methods and Procedures

Accordingly, this present study undertook a replication and extension of the research work on the process of reading and responding to written texts. Specifically, it replicated and extended the recent research by Barnes (1990) by using six essays for each reader and connecting subjective rating scales of readers' impressions of writers. The study looked at how teachers respond to student essays, explored the content of their comments and expectations, and examined their subjective impression of writers. More precisely, the following research questions were examined:

1. How do readers respond to male and female writers along the attitudinal dimensions of the Speech Dialect Attitudinal Scale (SDAS) and the Rhetorical Stance Scale (RSS) across all three language/stereotype conditions?
2. Are there differences between male and female readers' responses to male and female writers?
3. How are the readers' comments distributed among the essays?

Participants, Language Stimuli, and Procedures. The study examined the responses of 90 (46 female and 44 male) midwestern writing teachers between the ages of 25 and 50 years who taught either undergraduate composition courses or secondary English/writing during the school year 1991–1992.

The language samples used as stimuli for this investigation came from essays written by undergraduate students in a freshman writing program at a midwest college. Approximately 70 students (ranging in age from 17 to 25 years) wrote an essay responding to a moral dilemma entitled "What should Chris do?". In summary, Chris is a 12-year-old who has worked to save money to see a rock concert. However, her mother wants Chris to buy school clothes with the money instead of concert tickets. Students were asked to write an essay in which they discuss the problem and give their opinion as to what Chris should do. They were further instructed to express themselves as openly and sincerely as possible as there was no "right" or "wrong" answer to the problem. Finally, they were told no signature was required, only the information sheet asking for their gender and age.

To select writing samples that would be evaluated by the larger group of teachers, three raters (two female and one male), naive to the purpose of the study, first read and rated the essays on a subjective impression scale according to three levels (3 = high, 2 = middle, 1 = low) of overall writing quality. Six essays (3 by men, 3 by women) were randomly selected from among the group of 35 student essays rated as middle level. Each of the six essays was printed along with differences in accompanying information to constitute three different writing conditions: (a) language effect only (no name or gender attributed to writer), (b) language effect plus stereotype effect (correct name/gender attributed to writer), and (c) language effect versus stereotype effect (incorrect name/gender attributed to writer). The same six essays were used in all three conditions. The order of the essays was counterbalanced so that three different ordered sets of the essays were formed.

The participant raters (the writing teachers) each received a complete booklet containing the six essays from one language condition only along with written and oral directions on how to fill out the rating forms. Essay booklets representing all three conditions were distributed, with each rater's condition determined by randomization. All respondents were asked to make judgments based on their subjective impressions of the person who wrote the essay using the semantic differential scales located at the end of each essay. The raters were further instructed to treat the papers as if they were papers they had received in their English/writing class. They were to mark and comment upon them as they would normally, and to assign a letter grade. The purpose was to see the variety of ways teachers approach student papers, the range of teachers' comments, and the impression the writers had on the teachers.

Measurement Instruments. In each condition readers responded to the SDAS and to an RSS. The SDAS is comprised of 12 pairs of bipolar adjectives, each separated by a 7-point semantic differential scale. These were randomly assigned alternating polarities. The SDAS, consistent with previous studies (Mulac, 1976) in which it has been employed, revealed a factor structure (details of the factor analysis are available from the author on request) that included a Socio-Intellectual Status factor (illiterate/literate, low social status/high social status, blue collar/white collar), an Aesthetic Quality factor (awful/nice, unpleasant/pleasant, ugly/beautiful, sour/sweet) and a Dynamism factor (weak/strong, unaggressive/aggressive, passive/active, soft/loud).

The RSS revealed an underlying factor structure dominated by a Cooperative factor (socially autonomous/socially interconnected, uncooperative/cooperative, focused on self/focused on other) and a Competitive factor (nonassertive/assertive, noncompetitive/competitive, dependent/independent).

An additional measure was employed to analyze teachers' comments. This was the scheme used by Barnes (1990) for classifying teachers' comments in terms of speech-act theory. Comments were classified into two categories of speech acts. *Directive speech acts* tell someone what to do. Directives are then broken down into two subtypes depending on the revision requested. The first subtype is the *editive*; this is when the teacher suggests lower order revisions (mechanical, syntactical, grammatical, lexical). The second subtype is the *revisional*, when the teacher asks the students to make higher order revisionals (informational, organizational, holistic alterations). The second speech-act type is the *verdictive* (comments used to praise or to criticize). The intent here was to see if male and female students get different feedback/responses to their writing as illustrated in previous gender studies in oral discourse (Caywood & Overing, 1987; Gabriel & Smithson, 1990). Last, letter grades for essays were assigned points (ranging from A = 8 to C– = 1) in order to calculate mean scores for each male and female writer in the three conditions.

Analysis. To address the interdependence of a gender-linked language effect (psychologically real, identifiable gender differences in language use) and a sex role stereotype effect (attributes of differences based on readers' presumed stereotypes associated with male and female performances), a series of $2 \times 2 \times 3$ analyses of variance (writer sex × rater sex × condition) were employed. In addition to the principal focus of the study (the effect of writer sex under three conditions), rater sex was included as an independent variable because of its possible interaction with writer sex. SDAS and RSS factor scores for each rater's judgment of each writer were computed within each condition and compared across all three conditions. In cases where main or interactional effects were found, least significant difference (LSD) tests were conducted to locate these differences.

To address whether men and women receive different responses on their writing, separate statistical analyses were performed on the coded comments according to the two speech acts (directives and verdictives) made by readers on each essay. By using a series of $2 \times 2 \times 3$ (writer gender × rater gender × condition), ANOVAs (analyses of variance) were employed. When significant results were found in the ANOVAs, LSDs were employed to test for differences among the groups. The total number of words was used to statistically adjust for effects of varying composition length when considering mean differences in the frequencies of the two speech-act types.

Results

How Do Readers Respond to Male and Female Writers Along the Three Attitudinal Dimensions of the Speech Dialect Attitudinal Scale Across the Three Language/Stereotype Conditions? The results demonstrated significant differences in readers' responses to male and female writers along the three attitudinal dimensions of the SDAS across the three language conditions. The mean scores and standard deviations for the SDAS in all three conditions can be seen in Table 8.1.

The ANOVA for the Socio-Intellectual Status factor demonstrated a main effect for writer gender, $F(1, 522) = 69.70$, $p < .001$. Male writers were rated significantly higher than were female writers ($M_{male} = 4.65$, $M_{female} = 4.08$). A main effect for condition also emerged, $F(2, 522) = 6.94$, $p < .001$ with $M_{condition\ 1} = 4.55$, $M_{condition\ 2} = 4.26$, $M_{condition\ 3} = 4.27$. Post hoc analyses using LSD procedures, with $p < .05$ making planned pair-wise comparisons revealed that Condition 1 was significantly different from both Condition 2 and Condition 3. Further examination revealed a two-way interaction between condition and writer gender, $F(2, 522) = 5.55$, $p = .004$. In Condition 1, unidentified male writers were rated higher than were unidentified female writers ($M_{male} = 4.96$, $M_{female} = 4.15$); in Condition 2, correctly identified male writers were rated significantly higher than were correctly identified female writers ($M_{male} = 4.38$, $M_{female} = 4.14$); in Condition 3, male writers (falsely labeled female writers, $M_{male} = 4.61$) were rated significantly higher than were female writers (falsely labeled male writers, $M_{female} = 3.93$).

TABLE 8.1
Writer Sex by Rater Sex Cell Means and Standard Deviations
for SDAS Factor Scores

Dependent Variable	Socio-Intellectual Status		Aesthetic Quality		Dynamism	
Writer Sex:	m	f	m	f	m	f
LANGUAGE ONLY CONDITION						
Female Raters						
M	4.83	4.25	4.38	4.52	4.78	3.96
SD	0.87	1.02	0.65	1.15	0.73	0.82
Male Raters						
M	5.08	4.06	4.29	4.51	4.93	3.91
SD	0.93	1.03	0.46	1.06	0.80	0.79
LANGUAGE PLUS STEREOTYPE CONDITION						
Female Raters						
M	4.82	4.30	3.94	4.68	5.21	3.72
SD	0.53	0.51	0.58	0.58	0.78	0.60
Male Raters						
M	5.10	3.98	4.30	4.62	4.80	3.77
SD	0.62	0.53	0.56	0.95	0.55	0.89
LANGUAGE VS. STEREOTYPE CONDITION						
Female Raters						
M	4.51	3.95	4.66	4.30	4.46	4.43
SD	0.89	1.04	0.79	1.10	0.97	1.05
Male Raters						
M	4.71	3.92	4.88	4.03	4.48	4.57
SD	0.87	1.04	0.78	1.37	0.86	1.25

Note. Level of significance $p < .05$.

A two-way interaction also emerged on this variable between reader gender and writer gender, $F(1, 522) = 4.42$, $p = .036$ with female readers scoring male writers significantly higher than female writers ($M_{male} = 4.59$, $M_{female} = 4.17$) and male readers scoring male writers significantly higher than female writers ($M_{male} = 4.71$, $M_{female} = 3.98$). There was no main effect for reader gender.

The ANOVA for the Aesthetic Quality factor demonstrated a main effect for condition, $F(2, 522) = 6.97$, $p < .001$ with $M_{Condition\ 1} = 4.35$, $M_{Condition\ 2} = 4.25$, $M_{condition\ 3} = 4.26$. Post hoc analyses revealed that means scores in Condition 1 were significantly different from Condition 2 and Condition 3. A main effect for writer gender emerged, $F(1, 522) = 59.70$, $p < .001$. Female writers were rated significantly higher than were male writers ($M_{female} = 4.56$, $M_{male} = 4.09$).

There was no main effect for reader gender; however, there was a two-way interaction on this variable for reader gender by writer gender, $F(2, 522) = 5.74$, $p < .017$. Female readers scored female writers significantly higher than male writers ($M_{female} = 4.51$, $M_{male} = 4.31$) and male readers scored male writers significantly higher than female writers ($M_{male} = 4.57$, $M_{female} = 4.39$).

There was also a two-way interaction on this variable with condition by writer gender, $F(1, 522) = 19.43$, $p < .001$. In Condition 1, unidentified female writers were rated significantly higher than were unidentified male writers ($M_{female} = 4.51$, $M_{male} = 4.28$); in Condition 2, correctly identified female writers were rated significantly higher than were correctly identified male writers ($M_{female} = 4.65$, $M_{male} = 4.09$); and in Condition 3, male writers (falsely labeled female, $M_{male} = 4.77$) were rated significantly higher than were female writers (falsely labeled male, $M_{female} = 4.17$).

The ANOVA for the Dynamism Quality factor demonstrated a main effect for writer gender, $F(1, 522) = 101.84$, $p < .001$. There were no main effects for reader gender or for condition. However, there was a two-way interaction for condition by writer, $F(1, 522) = 26.86$, $p < .001$. In Condition 1, unidentified male writers were rated significantly higher than were unidentified female writers ($M_{male} = 4.85$, $M_{female} = 3.93$); in Condition 2, correctly identified male writers scored significantly higher than did correctly identified female writers ($M_{male} = 5.01$, $M_{female} = 3.74$); there were no significant differences in Condition 3, because male writers (falsely labeled female, $M_{male} = 4.47$) and female writers (falsely labeled male, $M_{female} = 4.50$) were rated similarly. No conditions on the Dynamism factor were significantly different from each other.

There were no three-way interactions for any of the three SDAS factors.

How Do Readers Respond to Male and Female Writers Along the Two Attitudinal Dimensions of the Rhetorical Stance Scale (RSS) Across the Three Language/Stereotype Conditions?

The results of the RSS demonstrated significant differences in readers' responses to male and female writers along the two attitudinal factors. The mean scores and standard deviations for the two RSS factors can be seen in Table 8.2.

The ANOVA for the Cooperative factor on the RSS revealed a main effect for writer gender, $F(2, 522) = 30.31$, $p < .001$. Female writers were rated significantly higher than were male writers on the Cooperative factor ($M_{female} = 4.78$, $M_{male} = 4.15$). There were no main effects for reader gender or for condition. However, there was a two-way interaction between condition and writer gender, $F(2, 522) = 30.02$, $p < .001$. In Condition 1, unidentified female writers were rated significantly higher than were unidentified male writers ($M_{female} = 5.24$, $M_{male} = 3.91$); in Condition 2, correctly identified female writers were rated significantly higher than were correctly identified male

TABLE 8.2
Writer Sex by Rater Sex Cell Means and Standard Deviations
for RSS Factor Scores

Dependent Variable:	Cooperative		Competitive	
Writer Sex:	m	f	m	f
LANGUAGE ONLY CONDITION				
Female Raters				
M	3.91	5.02	5.11	3.44
SD	0.92	1.22	0.88	1.25
Male Raters				
M	3.91	5.47	4.76	3.76
SD	0.85	1.32	0.91	0.96
LANGUAGE PLUS STEREOTYPE CONDITION				
Female Raters				
M	3.96	5.04	5.13	3.75
SD	1.03	1.03	0.79	0.81
Male Raters				
M	4.11	5.48	4.88	3.78
SD	1.03	1.17	0.82	1.13
LANGUAGE VS. STEREOTYPE CONDITION				
Female Raters				
M	4.86	4.19	4.5	4.17
SD	1.35	1.78	1.15	1.32
Male Raters				
M	4.52	3.86	4.53	4.36
SD	1.8	1.87	1.12	1.43

Note. Level of significance $p < .05$.

writers ($M_{female} = 5.00$, $M_{male} = 3.89$); in Condition 3, male writers (falsely labeled female, $M_{male} = 4.69$) were rated significantly higher than were female writers (falsely labeled male, $M_{female} = 4.02$).

The ANOVA for the Competitive factor on the RSS revealed a main effect for writer gender, $F(2, 522) = 103.93$, $p < .001$. Male writers received significantly higher scores than did female writers ($M_{male} = 4.78$, $M_{female} = 3.84$). There were no main effects for reader gender or for condition. Further examination revealed a two-way interaction for reader gender with writer gender, $F(1, 522) = 5.25$, $p = .022$. Female readers rated male writers significantly higher than female writers ($M_{male} = 4.93$, $M_{female} = 3.78$). Male readers rated male writers significantly higher than female readers ($M_{male} = 4.63$, $M_{female} = 3.91$). There was also a two-way interaction between condition by writer gender, $F(2, 522) = 16.58$, $p < .001$. In Condition 1, unidentified male writers were rated significantly higher than were unidentified female writers (M_{male} = 4.93, M_{female} = 3.60); in Condition 2, correctly identified male writers were rated higher than were correctly identified female writers (M_{male} = 4.42, M_{female} = 4.26); in Condition 3, male writers (falsely labeled female, M_{male} = 4.42) were rated significantly higher than were female writers (falsely labeled male, M_{female} = 4.26).

There were no three-way interactions for either of the two RSS factors.

How Are Readers' Comments Distributed Among the Essays? The means scores and standard deviation for the two types of speech-act theory across all three conditions can be seen in Table 8.3.

The ANOVA results for the Editive factor revealed a main effect for reader gender $F(1, 521)$ = 22.60, $p < .001$). Female writers received significantly higher scores than did male writers (M_{female} = 8.40, M_{male} = 6.11). A main effect for condition emerged, $F(2, 521)$ = 36.45, $p < .001$ with $M_{Condition\ 1}$ = 8.78, $M_{Condition\ 2}$ = 8.54, $M_{Condition\ 3}$ = 4.26. Mean scores revealed that Condition 1 was statistically different only from Condition 3. There was also a main effect for writer gender, $F(2, 521)$ = 117.56, $p < .001$. Female writers were rated significantly higher than were male writers (M_{female} = 9.85, M_{male} = 4.61).

Further examination revealed a two-way interaction on this variable between reader gender and writer gender, $F(1, 521)$ = 4.25, p = .040 with female readers scoring female writers (M_{female} = 11.47) significantly higher than male writers (M_{male} = 5.33). Similarly, male readers rated female writers significantly higher (M_{female} = 8.20) than male writers (M_{male} = 4.01). A two-way interaction also emerged between condition and writer gender, $F(2, 522)$ = 9.43, $p < .001$. In Condition 1, unidentified female writers were rated significantly higher than were unidentified male writers (M_{female} = 12.72, M_{male} = 6.21); in Condition 2, correctly identified female writers were rated significantly higher than were correctly identified male writers (M_{female} = 10.84, M_{male} = 4.84); in Condition 3, female writers (falsely labeled male, M_{female} = 5.68) were rated significantly higher than were male writers (falsely labeled female, M_{male} = 2.83).

The ANOVA results for the Revisional factor revealed a main effect for condition, $F(2, 521)$ = 27.76, $p < .001$ with $M_{Condition\ 1}$ = 1.02, $M_{Condition\ 2}$ = 1.84, $M_{Condition\ 3}$ = 3.09. LSD procedures revealed that mean scores in Condition 3 were significantly higher than mean scores in Condition 1 and in Condition 2. There was likewise a main effect for writer gender, $F(1, 521)$ = 20.09, $p < .001$; results demonstrated that male writers received significantly higher scores than did female writers (M_{female} = 1.45, M_{male} = 2.46).

A two-way interaction between condition by writer gender emerged for this variable, $F(2, 521)$ = 3.16, p = .043. In Condition 1, unidentified male writers were rated significantly higher than were unidentified female writers (M_{female} = 1.03, M_{male} = 1.71); in Condition 2, correctly identified male writers

TABLE 8.3

Writer Sex by Rater Sex Cell Means and Standard Deviations for Teachers' Comments

Dependent Variable:	Directives				Verdictives				Grade	
	m		*f*		*m*		*f*		*m*	*f*
Writer Sex:	editive	revisional	editive	revisional	criticism	praise	criticism	praise		
LANGUAGE ONLY CONDITION										
Female Raters										
M	5.69	1.58	13.78	1.03	0.66	1.36	0.84	0.56	3.20 (C+)	2.98 (C)
SD	4.50	1.27	4.71	1.68	0.86	0.91	0.82	0.76	0.81	1.00
Male Raters										
M	5.00	1.84	11.67	1.03	0.57	0.89	0.71	0.60	5.95 (B+)	3.88 (B−)
SD	3.67	1.15	5.33	1.48	0.79	0.82	0.95	0.84	0.86	0.98
LANGUAGE PLUS STEREOTYPE CONDITION										
Female Raters										
M	5.42	2.31	12.83	1.04	0.79	1.44	1.41	0.35	4.12 (B−)	3.23 (C+)
SD	5.46	1.52	7.40	1.32	0.97	0.68	0.92	0.64	0.96	1.14
Male Raters										
M	4.98	2.75	8.71	2.27	0.72	1.02	1.11	0.89	6.23 (B+)	3.35 (C+)
SD	5.53	1.30	4.79	1.88	1.10	0.93	1.03	0.75	0.90	1.02
LANGUAGE VS. STEREOTYPE CONDITION										
Female Raters										
M	3.71	2.24	7.43	3.50	1.21	0.43	0.98	0.43	4.98 (B)	4.23 (B−)
SD	6.74	2.91	8.03	3.58	1.91	0.89	1.73	0.97	0.94	0.95
Male Raters										
M	2.95	2.10	3.93	4.52	1.62	0.79	1.81	0.71	5.12 (B+)	3.98 (B−)
SD	3.12	4.55	4.57	5.02	2.15	1.69	2.00	1.22	0.79	0.93

were rated significantly higher than were correctly identified female writers (M_{female} = 1.15, M_{male} = 2.52); in Condition 3, female writers (falsely labeled male, M_{female} = 4.01) were rated higher than incorrectly identified male writers (falsely labeled female, M_{male} = 2.17).

The ANOVA results for the Criticism factor revealed a main effect for reader gender, $F(1, 521) = 8.61$, $p = .003$, showing female readers scoring significantly higher (M_{female} = 1.19) than male readers (M_{male} = .75). A main effect emerged for condition, $F(2, 521) = 12.43$, $p < .001$ with $M_{Condition 1}$ = .69, $M_{Condition 2}$ = .98, and $M_{Condition 3}$ = 1.40. There was no main effect for writer gender; however, there was a two-way interaction between condition and reader gender, $F(1, 521) = 3.24$, $p = .040$. In Condition 1, female reader scores (M_{female} = .75) were significantly higher than male reader scores (M_{male} = .66); in Condition 2, female reader scores (M_{female} = 1.24) were significantly higher than male reader scores (M_{male} = .75); in Condition 3, female reader scores were significantly higher (M_{female} = 1.71) than male reader scores (M_{male} = 1.10).

The ANOVA results for the Praise factor demonstrated a main effect for reader gender, $F(1, 521) = 9.77$, $p < .002$ with male readers scoring significantly higher (M_{male} = .75) than female readers (M_{female} = .43). There were no main effects for writer gender or for condition. A two-way interaction emerged between condition by reader gender, $F(2, 521) = 5.79$, $p = .002$. In Condition 1 (language only effect), male readers (M_{male} = 1.54) scored significantly higher than did female readers (M_{female} = .66); in Condition 2 (language and stereotype effect), male readers scored significantly higher than did female readers (M_{female} = .70, M_{male} = 1.56); in Condition 3, male readers (M_{male} = .85) scored significantly higher than did female readers (M_{female} = .43).

Overall, Condition 1 (language effect only) demonstrated the highest number of directives, and within this group the highest number being editives rather than revisionals. Male and female readers gave unidentified female and unidentified male writers higher numbers of editives (feedback on form) than revisionals (feedback on content). Unidentified female writers received the highest number of directives from both male and female readers, whereas unidentified male writers received equal numbers of editives from male and female readers. Interestingly, female writers received twice as many directives as male writers. Although both unidentified female and male writers received the least amount of verdictives, unidentified male writers received more verdictives (praise) than did unidentified female writers. Female readers wrote more of each type of speech-act comments than did male readers. The mean grade for unidentified male writers was B and the mean grade for unidentified female writers was C+.

A Qualitative Examination of Readers' Comments. As in Barnes' (1990) findings, by looking at teachers' written comments more qualitatively there appeared to be subtle differences in the responses. In general, responses to essays in Condition 1 demonstrated more positive and supportive comments for unidentified male writers than for unidentified female writers.

Essay 2 (unidentified female writer) was the exception, perhaps because it was written more in the standard male-rhetorical style. Although this essay received many editives, overall the comments were positive, and suggestions reflected standards appropriate to problem-solving strategies. Two comments from male readers supported the writer's reasoning and strategy, "A good analysis of both sides of the issue"; and, "Your writing attacks the problem completely and methodically." This essay, written by a woman, did not employ the *I* pronoun, rather followed a sequence of thought-out steps and ideas that could be followed. In fact, one female reader commented on the use of the "if–then" logic of order making it so sensible.

On the other hand, Essays 4 and 6 (both unidentified female writers) consistently received the highest editives, the lowest grades, and the harshest comments from female and male readers alike. Female readers asked: "Why do you talk about Chris and then yourself? Can't you make a distinction?"; or "What kind of title is that for a plan, please show some logic"; or "This is not the type of problem-solving for a young girl; it's OK to use the personal examples but don't assume parallels. Where is the objectivity?"; or "You have considered the subject somewhat and come up with partial solutions." Male readers also commented on the personalized references in the essay: "Why do you feel the need to put yourself in the story. Give concrete directions. . . . The paper would sound a lot better if you steered away from the pronoun *I*"; or "Perhaps you could rely a little less on your emotions and more on Chris' dilemma." Both of these essays used a personalized, open format that involved feelings and anecdotes, that is, stylistic features more closely associated with the female rhetorical style.

In contrast, Essay 3 (unidentified male writer) received the highest number of editives, yet comments on the paper demonstrated a positive response and addressed specific points. Male readers commented on the strength of the argument: "This is a strong and well-developed argument; start to consider all options"; or "You defended your point and tested some details"; or "You produced some excellent writing." Essay 7 (unidentified male writer) also received editives coupled with revisional comments pertaining to strategy. Although the essay contained personal references, female readers commented with suggestions: "You have a good foundation. You know how to give good advice"; or "Try to add more details to your thoughts so that your good advice is not wasted." Finally, Essay 9 (unidentified male writer) received the highest grade overall from all readers and had the least number of comments. Moreover, comments demonstrated both male and female readers perceived a strong writer who made valid points to support the advice being given: "This is a well-written, well thought-out essay. You are a good communicator"; "Your thoughts are clear, direct and logical to follow."

In Condition 2 (language effect plus stereotype effect), each essay was labeled with correct writer sex by using a specific name. Overall, when the readers' comments were analyzed, results demonstrated that male and female writers again received more directives than any other comment. Interestingly, the directives were again divided so that correctly identified female writers received on average higher numbers of directives than did correctly identified male writers. The average grade for female writers was C+ whereas the average grade for male writers was B. In this condition, comments from female readers clearly addressed more mechanics and idea development for female writers than for male writers. Essay 2 (correctly identified female writer) again received the least number of negative comments and those given centered totally on organization or problem solving: A female reader suggested, "How about looking at more specific points to strengthen your organization and your logic . . . you have good opening and closing statements." A male reader noted, "You are coherent and logical." On the other hand, Essays 4 and 6 (correctly identified female writers) received the bulk of comments criticizing style and thought patterns from both male and female readers: "Must you continuously reference yourself?"; "You give advice like a good mom"; "Why is your introduction at the end?"; "These are your feelings, not your advice to Chris." Two female readers wrote in large print "THIS NEEDS TO BE REWRITTEN." Male readers also addressed female stylistic features in these essays with comments such as, "You don't remain objective. You turn it into *your* problem"; "You start out with a mature approach to the problem and by the end, your argument deteriorated"; "Be careful about assumptions and exaggerations (would, always, never, etc). Try to remain more objective."

Comments from male readers to identified male writers tended to be more specific and offered more positive support. For example, Essay 3 (correctly identified male writer) had numerous editives and also comments such as: "What is a responsible decision?"; "How old should people be when they make decisions such as this?"; "What would have been other reasons for the change of mom's mind?" Female readers responded with similar comments to this essay. Essay 7 (correctly identified male writer) also received more comments from male and female readers on the logic of the advice given: "Good rationale and thought-provoking"; "Enhance your good ideas with stronger sentence structure. Do you need to do more proofreading?"; "Consider the justice aspect of your essay; write more to that in your next draft." Again, Essay 9 (correctly identified male writer) received the highest grades and the highest number of verdictives from male and female readers: "I could easily follow the sequence of your thought"; "You give excellent advice to Chris and back it up with a strong argument"; "You use the English language very well." One female reader actually outlined on the margins the order of the argument presented and gave the paper an A+.

Although the grades ranged from D to A–, there were far more Bs and Cs than in Condition 1 (where the essays were not assigned any gender identity). The average grade for female writers was C whereas the average grade for male writers was B. Some general differences found for Condition 2 were: (a) Only female readers used actual students' names when writing comments at the end, (b) male readers tended to make more comments that asked for additional information, and (c) both male and female readers tended to make lengthier responses than in Condition 1.

In Condition 3 (language vs. stereotype), with incorrect writer sex attribution, the average number of directives was still higher for female writers (falsely labeled male) than for male writers (falsely labeled female), although the differences in number were considerably less than in Conditions 1 and 2. The average grade for female writers was B– whereas the average grade for male writers was B. In Essay 2 (female writer falsely labeled male), female readers comments tended to question organization: "You don't have a thesis statement and you jump from point to point"; "Introduce an overview in your work"; You need to demonstrate tighter control over your work and thought." Male readers addressed problem-solving strategies in their comments: "Your essay seems to work from a solution to reasons. Paragraphs need a more logical flow"; "Good discussion. You demonstrate a duality of vision—you take into account both sides of the story and you stress dependability, fairness and honesty." In Essays 4 and 6 (female writers falsely labeled male), however, readers' comments shifted, suggesting that the style was not appropriate rhetoric for a college essay. Female readers wrote: "Why are you telling us this about you?"; "Your authorial voice shifts in the middle of the essay ... WHY???"; "Generally, you have a nice, strong clear voice which is confused by your mechanics." Male readers responded with: "Although you present an honest answer, is it really productive?"; "Stay away from using too many 'I would's' "; "I hope you don't use this approach in your interaction with me!"

Essay 3 (male writer falsely labeled female) received clear directions concerning reorganization from both male and female readers: "You have a three-part structure that generally has a good train of thought, but where is the thesis statement?" Male readers again asked more questions concerning the clarification of definitions: "What is best for children—are you talking socially, economically?"; "Good thought process is shown when you ask for justification of decision-making." Essay 7 (male writer falsely labeled female) received comments such as: "You have a good line of reasoning that gets muddy—let your reader know where you are going"; "Get a logical sequence of thought going here"; "How are you defining a lie? Is there a difference in types of lies?"; "Find a better way to get to yes for both parties—some of your comments are nasty." Essay 9 (male writer falsely labeled female) still received the most positive comments and most number of verdictives—

"Your essay is clear, direct and to the point"; "Let's hear more of what you have to say. What does 'dishonesty breeds dishonesty' mean? How does Chris relate to honesty?"; "What consequences are there in obeying authority? Is it always right to obey authority?"

DISCUSSION

The present study replicated the work done by Barnes (1990) on the relationship between readers' (teachers') written comments and writers' (students') gender by extending the inquiry to a larger number of essays under three different language conditions and by employing additional sets of dependent measures. Thus, in this mode of discourse (problem solving, conflict/resolution), results demonstrate that readers reveal reliable differences in perceptions of male and female writers and a consistent set of underlying dimensions of response to writing.

The patterns of the SDAS demonstrate that in Condition 1 (language effect only) unidentified female writers are rated significantly higher on Aesthetic Quality whereas male writers were judged higher on Dynamism Quality and Socio-Intellectual Status. Consistent with Mulac's results (Mulac & Lundell, 1981, 1982; Mulac et al., 1983; Mulac et al., 1985), the present study demonstrated significant differences in readers' responses to male and female writers along three attitudinal dimensions of the SDAS along three language stereotype conditions with somewhat different patterns of responses.

Results suggest that the differences in readers' responses to male and female writers in Condition 1 (language effect only) are related to differences in the way men and women use language (Flynn, 1988; Brown & Gilligan, 1992). In Condition 2 (language plus stereotype effect), results demonstrated an additive effect in the patterns of readers' responses on all three SDAS dimensions. Again, female writers were rated significantly on Aesthetic Quality whereas male writers were rated significantly higher on Socio-Intellectual Status and on the Dynamism factor. The combinations of language and correctly attributed gender served to enhance readers' responses from Condition 1 to Condition 2.

The results are also consistent with previous research on sex role stereotypes (Broverman et al., 1972), which shows that women are perceived as nice, sweet, and pleasant whereas men are perceived as strong, assertive, and active.

Finally, the results from Condition 3 (language vs. stereotype) demonstrated that male writers (falsely labeled female) were rated significantly higher on the Aesthetic Quality factor whereas female writers (falsely labeled male) were rated significantly higher on the Socio-Intellectual Status factor. The results suggest that the stereotype effect was stronger for the Aesthetic

Quality factor (i.e., women perceived as sweet and nice) whereas the language effect was stronger for the Socio-Intellectual Status factor in this condition.

The findings of the RSS demonstrated that in Condition 1 (language effect only) unidentified female writers were rated significantly higher than unidentified male writers for the Cooperative factor whereas unidentified male writers were rated significantly higher on the Competitive factor. These results suggest that readers responded to male/female differences in the language used. Again, the pattern of results for Condition 2 (language and stereotype effect) showed an additive effect with correctly identified female writers rated significantly higher on the Cooperative factor and correctly identified male writers rated significantly higher on the Competitive factor. In Condition 3 (language effect vs. stereotype effect), results showed that male writers (falsely labeled female) were rated significantly higher on the Cooperative factor than were female writers (falsely labeled male). Again, the stereotype effect appears stronger in this condition for the Cooperative factor whereas the language effect appears stronger for the Competitive factor. Overall, the results from the RSS suggest that readers' responses to male and female writers are consistent with claims of difference in the male and female preferred rhetorical stances (Flynn, 1988; Gilligan et al., 1988; Stanley & Wolfe, 1983).

Examination of teachers' comments made on student papers employed a speech-act analysis adapted from Barnes (1990). It reveals a pattern of showing differences in responses based primarily on writer gender. The results suggest that readers responded to gender-linked stylistic differences in essays regardless of manipulated attributions of gender. That is, comments appeared linked with actual language condition and not with the male or female name ascribed to the writer. A qualitative analysis of the ways in which both male and female readers comment on each of the essays demonstrates a striking confirmation of male and female rhetorical styles as described in the literature (see collection in Caywood & Overing, 1987; see also Meisenhelder, 1985; Tannen, 1990; Tavris, 1992). For example, Essay 2, written by a female writer in a style more clearly associated with the male rhetorical mode, received fewer editives and fewer sharp negative comments than did the other two essays written by female writers using a definite interpersonal style in their response (e.g., Annas, 1987; Flynn, 1988). Readers' responses to male writers (Essays 3, 7, and 9), on the other hand, demonstrated more questions probing the thinking/planning process, more references to strategy even when the work was falsely labeled a female, and more positive, supportive comments. This can be seen, for example, in the way Essay 9 was treated across the three gender attribution conditions. It was consistently praised for its direct, assertive style in writing and in problem solving (e.g., Flynn, 1988; Gilligan et al., 1988; Tavris, 1992).

Some effects of rater gender were also apparent, however. Overall, female readers' comments included more editives, with fewer revisionals and minimal verdictives. Their comments focused more on the form than on the content of the material. Male readers, on the other hand, wrote fewer editives and revisionals, offered a good number of verdictives, and asked for more information from the writers.

Interestingly, the number of editives decreased slightly when actual names were added to the essay papers in Condition 2. Perhaps this suggests that an identified/named writer changes the teacher–student interaction in some way. When the language and stereotype effect were pitted against each other in Condition 3, the number of editives decreased even more than in Condition 2. The pattern of the comments in this condition would suggest that readers accord different values to male and female discourse strategies as essays following a standard linear development (e.g., Essays 2 and 9) received praise for assuming a clear, logical and strong stance. The comments also assign strong stereotypic standards to the criteria. For example, when Essays 2, 4, and 6 (written by female writers) were attributed to male writers, there tended to be more specific questions addressing writing features and more positive coaching to write more effectively. When the same essays were correctly attributed to female writers, the comments provided feedback that suggested that women should not write from their own experience or use a rhetorical voice that is tentative and illogical (Caywood & Overing, 1987).

Implications and Conclusions

Results further establish the psychological reality attaching to readers' perception of differences between male and female writing styles as hypothesized in the literature. Moreover, results provide evidence for the psychological reality of differences in readers' responses to male and female writers in problem-solving writing and therefore contributes support for claims of feminists and other researchers of male and female preferred rhetorical stances or styles. Although the study does not include specific analyses of linguistic or strategic differences employed by male and female writers, the reliability of differences in readers' responses provides at least lateral support for previous claims made on behalf of gender differences in the resolution of conflict and in the evaluation of voice (e.g., Barnes, 1990; Lamb, 1991; Schweickart, 1990). And to characterize these gender-related differences, as reflected by readers' comments, overall the male rhetorical tradition is preferred by both male and female readers, whereas the female rhetorical tradition is undervalued.

Finally, the results would appear to offer further challenge to traditional assumptions undergirding the evaluation of student writing. Implicitly those assumptions seem to be that the evaluation of student writing proceeds on abstract, socially or interpersonally neutral rhetorical linguistic grounds and that traditional practice likely hides or disrupts the social-psychological complexity of what, inherently, is a socially constituted action and judgment. Recent results from the National Assessment of Educational Progress (1980) suggest differences in the writing of 9-, 13-, and 17-year-old male and female students. More specifically, the results reveal that there is an influence of gender on writing quality in that girls wrote better papers and received higher ratings than did boys (Roen, 1992). These findings may suggest that differences in female and male students on writing tasks appear to be related to the level of writing task difficulty (narrative and descriptive vs. expository and problem solving) as well as writing style characteristics. As previously shown, feminist and gender and education research suggest personalized writing styles are congruent with female students' writing style, which may lead to higher assessment ratings (Belenky et al., 1986; Caywood & Overing, 1987; Flynn, 1988; Rubin & Greene, 1992). This implication invites another set of problems, which stem from teachers' stereotypical expectations of male and female students; that is, if writing tasks are congruent with teachers' expectations of writers, then higher ratings will be obtained. Furthermore, the ability to succeed in any writing task requires the time and opportunity for all students to engage in various types of writing. An examination of any limitations in the curriculum will be needed in order to determine if more time is being devoted to the type of writing task required in statewide assessments than to other types of writing. Future research could explore the interactions of the assessed quality of student writing, the influence of cognitive demands and writing styles, and the readers' expectations of writers (Engelhard, Gordon, & Gabrielson, 1992).

The issue of response becomes one of exploring styles and modes of assessment that define more precisely the concept of response rather than standardized, traditional assessments. The idea that teachers' comments are powerful messages to students that can result in a variety of interpretive stances is evidenced. How, then, can teachers respond to students' writing in a voice that is ethical and responsible? First, one way to begin is by asking what discourse practices and style do teachers use for works in progress; specifically, what voice do teachers assume? One that interrupts and overthrows the student's voice as in a gatekeeper stance (Anson, 1989) or one that probes and extends thought through an invitational dialogue as co-responders (Roulis, 1992) and ultimately encourages the making of new knowledge?

Second, and perhaps just as crucial, it is necessary to address the roles of the reader and writer in the response process; that is, to extend permission for students to respond to teachers' comments and to negotiate their interpretation of them (Beach, 1989). In this way they participate more fully in the process from all perspectives and authorize their own text from a different, powerful, rhetorical stance (Greenhalgh, 1992).

Accordingly, the response role of writing teachers would then look at students' work in the light of gender sensitivity (McCracken & Appleby, 1992) as well as explore the impact of the gender-based conceptions that may color teacher–student interactions and student-to-student interaction (Weiler, 1988)—a response role that cultivates a gendered reader (McCracken & Appleby, 1992) and not just an evaluator; one that perceives students' real intentions in their writing, makes connections, moves into the writer's language, and then facilitates the writer's pursuit of making new choices to enhance their writing.

Providing authentic feedback would work toward the development of a sense of responsibility and possibility for all students to write and to contribute effectively in a variety of discourse strategies. Equitable value of the gendered voice would allow students to see themselves as participants in a process, not outsiders in an elite academic community. The exchanges between reader and writer could work toward a more caring stance that is student centered, one that validates the role of gender in learning, thinking, reading, and writing (Schweickart, 1990). The gendered voice of the student/writer combined with the gendered voice of the teacher/reader could have multiple possible forms of thought and, therefore, result in more powerful interactions of responsiveness. In a reciprocity of care process, response would silence neither male nor female students, but would serve to link the experiences and voices of the students and teachers involved (Eichorn et al., 1992; Ellsworth, 1992).

Last, there is a need in future research to examine how the elements that are linked to male and female writers are perceived and evaluated differently by male and female readers through more deliberate and carefully controlled studies of male and female raters of male and female writing samples.

ACKNOWLEDGMENTS

I thank Don Rubin for his comments and support on earlier versions of this chapter.

I wish to thank my graduate assistants Heidi Kunde, Jill Erickson, Mary-Fred Bausmann-Watkins, and Carrie Clark for their assistance with gathering the data.

REFERENCES

American Association of University Women (1991). *Shortchanging girls, shortchanging America.* Washington, DC: American Association of University Women Educational Foundation.
Annas, P. (1987). Silences: Feminist language research and the teaching of writing. In C. Caywood & G. Overing (Eds.), *Teaching writing: Gender, pedagogy and equity* (pp. 3–18). Albany: State University of New York Press.

Annas, P., & Maher, F. (1992). Feminist pedagogies and differences in the classroom. *Radical Teacher, 42,* 2–4.

Anson, C. (Ed.). (1989). *Writing and response.* Urbana, IL: National Council of Teachers of English.

Applebee, A., & Langer, J. A. (1983). Instructional scaffolding: Reading and writing as natural language activities. *Language Arts, 60,* 168–175.

Ashmore, R. D., & Tumia, M. L. (1980). Sex stereotypes and implicit personality theory: A personality description approach to the assessment of sex role stereotypes. *Sex Roles, 6,* 501–518.

Barnes, L. (1990). Gender bias in written teachers' comments. In S. Gabriel & I. Smithson (Eds.), *Gender in the classroom* (pp. 140–159). Urbana & Chicago, IL: University of Illinois Press.

Beach, R. (1989). Evaluating writing to learn: Responding to journals. In B. Lawson, S. Ryan, & W. R. Winterowd (Eds.), *Encountering student texts* (pp. 183–198). Urbana, IL: National Council of Teachers of English.

Belenky, M., Clinchy, B., Goldberger, N., & Tarule, J. (1986). *Women's ways of knowing: The development of self, voice and mind.* New York: Basic Books.

Bereiter, C., & Scardamalia, M. (1982). From conversation to composition. In R. Glaser (Ed.), *Advances in instructional psychology* (Vol. 2). Hillsdale, NJ: Lawrence Erlbaum Associates.

Berryman-Fink, C. L., & Wilcox, J. R. (1983). A multivariate investigation of perceptual attributions concerning gender appropriateness in language. *Sex Roles, 9,* 663–681.

Broverman, I. K., Vogel, S. R., Broverman, D. M., Clarkson, F. E., & Rosenkrantz, P. S. (1972). Sex-role stereotypes: A current appraisal. *Journal of Social Issues, 28,* 59–78.

Brown, L. M., & Gilligan, C. (1992). *Meeting at the crossroads. Women's psychology and girls' development.* Cambridge, MA: Harvard University Press.

Burkhart, F. N., & Sigelman, C. (1990). Byline bias? Effects of gender on news article evaluation. *Journalism Quarterly, 67,* 492–500.

Caywood, C., & Overing, G. (Eds.). (1987). *Teaching writing: Gender, pedagogy, and equity.* Albany: State University of New York Press.

Chodorow, N. (1978). *The reproduction of mothering: Psychoanalysis and the sociology of gender.* Berkeley: University of California Press.

Chodorow, N. (1989). *Feminism and psychoanalytic theory.* New Haven, CT: Yale University Press.

Coates, J. (1986). *Women, men and language.* London: Longman.

Connors, R., & Lunsford, A. (1993). Teachers' rhetorical comments on student papers. *College Composition and Communication, 44,* 200–223.

Cooper, C., & Odell, L. (1977). *Evaluating writing.* Urbana, IL: National Council of Teachers of English.

Crosby, F., & Nyquist, L. (1977). The female register: An empirical study of Lakoff's hypotheses. *Language in Society, 6,* 313–322.

Daumer, E., & Runzo, S. (1987). Transforming the composition classroom. In C. Caywood & G. Overing (Eds.), *Teaching writing: Gender, pedagogy and equity* (pp. 45–62). Albany: State University of New York Press.

Delamont, S. (1990). *Sex roles and the school* (2nd ed.). New York: Routledge.

Dubois, B., & Crouch, I. (1975). The questions of tag questions in women's speech: They don't really use more of them, do they? *Language in Society, 4,* 289–294.

Edelsky, C. (1977). Acquisition of an aspect of communicative competence: Learning what it means to talk like a lady. In C. Mitchell-Kernan & S. Ervin-Tripp (Eds.), *Child discourse* (pp. 225–258). New York: Academic Press.

Eichorn, J., Farris, S., Hayes, K., Hernandez, A., Jarrett, S., Powers-Stubbs, K., & Sciachitano, M. (1992). A symposium on feminist experiences in the composition classroom. *College Composition and Communication, 43,* 297–322.

Ellsworth, E. (1992). Teaching to support unassimilated differences. *Radical Teacher, 42,* 4–9.

Elshtain, J. B. (1982a). Feminist discourse and its discontents: Language, power and meaning. *Signs, 7,* 603–621.

Elshtain, J. B. (1982b). Feminist political rhetoric and women's studies. In D. Keohane, R. Rosaldo, & A. Gelpi (Eds.), *Feminist theory, a critique of ideology* (pp. 319–340). Boston: Harvester Press.

Engelhard, G., Gordon, B., & Gabrielson, S. (1992). The influences of mode of discourse, experiential demand, and gender on the quality of student writing. *Research in the Teaching of English, 26,* 315–336.

Farr, M., & Daniels, H. (1986). *Language diversity and writing instruction.* Champaign-Urbana, Illinois: ERIC Clearing House.

Farrell, T. (1979). The female and male modes of rhetoric. *College English, 40,* 909–921.

Finke, L. (1993). Feminism, voice, and the pedagogical unconscious. *College English, 55,* 7–27.

Fishman, P. (1983). Interactions: The work women do. In B. Thorne, C. Kramarae, & N. Henley (Eds.), *Language, gender and society* (pp. 89–102). Rowley, MA: Newbury House.

Flynn, E. (1983, March). *Gender difference and student writing.* Paper presented at the annual meeting of the Conference on College Composition and Communication, Detroit. (ERIC Document Reproduction Service No. ED 233 399)

Flynn, E. (1988). Composing as a woman. *College Composition and Communication, 39,* 423–435.

Flynn, E. (1989). Learning to read student papers from a feminine perspective, I. In B. Lawson, S. Ryan, & W. R. Winterowd (Eds.), *Encountering student texts* (pp. 49–58). Urbana, IL: National Council of Teachers of English.

Freedman, S. (1987). *Response to student writing.* Urbana, IL: National Council of Teachers of English.

Gabriel, S. L. (1990). Gender, reading and writing: Assignments, expectations and responses. In S. L. Gabriel & I. Smithson (Eds.), *Gender in the classroom* (pp. 127–139). Chicago: University of Illinois Press.

Gabriel, S. L., & Smithson, I. (Eds.). (1990). *Gender in the classroom.* Chicago: University of Illinois Press.

Gearhart, S. (1979). The womanization of rhetoric. *Women's Studies International Quarterly, 2,* 195–201.

Gilligan, C. (1982). *In a different voice: Psychological theory and women's development.* Cambridge, MA: Harvard University Press.

Gilligan, C. (1990). *Making connections.* Cambridge, MA: Harvard University Press.

Gilligan, C., Ward, J. V., Taylor, J. M., & Bardige, B. (1988). *Mapping the moral domain.* Cambridge, MA: Harvard University Press.

Giroux, A., & Freire, P. (1988). Introduction. In K. Weiler (Ed.), *Women teaching for change* (p. xi). New York: Bergin & Garvey.

Goodwin, M. (1980). Directive response speech sequences in girls' and boys' task activities. In S. McConnell-Ginet, R. Borker, & N. Furman (Eds.), *Women and language in literature and society* (pp. 157–173). New York: Praeger.

Greenhalgh, A. M. (1992). Voices in response: A postmodern reading of teacher response. *College, Composition and Communication, 43,* 401–410.

Grossman, H., & Grossman, S. H. (1994). *Gender issues in education.* Boston, MA: Allyn & Bacon.

Hall, R. M., & Sandler, B. (1982). *The classroom climate: A chilly one for women. Project on the status and the education of women.* Washington, DC: Association of American Colleges.

Hargreaves, D. J., & Colley, A. (1987). *The psychology of sex roles.* London: Hemisphere.

Haswell, R., & Tedesco, J. (1991, November). *Gender and the evaluation of writing.* Paper presented at the annual meeting of the National Council of Teachers of English, Seattle.

Hiatt, M. (1977). *The way women write.* New York: Teachers College Press.

Hymes, D. (1974). Speech and language: On the origins and foundations of inequality among speakers. In E. Haugman & M. Bloomfield (Eds.), *Language as a human problem* (pp. 45–72). New York: Norton.

Keene, N. A. (1985). *Male/female language: A stylistic analysis of freshman compositions.* Unpublished doctoral dissertation, Illinois State University, Normal.

Keroes, J. (1986, March). *But what do they say? Gender and the content of student writing.* Paper presented at the annual meeting of the Conference on College Composition and Communication, Seattle, WA. (ERIC Document Reproduction Service No. ED 269 802)

Key, M. R. (1975). *Male/female language.* Metuchen, NJ: Scarecrow Press.

Kramarae, C. (1981). *Women and men speaking.* Rowley, MA: Newbury House.

Kramarae, C., Schultz, M., & O'Barr, W. (Eds.). (1984). *Language and power.* London: Sage.

Kramarae, C., & Treichler, P. (1990). Power relationships in the classroom. In S. Gabriel & I. Smithson (Eds.), *Gender in the classroom* (pp. 127–139). Chicago: University of Illinois Press.

Kramer, C. (1975). Women's speech: Separate but equal? In B. Thorne & N. Henley (Eds.), *Language and sex: Difference and dominance* (pp. 43–56). Rowley, MA: Newbury House.

Kramer, L. (1991). *The sociology of gender.* New York: St. Martin's Press.

Lakoff, R. (1975). *Language and woman's place.* New York: Harper & Row.

Lakoff, R. (1977). Women's language. *Language and Style, 10,* 222–247.

Lamb, C. E. (1991). Beyond argument in feminist composition. *College Composition and Communication, 42*(1), 11–24.

Lawson, B., Ryan, S., & Winterowd, R. (1989). *Encountering student texts. Interpretive issues in reading student text.* Urbana, IL: National Council of Teachers of English.

Lever, J. (1976). Sex differences in the games children play. *Sex Roles, 4,* 478–487.

Lewis, M., & Simon, R. (1986). A discourse not intended for her. *Harvard Educational Review, 56,* 457–472.

Liska, J., Mechling, E. W., & Stathas, S. (1981). Differences in subjects' perceptions of gender and believability between users of deferential and nondeferential language. *Communication Quarterly, 4,* 40–47.

Luke, C., & Gore, J. (1992). *Feminisms and critical pedagogy.* London: Routledge.

Lynch, C., & Strauss-Noll, M. (1987). Mauve washers: Sex differences in freshman writing. *English Journal, 76,* 90–94.

Maltz, D., & Borker, R. (1982). A cultural approach to male/female miscommunication. In J. Gumperz (Ed.), *Language and social identity* (pp. 196–215). New York: Cambridge University Press.

McConnell-Ginet, S., Borker, R., & Furman, N. (Eds.). (1980). *Women & language in literature & society.* New York: Praeger.

McCracken, N., & Appleby, B. (Eds.). (1992). *Gender issues in the teaching of English.* Portsmouth, NH: Boynton/Cook Heinemann.

Meisenhelder, S. (1985). Redefining powerful writing: Toward a feminist theory of composition. *Journal of Thought, 20,* 184–195.

Miller, J. B. (1986). *Toward a new psychology of women* (2nd ed.). Boston: Beacon Press.

Mulac, A. (1976). Assessment and application of the revised Speech Dialect Attitudinal Scale. *Communication Monographs, 43,* 238–245.

Mulac, A., & Rudd, M. J. (1977). Effects of selected American regional dialects upon regional audience members. *Communication Monographs, 44,* 185–195.

Mulac, A., Blau, S., & Bauqier, L. (1983, November). *Gender-linked language differences and their effects in male and female students' impromptu essays.* Paper presented at the meeting of the Speech Communication Association, Washington, DC.

Mulac, A., Incontro, C., & James, M. (1985). Comparison of the gender-linked effect and sex role stereotypes. *Journal of Personality and Social Psychology, 49,* 1098–1109.

Mulac, A., & Lundell, T. L. (1981, November). *Effects of gender-linked language differences in male and female written communication.* Paper presented at the meeting of the Speech Communication Association, Anaheim, CA.

Mulac, A., & Lundell, T. L. (1982). An empirical study the of the gender-linked language effect in a public speaking setting. *Language and Speech, 25,* 243–256.

National Assessment of Educational Progress (1980). *Writing achievement 1969–79: Results from the third national writing assessment* (Volume I—17 year olds). Denver: Education Commission of the States.

O'Barr, W., & Atkins, B. (1980). Women's language or powerless language? In S. McConnell-Ginet, R. Borker, & N. Furman (Eds.), *Women and language in literature and society* (pp. 93–110). New York: Praeger.

Olsen, T. (1978). *Silences.* New York: Dell.

Palinscar, A., & Brown, A. (1984). Reciprocal teaching of comprehension-fostering and monitoring activities. *Cognition & Instruction, 1,* 117–175.

Perry, W. (1970). *Forms of intellectual and ethical development in the college years.* New York: Holt, Reinhart & Winston.

Peterson, S. L. (1986). *Sex-based differences in English argumentative text: A tagmemic sociolinguistic perspective.* Unpublished doctoral dissertation, University of Texas, Arlington.

Phillips, S., Steele, S., & Tanz, C. (1987). *Language, gender and sex in comparative perspective.* London: Cambridge University Press.

Prior, P. (1991). Contextualizing writing and response in a graduate seminar. *Written Communication, 8,* 267–310.

Rasmussen, J., & Moely, B. (1986). Impression formation as a function of the sex role appropriateness of linguistic behavior. *Sex Roles, 14,* 149–161.

Rich, A. (1979). *On lies, secrets and silence.* New York: Norton.

Riddell, S. (1992). *Gender and the politics of curriculum.* New York: Routledge.

Roen, D. H. (1992). Gender and teacher response to student writing. In N. McCracken & B. Appleby (Eds.), *Gender issues in the teaching of English.* Portsmouth, NH: Boynton/Cook Heinemann.

Roulis, E. (1990). The relative effect of a gender-linked language effect and a sex role stereotype effect on readers' responses to male and female argumentative-persuasive writing. *Dissertation Abstracts International,* University of Minnesota, Minneapolis (Vol. 52-05, p. 1670). University Microfilm No. ADG 9122207.

Roulis, E. (1992, May). *Male and female gender-linked writing styles: Effective composing strategies for nontraditional learners.* Paper presented at the Minnesota Council of Teachers of English, St. Louis Park.

Rubin, D. L., & Greene, K. (1992). Gender-typical style in written language. *Research in the Teaching of English, 26,* 7–40.

Sadker, M., & Sadker, D. (1980). *Between teacher and student: Overcoming sex bias in classroom interaction.* Washington, DC: U.S. Department of Education.

Sadker, M., & Sadker, D. (1986). Sexism in the classroom: From grade school to graduate school. *Phi Delta Kappan, 56,* 511–515.

Scardamalia, M., & Bereiter, C. (1985). Fostering the development of self regulation in children's knowledge processing. In S. F. Chipman, J. W. Segal, & R. Glaser (Eds.), *Thinking and learning skills* (Vol. 2, pp. 563–577). Hillsdale, NJ: Lawrence Erlbaum Associates.

Scates, C. M. (1981). *A sociolinguistic study of male/female language in freshman composition.* Unpublished doctoral dissertation, University of Southern Mississippi, Hattiesburg.

Schweickart, P. P. (1990). Reading, teaching and the ethic of care. In S. Gabriel & I. Smithson (Eds.), *Gender in the classroom* (pp. 78–95). Chicago: University of Illinois Press.

Scott, K. (1980). Perceptions of communication competence: What's good for the goose is not good for the gander. *Women's Studies International Quarterly, 3,* 199–208.

Searle, J. (1974). Chomsky's revolution in linguistics. In G. Hartman (Ed.), *On Noam Chomsky: Critical essays* (pp. 2–33). New York: Praeger.

Smith, P. (1985). *Language, the sexes and society*. Oxford, England: Basil Blackwell.

Spear, M. (1989). Differences between the written work of boys and girls. *British Educational Research Journal, 15*, 217–277.

Spender, D. (1980). *Man made language*. London: Routledge & Kegan Paul.

Spender, D. (1989). *The writing or the sex*. Oxford, England: Pergamon.

Stanley, J., & Wolfe, S. (1983). Conscious as style: Style as aesthetic. In B. Thorne , C. Kramarae, & N. Henley (Eds.), *Language, gender, and society* (pp. 125–143). Rowley, MA: Newbury House.

Sterkel, K. S. (1987). *The relationship between gender and writing style in business communications*. Unpublished doctoral dissertation, University of Northern Colorado, Greeley.

Stimpson, C. R. (1988). *Where the meanings are: Feminism and cultural spaces*. London: Routledge, Chapman, & Hill.

Tannen, D. (1990). *You just don't understand*. New York: Morrow.

Tavris, C. (1992). *The mismeasure of woman*. New York: Simon & Schuster.

Thorne, B. (1983). Rethinking the way we teach. *Women and Language News, 7*, 15.

Thorne, B., & Henley, N. (1975). Difference and dominance: An overview of language, gender and society. In B. Thorne & N. Henley (Eds.), *Language and sex: Difference and dominance* (pp. 3–40). Rowley, MA: Newbury House.

Thorne, B., Kramarae, C., & Henley, N. (1983). *Language, gender, and society*. London: Newbury House.

Walker, B. A., & Mehr, M. (1992). *The courage to achieve*. New York: Simon & Schuster.

Waters, B. L. (1975, November). *She writes like a woman*. Paper presented at the Southeast Conference on Linguistics, Atlanta. (ERIC Document Reproduction Service No. ED 115 113)

Weiler, K. (1988). *Women teaching for change*. New York: Bergin & Garvey.

Weis, L. (1988). *Class, race and gender in American education*. Albany, NY: State University Press.

West, C., & Zimmerman, D. (1985). Gender, language, and discourse. *Handbook of discourse analysis, 4*, 113–118.

Whaley, L., & Dodge, L. (1993). *Weaving in the women: Transforming the high school English curriculum*. Portsmouth, NH: Boynton/Cook Heinemann.

Wiley, M. G., & Eskilson, A. (1985). Speech style, gender stereotypes, and corporate success: What if women talked more like men? *Sex Roles, 12*, 993–1007.

Wilson, K., & Gallois, C. (1985). Perceptions of assertive behavior: Sex combination, role appropriateness and message type. *Sex Roles, 12*, 125–141.

Wrigley, J. (1992). *Education and gender equality*. London: Falmer Press.

Zahn, C. (1989). The bases for differing evaluations of male and female speech: Evidence from ratings of transcribed conversation. *Communication Monographs, 56*, 59–73.

Zimmerman, D., & West, C. (1975). Sex role, interruptions and silences in conversations. In B. Thorne & N. Henley (Eds.), *Language and sex: Difference and dominance* (pp. 105–129). Rowley, Massachusetts: Newbury House.

PART THREE

COMPOSING WRITER–AUDIENCE ROLE RELATIONS

CHAPTER NINE

The Developmental Stylistics of Young Writers' Communicative Intentions

Marion Crowhurst
University of British Columbia

Research over the past 30 years indicates that even young children are able to use oral language to communicate effectively in a variety of situations (Warren-Leubecker & Bohannon, 1989). In their conversation, preschoolers can maintain topics, take turns appropriately, and elicit replies from conversational partners. They simplify their sentences when speaking to very young children. When asked to adopt various roles, they can adapt their language according to their role as speaker and the role of their partner. They can understand indirect requests made by peers or parents. They can judge between the "niceness" of pairs of requests like *I want a candy* and *I would like a candy*; and even 2-year-olds can increase the politeness of their requests when prompted to do so. Of course, their ability to adjust their speech to the situation improves with age.

Their ability to communicate effectively is greatly influenced by context. Early experimental studies (e.g., Glucksburg & Krauss, 1967) reported that children in the late preschool period failed to adapt their messages to the needs of their listeners. However, this failure has been attributed, at least in part, to the artificiality of the experimental situation (Warren-Leubecker & Bohannon, 1989). Children are most likely to show sophisticated adjustment of their spoken language when passing on well-known information in familiar situations.

Early studies of written language indicated some ability by quite young students to adapt their language according to the rhetorical situation. Many studies, for example, have found large differences in syntactic complexity due to mode of discourse or language function for Grades 3 and upwards (e.g., Crowhurst & Piché, 1979; Langer, 1986; Perron, 1977). Early studies, however, failed to find much evidence that young students' writing showed adaptation for other aspects of the rhetorical situation such as audience.

Recent studies of children's writing suggest that those earlier studies underestimated children's rhetorical ability. The purpose of this chapter is to review a group of studies that examined students' language variation as influenced by two aspects of the rhetorical situation, namely, audience and language function (or genre).

AUDIENCE

Early studies of the ways students adapted their writing for different audiences found little evidence of audience adaptation by elementary students (Crowhurst, 1978; Crowhurst & Piché, 1979; Rubin & Piché, 1979; Smith & Swan, 1978). Smith and Swan asked sixth-graders and college students to rewrite a stimulus passage three times: so that it "sounded better"; so that it could be read by a third-grader; and so that it would be appropriate for an adult reader. Their college students wrote significantly shorter clauses for third-graders than for either of the other two conditions; there were no significant differences among the three versions written by sixth-graders, although cell means show a trend toward longer T-units for the older audience (8.53 words/TU) than for the younger (7.84 words/TU).

Crowhurst (1978; Crowhurst & Piché, 1979) examined the extent to which 6th- and 10th-graders varied the syntactic complexity of writing addressed to two audiences: best friend and teacher. Students were assigned to write narrations, descriptions, or arguments—40 students writing in each mode at each grade level—and wrote six compositions, three for each audience. Clause length was significantly greater for the teacher audience than for the best friend. The trend toward longer clauses for the teacher audience was evident in all three modes and at both grade levels; however, the difference between audiences was significant only for Grade 10 and only in the mode of argument. Like Smith and Swan's (1978) 6th-graders, those in Crowhurst's study made no significant adjustments in syntactic complexity when writing for different audiences, although there was a trend toward shorter T-units and clauses for the younger audience as was the case for Smith and Swan.

Rubin and Piché (1979) looked at the persuasive strategies used for different audiences by 4th-, 8th-, and 12th-graders and expert adults. Only the expert adults showed substantial differences in the types of persuasive strategies they used for different target audiences.

Early studies, then, looking mainly at the effect of audience on syntactic complexity, did not find significant adaptation for audience in the writing of elementary students. However, a small set of more recent studies has found interesting kinds of audience adaptation by fifth- and sixth-grade writers, and even by second-graders (Craig, 1986; Crowhurst, 1992; Frank, 1992; Greenlee, Hiebert, Bridge, & Winograd, 1986; Kroll, 1985).

Craig (1986) had students in Grades 6 and 11 write arguments for teacher and best friend. Craig, having noted evidence of audience effects on children's oral language, surmised that measures previously used in written-language studies might be too insensitive to detect differences. She used, as her measures, a set of language functions derived from oral-language studies. She found significant audience effects at both grades. Two functions were used more for best friend than for teacher, namely, requests for collaboration (e.g., *I hope you agree with me Janie because I couldn't do it without you*), and rhetorical requests for opinion or direction (e.g., *The money should go toward things that we need. Don't you agree?*). One function was used more for teacher than for best friend, namely, the function described as "surveying possibilities, anticipating problems and solutions, drawing conclusions" (e.g., *I know five hundred dollars wouldn't be enough for an expensive computer but we could get a simple one. Then in the future we could expand and get more things for the computer*). The effect of these differences was that compositions addressed to the teacher sounded more objective, whereas those addressed to best friends sounded more conversational and personal.

Kroll (1985) had students in Grades 5, 7, 9, and 11 and college freshmen rewrite a linguistically complex story for a third-grade reader. Students became progressively better with age at simplifying the story, with a major improvement occurring somewhere between Grades 7 and 9. This major change was especially evident in the number of students who reformulated and simplified the complex moral of the story. More than 90% of students from Grade 9 on made major changes to the moral whereas only a quarter of the fifth-graders did so. Students at all grade levels reduced the lexical and syntactic complexity of the original. The simplification of syntax by young students (Grades 5 and 7) in Kroll's study appears to contradict findings by Crowhurst (1978; Crowhurst & Piché, 1979) and by Smith and Swan (1978), each of whose studies found only a slight trend for sixth-graders to produce syntactic differences for different audiences.

However, the difference between Kroll (1985), on the one hand, and Crowhurst (1978; Crowhurst & Piché, 1979) and Smith and Swan (1978) on the other is likely due to differences in experimental conditions and especially to differences in the specified younger audience. Kroll specified that his subjects rewrite for a third-grade audience; Crowhurst specified that her subjects write for a teacher (an older, more distant audience) and for a best friend (a younger, more intimate audience who would presumably have been about the same age as the sixth-grade subjects); and Smith and Swan's younger audience was described as "someone who has just learned to read," which may or may not have been interpreted, by all their sixth-grade writers, to mean someone in about the third grade. In oral language, even very young children simplify their syntax for younger children (Shatz & Gelman, 1973); it is reasonable to think that the best way to obtain simplified syntax in writing is to specify an audience younger than the writer.

Frank (1992) had fifth-grade students compose a newspaper advertisement and then revise it for a distinctly different audience. They were to try to sell something that they owned to either an adult or a third-grader. A few days later they were asked to rewrite the advertisement to persuade the audience not addressed originally. Adult and third-grade readers who were asked to judge which version addressed which audience were able to do so. Students wrote successfully for both audiences, but were more successful writing for third-graders than for adults as evidenced by the fact that more third-graders than adults were able to identify the audience addressed in the fifth-graders' writing, even though the adults were, presumably, more sophisticated readers than the third-graders. Some examples of the adaptations used were: lower prices, more colloquial language, shorter texts, and simpler adjectives for the younger audience (e.g., "old chairs" vs. "antique Spanish chairs"; "terrific computer" vs. "sophisticated computer"); different forms of address and different selling tactics to appeal to the different audiences.

Crowhurst (1991b, 1992) had students in a Grade 5/6 class correspond weekly for a period of nearly 3 months with preservice teachers enrolled in a language arts methods class. The project was set up for pedagogical rather than research purposes. However, over time, the young students showed remarkable ability to communicate in appropriate ways with their correspondents. A comparison between their first letter and later letters showed interesting differences. (Note that the first letter was written to a remote, unfamiliar correspondent; writing this letter was thus similar to a large number of writing tasks assigned in school.) As compared with first letters, later letters were longer, syntactically more varied and more interesting, and altogether more "communicative." Whereas many first letters began and ended abruptly, most students later adopted more audience-centered ways of beginning and ending—some of them clearly modeled on the beginnings and endings of their older correspondents. They showed developing skill in ways of taking up topics, and of interspersing comments about themselves with inquiries about their correspondents. The kinds of differences noted in the writing of many students is well illustrated by the following pair of letters by "Eric" below, and by comments Carolyn wrote in her journal about her sixth-grade correspondent, "Neil," that follow the letters:

Eric's First Letter

September 15

Dear Pen Pal,

My name is Eric. I go to General Gordon School. I'm a Grade 6 student. My teacher's name is Miss X. The things I like are rock music, sports and science. I'm hoping to be a lawyer when I grow up so I can makes lots of money.

Your Pen Pal

Eric

Eric's Fourth Letter

November 5

Dear T,

I sure have a lot to write after all those weeks. I guess I should start asking questions about your teaching. [NOTE: The student teacher had just completed a 3-week practicum.] How was it? Do you have a good class? What grade are you teaching? Is it a lot of work teaching? Well that's all I have to say about you.

I have lot's of things to tell you about me. I really had a good time at Halloween. I got lots of candy. I lit lots of fireworks and firecrakers with my dad at night, then I went to the Kits Community Centre at the dance. It was realley fun and at the end I was so tired I almost fell asleep. When I went home, I couldn't catch T.V. because every channel I changed, all the movies were gorey. After Halloween it was time for school again and we sure had a lot of tests coming up, so I didn't have very much time to play with my friends because I had to get good marks for the tests.

I really liked your last letter you wrote me and all the places you visited at Greece and I really liked the drawing you drew of your hut you made with your sister on the island. It was pretty well thought out and I liked the inside a lot. It must of bin really fun living in a nice place that you've made. What did you do with it when you left? Did you leave it there?

Love from your

friend, Eric.

(Crowhurst, 1991b, p. 218)

Carolyn's Journal Entry

Neil has become remarkably more enthusiastic about letter exchanges. The first letter he sent me was disappointing . . . only four sentences in total. . . . [H]e was probably looking at our letter writing as an assignment for school. His next letter was a big improvement. He wrote . . . almost a full page . . . and answered some of my questions. . . . To my surprise, on this past Thursday, I received a wonderful card from him which included jokes and, for the first time, questions for me to answer. . . . In addition, . . . he communicated a great deal about himself and his feelings. He explained that he has a weak eye and that he wears glasses. Like most children, Neil would rather not have to wear them. . . . Neil was inexperienced at writing letters and still spells poorly, but in only three letters, he is communicating effectively. (Crowhurst, 1991b, p. 217).*

Greenlee et al. (1986) found audience effects for much younger students. They had second-graders write either letters to a real audience (preservice elementary teachers) or letters of the kind commonly assigned in language arts textbooks. The preservice teachers responded; the textbook assignments were marked by the teacher. Later letters written to the real audience were significantly longer, and had significantly longer T-units than did responses to the textbook assignments.

What, then, is to be made of this set of studies and the various audience effects reported? The first implication is that, contrary to conclusions drawn from early research studies, the writing of elementary-age students undoubtedly reveals evidence of audience adaptation. Second, as with oral language, the ability to adapt to different audiences improves with age (Kroll, 1985). Third, audience effects are especially likely to be observed if one or more of the following conditions exist: (a) One of the audiences students write for is notably younger (Frank, 1992; Kroll, 1985), (b) they write for real rather than imagined audiences (Crowhurst, 1991a, 1992; Greenlee et al., 1986), (c) they write in a genre that encourages a focus on the audience, notably, persuasion (Craig, 1986; Crowhurst & Piché, 1979; Frank, 1992), (d) the measures used are sensitive to the text as a communicative instrument (Craig, 1986).

LANGUAGE FUNCTION

Language function (i.e., persuading, reporting, narrating, etc.) in the written mode may be roughly equated with genre or mode of discourse.[1] Young students' ability to write effectively in various genres has been the subject of considerable discussion. Expository and argumentative discourse have long been regarded as difficult modes for young writers (e.g., Moffett, 1968; Wilkinson, Barnsley, Hana, & Swan, 1980). In recent years, however, compelling voices have asserted that the precursors of exposition and argument appear in the writing of children in the primary grades and that children's ability to write in various genres is both underestimated and undercultivated (Martin & Rothery, 1981; Newkirk, 1985, 1987; White, 1989). The purpose of this section is to consider, briefly, the performance of young students writing in two non-narrative genres: persuasive/argumentative discourse, and reports.

---

*From "Two-Way Learning in Correspondence Between Pen-Friend Pairs," *English Education, 23*(4). Reprinted by permission of the National Council of Teachers of English.

[1]The distinctions that can and should be made among the three terms *language function, genre,* and *mode of discourse* are omitted here for lack of space (cf. Rubin, 1984).

Persuasive/Argumentative Discourse

It has generally been held that students do not perform well in persuasive/argumentative discourse. This belief is based partly on theoretical arguments (e.g., Moffett, 1968), partly on teachers' experience, and partly on research evidence. For example, students' performance on persuasive writing tasks in National Assessments of Educational Progress has been consistently poor at all grade levels (4, 8, and 11) (Applebee, Langer, & Mullis, 1986).

A number of specific weakness have been described by researchers. Persuasive compositions are short and thin on content, especially on support for points of view (Bereiter & Scardamalia, 1982; Crowhurst, 1990; Gorman, White, Brooks, MacLure, & Kispal, 1988; Pringle & Freedman, 1985).

A second kind of weakness is poor or inappropriate organization (Gorman et al., 1988; Pringle & Freedman, 1985). In national assessments conducted at ages 11 and 15 years in the United Kingdom, even high-rated scripts by 15-year-olds were apt to exhibit "the sudden appearance of illogically placed information" (Gorman et al., 1988, p. 146). Many compositions by students in the 11–13 year age range begin formulaically with the statement of an opinion ("I think . . ."), and lack a conventional conclusion. Some have no ending at all, but stop abruptly after the final point is made. Those that do have an ending are likely to have some kind of blunt appeal ("So please don't let that rule go into effect"; "So please let us have pools. DECIDE QUICK.") or a comment that clearly ends the composition, though in an inappropriate way ("Thank you"; "I guess that's all I can think of") (Crowhurst, 1990, 1991a). In some cases, young students, when asked to persuade, write narratives (almost always the story of an attempt to persuade) or dialogues recording an exchange between people having a disagreement (Craig, 1986; Crowhurst, 1978, 1990; Gorman et al., 1988; Wilkinson et al., 1980).

A further characteristic weakness is stylistic inappropriateness. Compositions, especially by students aged 12 years and under, often use informal or familiar language, language reminiscent of spoken language. They tend to overuse connectives such as *so, another thing*, and *also*, and make less use than older students of the kinds of phrases typically used to mark the development of an argument (e.g., *first of all, finally, on the other hand, however, therefore*) (Crowhurst, 1987; Gorman et al., 1988).

The ability to write persuasive/argumentative discourse improves with age (Crowhurst, 1987; Gorman et al., 1988; McCann, 1989). White (1989), comparing good writing at age 11 years with good writing at age 15 years, pointed out that the writing of the younger students reflected the conventions of speech, whereas that of the older students revealed considerably more knowledge both about written argument and about the text-forming devices of language.

The description somewhat sketchily available from research allows some interesting conclusions about what students know about writing arguments and interesting speculation about how they know what they know. Clearly, no matter what the inadequacies of their written arguments, young students in the upper elementary school know a good deal about this genre. Even those responses that must be categorized as other than arguments (most commonly, narrative and dialogue compositions) show the rudiments of argument. The narratives virtually always contain the embryo of an argument—a statement of opinion and at least one reason (see Appendix A, e.g.)—whereas the dialogues read like oral persuasive exchanges and, likewise, contain elements of written argument (see Appendix B, e.g.). Moreover, even though young students may not be able to produce sophisticated written arguments, they reveal, when questioned, a good deal of knowledge about argument. McCann (1989) asked 6th-, 9th-, and 12th-graders and adults to judge whether or not seven prose passages were arguments, and found no difference among judgments made by the four groups. Bereiter and Scardamalia (1982) found that students aged 10–12 years were able to predict a good number of the discourse elements that would be found in argument (e.g., statement of belief, reason, elaboration). Bereiter and Scardamalia suggested that students get their knowledge from their experience with oral persuasion.

The indebtedness of young students to oral language is evident in a variety of ways—in the conversational nature of the appeals with which they often conclude their persuasive writing, and in the informality of their language. White (1989) pointed out that they sometimes use capitals, underlining, and exclamation marks in an attempt to represent the prosodic features of spoken language. She pointed out, further, that the echoes of spoken language in written arguments may be a strength: "[M]uch of the best writing from 11-year-olds (i.e., in the assessments of performance in the United Kingdom) gains force and immediacy from the adaptation of spoken language exchanges" (p. 20). Students of this age understand a lot about persuading. Indeed, children start persuading, in the oral mode, at a very early age, as any parent knows well.

Three aspects of written argument that students often fail to manage well are: the use of conventional text features, locating relevant content, and organizing content in a logical manner. These are aspects of written argument that do not transfer from students' experience with oral language. Many of the logical connectives that facilitate the development of written argument (e.g., *however, nonetheless, therefore, although* . . . , *unless* . . .) are much less common in spoken language than in written and are late acquired (Nippold, 1988; Perera, 1984). In oral exchanges, finding appropriate content is facilitated by the input of other participants, which serves to prompt the speaker in searching for appropriate contributions to an argument; writers of argument have no such help in locating content (Bereiter & Scardamalia, 1982). In writing narrative, students may draw on the entire body of their real and vicarious experience for content because story writers have great latitude in selecting content; the constraints on the writer of argument are much greater. Finally, the organization of oral exchanges is far different from the logical organization required in written argument.

In summary, then, by the end of elementary school, students know that arguments state a point of view and reasons to support it; their written arguments echo spoken language both in expression and in the strategies they use (e.g., appeals); they are likely to have difficulty producing the more distanced, impersonal language and logical organization that are characteristic of written argument; and, in common with many older students, they have difficulty finding relevant content. Their performance can be improved by instruction; but it is easier to teach them to use appropriate connectives (e.g., *in the first place, finally*) and to end with appropriate summary statements than it is to help them with the difficult tasks of locating content and organizing compositions logically and coherently (Crowhurst, 1991a).

Reports

Report writing has been most thoroughly examined by Langer (1986), who examined stories and reports written by third-, sixth-, and ninth-graders. As early as Grade 3, students had a concept of report that was different from their concept of story: Reports are informative, whereas stories are make-believe; reports are differently structured (they do not have to follow a rigid order as stories do) and end differently from stories. There were notable changes in report writing from Grade 3 to Grade 9 whereas changes in the structure of stories were much less dramatic. Reports became "considerably longer, more content-laden, better elaborated, and more highly structured across the years" (pp. 42–43); the reports of older students used more complex syntax, and had more sophisticated beginnings and endings—thesis statements to begin and summaries or evaluations to end—than those of younger students. Most third- and sixth-graders began, formulaically, with statements like "This is a report about . . ." or "Horses are animals"; many of them ended abruptly with their last stated fact.

Report writing, of course, is the genre of school writing most often demanded by content area classes. Some interesting work on report writing in content area classes was done by Early, Mohan, and Hooper (1989). Given research evidence that it takes immigrant children several years to master the language of academic discourse (Cummins, 1981), they have been trying to assist teachers to help second-language students to improve both their academic achievement in content areas and their English proficiency. A major feature of their approach is the use of graphics for a variety of purposes: to prepare students to read an academic text, to support a teacher's oral presentation, to revise previously presented material, and to develop language skills. One means of developing language skills is having students translate graphics into words, either orally or in writing.

Much of the writing produced by students in the project—writing produced with the support of graphics—is considered remarkable by many second-language teachers outside the project who have experienced difficulty getting their students to produce acceptable writing. The report by a sixth-grade second-language student shown in Appendix C is typical of the writing of students in the project. It is notable in several ways: in its organization, in its use of appropriate beginning and ending, and in its syntax. Note the writer's use of the following syntactic constructions: the appositive *my specimen, a spider*; several noun phrases with post modification of the head word, for example: *a mouth at the bottom, near the stomach; eight legs, four on each side of the head; two black, pointy fangs to suck the blood out from their prey; all of the inside body parts such as the head and spinneret*[2]; the fronting of *attached to the head*; the concessive clause, *Although* . . .

The development of report writing suggested by Langer's (1986) study shows similarities with the development of persuasive/argumentative writing. Students improve with age. Weaknesses of young students are: slim content, organization, formulaic or inadequate beginnings and endings. As with argument, even young students have knowledge about what a report is and how reports differ from stories. The writing of students in the second-language project of Early et al. (1989) illustrates effects of both instruction and "scaffolding." The students had received instruction in report writing—ways of beginning and ending, for example. The varied visuals used in the project (e.g., pictures, diagrams, tables, graphs, models) provided important scaffolding or support by providing students with visual content organized spatially to be translated into written prose. The content of the student's writing shown in Appendix C was provided and organized in the diagram she was describing. Thus supported in two of the most difficult tasks of writing—finding content and organizing it—she was able to concentrate on other aspects of writing.

CONCLUSION

Recent research challenges earlier conclusions that young students have little ability to adapt their writing style to suit their communicative intentions. Students in the elementary years show considerable ability to adapt their writing for different audiences and to write appropriately for a wide variety of purposes. They can make good attempts at genres formerly considered very difficult like argument. Even failures to conform to the required form

---

[2]It has been noted elsewhere (Crowhurst, 1978) that describing visuals tends to cause students to produce many long noun phrases with considerable postmodification of the head noun, a kind of syntactic structure not usually much used by young writers (see summary in Perera, 1984).

(like dialogue and narrative responses to argument assignments) reveal students' knowledge about argument.

Students bring to writing tasks the knowledge they have acquired from their life experience. They know how to persuade and how to pass on information (i.e., to report). They have been using spoken language to perform these functions since their early preschool years. They also learn early that persuading a parent and persuading a younger sibling, for example, require different strategies. That is to say, they have developed some skill in assuming different role identities vis-à-vis their listeners. This well-established knowledge they call into play when tackling writing tasks.

Of course, elementary students have much to learn both about ways of influencing different audiences and about the requirements of written language. Their performance in audience adaptation and in writing for different purposes improves with age and experience. It behooves teachers to see that young writers have many experiences reading varied texts and writing to varied audiences for varied purposes. We should beware of underestimating students on the basis of ill-informed conclusions about their supposed limitations.

APPENDIX A
Example of a Narrative in Response to a Persuasive Assignment

It was one day and a substitute came in to are classroom and said that are teacher was sick and she was going to be away for the whole day. The substitute said we are going to start reading so the boys and girls took out there reading books. Everyone in the classroom read a paragraph. It was Billys turn to read and he didnt start reading and everybody was looking at Billy. The substitute walked over and was staring at him. Billy was using a sling shot and using that he was throwing paper around the room. It is a rule in our classroom and *I think he should be punnished like having a detention every day for a month and write 60 lines every recess and lunch. I think we should do it because it is important to convince him not to do it again. Just because there is a substitute doesn't mean that he can do whatever you want.* Then I gave it to the teacher and she said if there is supposed to be a response I will give it to you tomorow. (Grade 5)

APPENDIX B
Example of a Dialogue in Response to a Persuasive Assignment

"Well I myself think that he should be confined to the chalkboard to write 4000 lines of 'I shall not shoot another elastic band'," I said to my teacher as we were argueing about punishment for the situation.

The teacher said, "I think that's a bit much, Dave. I think 50 lines is enough."

"Maybe so," I said, "but he broke our biggest class rule. You even said that the number one rule was never to throw anything at anyone."

"I still say 4000 lines is going overboard!"

Miss Dalton tried reasoning with me, but I stuck with 4000 lines. Nothing—no nothing—would change that!

Finally, after staring at her for a long time I said, "You picked me for leader of this group! Now, its either 4000 lines *or nothing!*"

"Okay, okay," Miss Dalton said, but only 1000 a day."

"Fine with me."

Then she said, "Now that that's settled go out for your recess." (Grade 5)

APPENDIX C
Report by a Sixth-Grade ESL Student—
Parts of a Spider

My Specimen, a spider, has two main body segments, and no exoskeleton. The two main body segments are the head and the abdomen.

The head of a spider is oval shaped and hairy. On the head there is eight smooth, dark, black eyes. Two of the eyes are at the top, two underneath, and four just beneath the others in a semicircle. It also has a mouth at the bottom, near the stomach. The mouth is kind of tube-shaped, and has a dull point. Although it has a mouth, spiders cannot chew on their food because they don't have a jaw! Instead they have two black, pointy fangs to suck the blood out from their prey. Spiders have eight legs, four on each side of the head. They are also hairy. These legs are excellent to walk forward fast. Attached to the head, is the abdomen. The abdomen contains all of the inside body parts, such as the heart and spinneret. The spinneret is also used in many ways. They are used for making the web and wrapping their prey before they eat it. The spiders also puts its victim into sleep by sending a sleeping liquid through their bodies. This is my description of spider's two main body segments, the head and the abdomen.*

REFERENCES

Applebee, A. N., Langer, J. A., & Mullis, I. V. S. (1986). *Writing: Trends across the decade, 1974–1984.* Princeton, NJ: National Assessment of Educational Progress.

Bereiter, C., & Scardamalia, M. (1982). From conversation to composition: The role of instruction in a developmental process. In R. Glaser (Ed.), *Advances in instructional psychology* (Vol. 2, pp. 1–64). Hillsdale, NJ: Lawrence Erlbaum Associates.

---

*From p. 278 of M. Crowhurst, *Language and Learning Across the Curriculum*, 1994. Reprinted by permission of Allyn & Bacon, Canada.

Craig, S. (1986). *The effect of intended audience on language functions in written argument at two grade levels.* Unpublished doctoral dissertation, University of British Columbia, Vancouver.

Crowhurst, M. (1978). The effect of audience and mode of discourse on the syntactic complexity of the writing of sixth and tenth graders. *Dissertation Abstracts International, 38*, 7300A–7301A.

Crowhurst, M. (1987). Cohesion in argument and narration at three grade levels. *Research in the Teaching of English, 21*, 185–201.

Crowhurst, M. (1990). The development of persuasive/argumentative writing. In R. Beach & S. Hynds (Eds.), *Developing discourse practices in adolescence and adulthood* (pp. 200–223). Norwood, NJ: Ablex.

Crowhurst, M. (1991a). Interrelationships between reading and writing persuasive discourse. *Research in the Teaching of English, 25*, 314–338.

Crowhurst, M. (1991b). Two-way learning in correspondence between pen-friend pairs. *English Education, 23*, 212–224.

Crowhurst, M. (1992). Some effects of corresponding with an older audience. *Language Arts, 69*, 268–273.

Crowhurst, M., & Piché, G. L. (1979). Audience and mode of discourse effects on syntactic complexity in writing at two grade levels. *Research in the Teaching of English, 13*, 101–109.

Cummins, J. (1981). Age and rate of acquisition of second language learning in Canada: A reassessment. *Applied Linguistics, 2*, 132–149.

Early, M., Mohan, B., & Hooper, H. (1989). The Vancouver school board language and content project. In J. H. Esling (Ed.), *Multicultural education and policy: ESL in the 1990's* (pp. 107–124). Toronto: O.I.S.E. Press.

Frank, L. A. (1992). Writing to be read: Young writers' ability to demonstrate audience awareness when evaluated by their readers. *Research in the Teaching of English, 26*, 277–298.

Glucksberg, S., & Krauss, R. (1967). What do people say after they have learned how to talk? Studies of the development of referential communication. *Merrill–Palmer Quarterly, 13*, 309–316.

Gorman, T. P., White, J., Brooks, C., MacLure, M., & Kispal, A. (1988). *A review of language monitoring 1979–83.* London: Assessment of Performance Unit, HMSO.

Greenlee, M. E., Hiebert, E. H., Bridge, C. A., & Winograd, P. N. (1986). The effects of different audiences on young writers' letter writing. In J. A. Niles & R. V. Lalik (Eds.), *Solving problems in literacy: Learners, teachers and researchers* (Thirty-fifth Yearbook of the National Reading Conference) (pp. 281–289). Rochester, NY: National Reading Conference.

Kroll, B. M. (1985). Rewriting a complex story for a young reader: The development of audience-adapted writing skills. *Research in the Teaching of English, 19*, 120–139.

Langer, J. A. (1986). *Children reading and writing: Structures and strategies.* Norwood, NJ: Ablex.

Martin, J., & Rothery, J. (1981). The ontogenesis of written genre. In J. R. Martin & J. Rothery (Eds.), *Working papers in linguistics, No. 2* (pp. 1–59). Sydney, Australia: Sydney University, Linguistics Department.

McCann, T. M. (1989). Student argumentative writing, knowledge and ability at three grade levels. *Research in the Teaching of English, 23*, 62–76.

Moffett, J. (1968). *Teaching the universe of discourse.* Boston: Houghton Mifflin.

Newkirk, T. (1985). The hedgehog or the fox: The dilemma of writing development. *Language Arts, 62*, 593–603.

Newkirk, T. (1987). The non-narrative writing of young children. *Research in the Teaching of English, 21*, 121–144.

Nippold, M. A. (1988). The literate lexicon. In M. A. Nippold (Ed.), *Later language development: Ages 9 through 19* (pp. 29–48). Boston: Little, Brown.

Perera, K. (1984). *Children's writing and reading: Analysing classroom language.* Oxford, England: Basil Blackwell.

Perron, J. D. (1977). *The impact of mode on written syntactic complexity, Parts I–III* (Studies in Language Education, Report Nos. 24, 25, 27). Athens: University of Georgia.

Pringle, I., & Freedman, A. (1985). *A comparative study of writing abilities in two modes at the grade 5, 8, and 12 levels.* Toronto: Ministry of Education.

Rubin, D. (1984). Social cognition and written communication. *Written Communication, 1,* 11.

Rubin, D., & Piché, G. L. (1979). Development in syntactic and strategic aspects of audience adaptation skills in written persuasive communication. *Research in the Teaching of English, 13,* 293–316.

Shatz, M., & Gelman, R. (1973). The development of communication skills: Modifications in the speech of young children as a function of listener. *Monographs of the Society for Research in Child Development, 38* (Serial No. 152).

Smith, W. L., & Swan, M. B. (1978). Adjusting syntactic structures to varied levels of audience. *Journal of Experimental Education, 46*(4), 29–34.

Warren-Leubecker, A., & Bohannon, J. N., III (1989). Pragmatics: Language in social contexts. In J. B. Gleason (Ed.), *The development of language* (2nd ed., pp. 327–368). Columbus, OH: Merrill.

White, J. (1989). Children's argumentative writing: A reappraisal of difficulties. In F. Christie (Ed.), *Writing in schools: Reader* (pp. 9–23). Geelong, Australia: Deakin University Press.

Wilkinson, A. M., Barnsley, G., Hana, P., & Swan, M. (1980). *Assessing language development.* Oxford, England: Oxford University Press.

CHAPTER TEN

Ultimatum and Negotiation: Gender Differences in Student Writing

Kathryn Heltne Swanson
Augsburg College

For several decades the relationship between social cognition and communication has been thought to be critically important to those working within a wide range of cognitive, developmental, and interactionist theoretical frameworks (see Feffer, 1959; Kelly, 1955; Piaget, 1926/1955; Werner, 1957). In one way or another, all of these theoretical positions view social cognition—"the intuitive or logical representation of others . . . [including] inferences about their covert, inner psychological experiences" (Shantz, 1975, p. 1)—and communication as processes somehow dependent on speakers' and hearers' individual abilities.

The concept of social cognitive complexity is most closely associated with Kelly's (1955) personal construct psychology. Soon after the publication of Kelly's work, Bieri, a social psychologist, introduced the specific concept of "cognitive complexity" as a variable that defines an individual difference in a person's social-cognitive system. According to this theory, individuals understand the social world on the basis of social constructs derived from various pieces or elements of information about other people and their attitudes. A construct system is considered complex in structure if it contains a relatively large number of elements and if the elements are integrated hierarchically by relatively "extensive bonds of relationship" (Crockett, 1965, p. 49). Further, according to construct theory, a person construes another's construction processes and formulates and interprets messages in terms of his or her understandings of the other's perspective (O'Keefe & Delia, 1982).

During the last decade, researchers following in the tradition of Kelly's (1955) theory (e.g., Clark & Delia, 1977; Crockett, 1965; Delia & Crockett, 1973;

Hale & Delia, 1976; O'Keefe & Delia, 1979, 1982, 1985) have extended the constructivist perspective to study the relationships between social cognitive complexity and a variety of functional communication skills. These researchers have maintained the central role that communicators' social cognition plays in their composing process (see Rubin, 1984; Rubin & Rafoth, 1986).

In general, this research has centered on speakers' ability to directly accommodate or adapt their messages to their audiences with results showing that individuals with more differentiated social constructs were generally better able to accomplish such adaptations. As extended to written communication, the research has shown the same general pattern of results, including a generally positive relationship between interpersonal cognitive complexity and the judged overall quality of the writing.

For example, investigating audience adaptation in persuasive writing by 4th-, 8th-, and 12th-grade students, Rubin and Piché (1979) affirmed the relation between measured interpersonal cognitive complexity and the tendency of persuasive writers to alter syntactic and strategic properties of messages in response to perceptions of varying degrees of intimacy with their audience. In further studying 4th-, 8th-, 12th-graders, and expert adults, Rubin (1982) found developmental effects in construct differentiation that were related to both clause length and fluency and that increased with the writer's age. Thus, to a greater extent than did the younger writers, mature writers adapted their texts in accordance with their perceptions of a particular audience.

Studying persuasive letters written by 11th-graders, Piché and Roen (1987) found a significant positive relationship between writers' levels of interpersonal cognitive complexity and abstractness with the quality of their writing, overall persuasiveness, appropriateness of tone, and level of persuasive strategy employed. That is, writers who were rated cognitively complex received higher ratings on their writing than did their peers who also had received lower ratings of cognitive complexity.

In some ways paralleling these developments in composition theory, more recent research on social cognition and communication has shifted to study the use of alternative message design logics and the means–ends relationships holding between those message design logics and communicators' goals. This new line of research is centered on the belief that one's interpersonal construct system influences message production by advancing the message producer's knowledge of *messages* rather than the message producer's knowledge of message *recipients*.

Recent Research on Interpersonal Cognitive Complexity and Message Production and Evaluation

Specifically, the work of O'Keefe (1988), O'Keefe and Delia (1988), and O'Keefe and McCornack (1987) has centered on the use of alternative message design logics and the means–ends relationships holding between those message design logics and communicators' goals. Thus, the theoretical concern has shifted from more or less exclusive focus on audience and audience accommodation to attention to the discourse produced by speakers and writers and to the reasoning about communication that somehow underlies and shapes the messages that are actually produced.

O'Keefe (1988) categorized communicators' messages according to what she called differences in their message design logic. For regulative communication, communication by which the speaker or writer seeks to influence or control the thoughts and actions of the recipient, O'Keefe defined three message design logics: *expressive, conventional,* and *rhetorical* (see Table 10.1). If the message design logic is expressive, it simply expresses the communicator's thoughts or feelings at the moment, with little attention to the precise context of the particular message. The expressive message is generally literal, direct, and subjective. The communicator is motivated primarily by a need for self-expression, regardless of rules and conventions that may be known by the audience. A conventional message design logic is based on the premise that communication is a "game played cooperatively by social rules" (p. 79) and it is thus generated by a specific context to secure a desired response. It is constructed with consideration for discourse rules, forms of politeness, and other conventions that reflect an awareness of the audience and the parameters of appropriateness within a particular communicative context. A rhetorical message design logic is one that incorporates negotiation to achieve social consensus. Here, the context is created by the communication process itself. Thus, the social structure is seen as flexible and is, in fact, created through the act of communication. The rhetorical communicator, then, designs messages to "portray a scene that is consistent with one's wants; the discourse of others is closely interpreted to determine the nature of the drama and the perspective they are enacting" (p. 80).

For O'Keefe (1988), the three forms of message design logic form a natural developmental progression, with the "mechanism of development being the progressive accumulation and integration of information about communication" (pp. 88–89). Thus, the expressive premise is a logical prerequisite to conventional functioning, and the conventional premise is a logical prerequisite to rhetorical functioning. Also important to note, because communication is not necessarily a uniform process, communicators are affected by the message design logics used by those with whom they are most often in contact. For example, people who are surrounded by others who use negotiation as a primary means of communication are more able to construct rhetorical messages easily and readily than those who are not in frequent contact with this mode of communicating. In contrast, people who "live in a world where power and resource control are used to fix meaning and social arrangements (e.g., people who are surrounded by others who have

TABLE 10.1
Message Design Logics

Characteristic	Expressive	Conventional	Rhetorical
Fundamental Premise	Language is a medium for expressing thoughts and feelings	Communication is a game played cooperatively by social rules	Communication is the creation and negotiation of social selves and situations
Key Message Function	Self-expression	Secure desired response	Negotiate social consensus
Temporal Organization of Messages	Reaction to prior event	Response specified by present context	Initiate movement toward desired context
Message/Content	Little attention to context	Action and meaning are context-determined	Communication process creates context
Internal Message Coherence	Subjective and Associative	Intersubjective and rule-focused	Intersubjective and style-centered
Method of Managing Face Goals	Editing	Politeness forms	Context redefinition

Note. From B. O'Keefe, "The Logic of Message Design: Individual Differences in Reasoning About Communication," 1988, p. 85. Copyright © 1988 by The Speech Communication Association. Reprinted by permission.

achieved only a conventional communication system) may find it difficult to develop a belief in the social constitution of reality and the power of language to reorder social life" (p. 89). Thus, although O'Keefe maintained a developmental position (and thus aligned herself with the cognitive developmentalists noted earlier), she also allowed for the importance of social context and situation as determinants of message production.

O'Keefe (1988) also maintained that in addition to employing different message design logics, communicators differed in the number and type of goals their messages were designed to serve. She described three categories of goal structures: *minimal, unifunctional,* and *multifunctional.* If a goal set is minimal, the communicator has an unclear or empty set of goals. A unifunctional goal set occurs when the message producer is pursuing one dominant objective to the exclusion of others, and a multifunctional goal set is apparent when the communicator is pursuing two or more competing objectives in the same message production. Each message design logic offers means for managing minimal, unifunctional, and multifunctional goal sets. The complexity of the goal set being pursued as the communicator designs the message can vary independently of the message design logic used by the message producer. The more complex a social situation the greater the possibility for variation in messages due to variations in goal sets; the specific use of a message design logic and a particular goal set is situational determined.

Links With Studies of Language and Gender

In her landmark study that investigated the composing processes of 12th-graders, Emig (1971) found that girls were most comfortable using the "reflexive mode," which enabled them to focus on thoughts and feelings, whereas boys preferred the "extensive mode" as the means for them to most effectively convey their messages to readers.

Further studying links between gender and writing, Waters (1975) found that experienced readers (English teachers) could correctly identify the sex of essay writers based on their prose style; she determined that male writers used a detached prose style, whereas female writers used a more personal style. Similarly, Flynn (1983) found that male and female writers differed in the topics they chose. Male writers more often described experiences involving leadership and rebellion against authority, but female writers often wrote about experiences involving accommodation, nonassertiveness, and personal interaction.

Additional research has further noted differences in a male pugilistic/phallocentric rhetorical stance and a female cooperative/nurturing rhetorical stance (Caywood & Overing, 1987; Flynn, 1986, 1988; Meisenhelder, 1985; Spender, 1980). Gilligan's (1982) metaphors of the web and the ladder illustrate gender differences as women's webs suggest interconnectedness whereas men's ladders depict independence and hierarchy. Analysis of texts produced by men and women in response to a similar writing task also revealed that men wrote texts in which they adopted the role of an independent, active individual who is relatively self-centered, whereas women produced texts in which they adopted the role of a nurturing, empathetic individual who is focused on others (Keroes, 1986).

Thus, a substantial body of research has revealed that men more often than women write messages that tend to be task oriented and self-centered and that women are more likely than men to produce messages that reflect awareness of audience and that are other-centered. There is an important link here with writers' levels of social cognitive complexity. Although it is generally believed that women write more "connected" and "relational" texts (Flynn, 1988), recent research has shown that women also demonstrate higher levels of social cognitive complexity on the Crockett Role Category Questionnaire (Swanson, 1990).

Women, therefore, choose specific strategies of composition, specifically here, a particular level of message design logic, in accordance with their gender and their level of social cognition. The conventional and, especially, the rhetorical strategies are used by women to negotiate and collaborate with their readers.

METHODS AND PROCEDURES

Accordingly, the present study undertook a replication of earlier research by O'Keefe (1988) and O'Keefe and McCornack (1987) and extended this research by investigating the relationship between message design logic and goal structure and the gender of writers producing regulative messages. Participants in the study were students at Augsburg College, a private liberal arts college in Minneapolis, Minnesota, who were enrolled in Effective Writing (EW), a general writing course required of all students. Five sections (100 students) completed the Crockett Role Category Questionnaire (RCQ) and a regulative writing task; non-native speakers of English were not included in the study. Subjects were in intact classes, and so it was not possible to control for exact balance between male and female students or for precise parameters of age. In the classes used, there were 46 female and 54 male message writers. All except 2 of the students were between 18 and 25 years old and all of the students were commonly enrolled in their first-level college writing course.

Approximately 1 week before they were asked to complete the regulative writing task, student writers were asked to write descriptions of two peers, one whom they liked and one whom they disliked. This two-peer version of the Crockett (1965) RCQ is a measure based on the assumption that the number of constructs employed in students' written descriptions of their peers reflects the degree of differentiation of the subjects' personal construct systems, that is, their level of social cognitive complexity. The number of constructs contained in each written impression was tabulated, following the scoring procedures detailed in Crockett, Press, Delia, and Kenny (1974).

After discussing procedures and practicing scoring of sample messages, two raters independently scored 35 randomly selected peer descriptions (with approximately equal numbers of male and female student writers). After establishing an agreement rate of 98%, the author scored the remaining RCQ descriptions.

A single regulative writing task (see Appendix) was designed to include a fairly high level of interpersonal imposition among persons who are interpersonally proximate or close. Moreover, the writing task was intended to define a hypothetical situation of communicative exigence with which writers could closely identify. The task was one in which students wrote a regulative message to their roommate following a dispute over dorm room rights. The roommate's name, Chris, was selected as one that could be read as gender-neutral. The idea for the problem originated with one of my former students who, in casual conversation, recalled a frustrating experience from his first year as a college student. Pretesting with students not involved in the final study established that the stimulus was believable and that it created sufficient immediate imposition to elicit differential responses. Accordingly, students participating in the final study were given the following task during a regular EW class session and were allowed 20 minutes to complete it.

Response Measures

Message Design Logics. Each writer's response to the task was classified in terms of the dominant level of message design logic employed, that is, expressive, conventional, or rhetorical. In order to score messages consistently, the raters had to agree on criteria that would define each of the message design logics. Thus, following O'Keefe's (1988) system for analyzing regulative messages, we described expressive messages as those that were reactive, relatively incoherent, and unable to engage the immediate task to be accomplished in the given situation; conventional messages as context-bound, socially polite and appropriate, and initiated to elicit a particular response from the message recipient to the situation; and rhetorical messages as organized to obtain assent to a plan or consensus on a goal, or to negotiate a mutually acceptable solution to the problem. The author and a second coder independently scored 50% of the messages, which were randomly selected. Following a 96% rate of agreement, the author coded the remaining messages.

Writers of expressive messages were angry, but not specifically about the immediate situation. Expressive message design logic, then, was that used by the writer to express affect, to complain about Chris' past transgressions, and to deliver insults to Chris. There was a noticeable absence of information about actions needed to remedy the particular situation; Chris was not told via an expressive message what to do to correct the error. These messages were subjective, literal, and direct, and relatively context-free, with the writer often attacking Chris personally. Following are examples of expressive messages:

> Everybody is out to get you—right. What are you, some kind of paranoid flake? O.K. quit being so unreasonable. Do you have some kind of a disorder or something?

> I'm sorry that you cannot get along with me. I'm a great person to be friends with. I'm a nice guy who is considerate and warm. You, on the other hand, are a conceited pig who only wants things your way and when you do not get them, you throw a temper tantrum. You seriously need to learn how to handle the fact that you're not the only person in the room, dorm, and college. You really need to grow up and be more outwardly caring to other people's feelings.

Conventional messages were written within the context of the situation. Thus, the writer addressed the issues of typing and sleeping and offered some remedy to the situation, usually by telling Chris what to do. There was a clear attempt by the writer to follow social norms to elicit the desired response and to correct the message recipient's error. Thus, the conventional messages were contextually appropriate, relatively polite, and context-bound. See the following examples of conventional messages:

> I know you need to get your paper typed and that it's just as important as my test tomorrow. But you're not being very sensitive towards me at all. I tried sleeping with you typing, but it's impossible. I need to sleep in my own bed so I can get a good night's sleep. Couldn't you *please* move out to the lounge? It's quiet out there and I'm sure you'll be able to get it done. I'm trying to think of you, but it's just a black and white situation. Either I don't sleep and you type here, or you type out there. Please move to the lounge. I have to do well on that test tomorrow!

> I understand that this room belongs to both of us. We should be able to have our own things and our own study and sleep habits. Tonight, however, your study habits are more disturbing than they would usually be. I am the kind of person who needs a lot of rest to do a good job and even if you aren't, I'd like you to respect this need. It's not very often that I ask you to leave our room. I think I've done a good job adjusting to respecting your different

habits. I would appreciate it if you could adjust to mine, if only for this one night. Thank you.

In contrast, a writer employing a rhetorical message design logic seeks to negotiate some consensus. This writer reshapes and transforms the problem to serve multiple communicative aims, in the course of attempting to change the situation. Thus, the student writing a rhetorical message has some skill in problem solving and in reaching goals through composing (cf. Bereiter, 1980; Bereiter & Scardamalia, 1982; Flower & Hayes, 1981; Newell & Simon, 1972; Voss, 1988). This writer is able to transform the message in terms of its social context and in accordance with the perceived audience (Ede & Lunsford, 1984). As experienced writers, the writer using rhetorical message design logic is composing reader-based prose rather than writer-based prose (Flower, 1979; Flower & Hayes, 1980). The writer of rhetorical messages seems to envision a real reader and is willing to negotiate and to adjust the goals and purposes for a particular message in accordance with a specific audience. This writer is better able to adapt strategies to the particular writing task and to be flexible in revising to meet particular goals of the writing problem. Thus, instead of telling Chris what to do to correct an error, this writer is also willing to act to find a new, mutually satisfactory solution to the problem. In the rhetorical message, then, there is greater flexibility and a redefinition of the situational context (cf. O'Keefe, 1988, pp. 87–88). The following are examples of rhetorical messages:

I am sorry about fighting with you earlier. My test means just as much to me as your term paper does to you. I think that you can get your paper done in the lounge just as fast, and you can do it just as well. I cannot sleep with all that noise. Please understand. You can still get your paper done and I can get some sleep. I'll be happy to do the same thing for you. From now on, let's talk out our problems and conflicts instead of getting in a major fight. We'll both have to compromise. If this still bothers you, I will be happy to see if I can sleep in someone else's room for a while, but I will not do this always. I hope that we can stay pals, and be more understanding. Let's try to understand the other one's problems more, compromise, and find the best solution in the future. Sorry.

I understand that you feel I treated you unfairly. I agree that this is your room also, but I did offer to help you move your things and I warned you in advance that I needed to sleep. Maybe both of us are just on edge because of all the work. Living in a cubicle like this makes me really grouchy. I didn't mean to take it out on you. Please try to understand that I'm not forcing you out of your room. I don't want to do that. I only want a little consideration for my feelings, just the same as you expect of me. Maybe next time something like this happens, we can pay attention to each other's feelings and needs instead of flying off the handle. I'm sorry about last night. Let's make sure it doesn't happen again!

Goal Structures.   Each writer's response to the regulative task was further analyzed to determine whether it reflected a minimal, a unifunctional,
or a multifunctional goal structure. Procedures were based on coding categories for message design logics and message goal structures as outlined in
O'Keefe (1988). Again, two raters discussed categorization criteria and practiced coding sample messages. The raters then independently scored 50
randomly selected messages; the agreement rate was 96%. The author then
coded the remaining messages.

Message goal structure and design logic are independent sources of message variation. Thus, examples of each type of goal structure can be found
within each of the three message design logics. A message with a minimal
goal structure is one that is unclear or empty. The writer is confused about
exactly what the message should accomplish. That is to say that these messages exhibit no clear, direct, or positive action. Following is an example
of minimal goal structure:

> You're my idol! I will move out to the study lounge and sleep. Please forgive
> me for asking you to let me sleep in my own room. I know it is asking a lot.
> I hope you do a good job on your paper. If you need help, you know where
> I will be. I am pulling a 1.5 in Chemistry, so don't worry about waking me
> up. I mean, I am passing by a whole 1.5, so please feel free to bug me for
> help.

A unifunctional message is one that is produced to serve one specific and
single goal, one relevant to the regulative task *or* to the maintenance of the
writer's face wants. The writer has one objective, to the exclusion of others.
Thus, the unifunctional message is clear and direct, free from confusion or
complexity of purpose. See the following examples of unifunctional goal
structure:

> Cool off. No big deal. Just move your stuff out into the hall, right outside the
> door. I've seen others sitting right outside their doors. I'll still help you if
> you'll agree to what I'm saying.

> You've got to understand my point. I have a huge Chem test tomorrow. If I
> don't do well on this test, I'm screwed. I've been studying for weeks, as you
> know. There is no reason why you can't move the typewriter and your notes
> to the study lounge. You would have more room to spread out and the
> lighting would be better. I don't think that's too much to ask. I'll help you
> move the stuff out and back. Just tonight. That's all I ask!

Messages with multifunctional goal structures are those in which the writer
is pursuing two or more competing objectives at the same time. That is, the
message producer intends to accomplish both the regulative task and the
maintenance of face wants. Thus, this writer employs conventional politeness

strategies while acknowledging the existence of multiple perspectives (i.e., those of the message recipient as well as those of the message producer). The following are examples of multifunctional goal structure:

> I need some sleep! Do you know how important this chemistry test is to me? About as important as your paper, right? Alright—tomorrow I will go out and buy some ear plugs so I won't hear your typing as much. Why don't we talk to each other about doing our homework at the same time or we could at least set a time period when we both should stop doing homework and go to bed. I will respect your schedule if you will respect mine. O.K.?

> I am sorry that we are not getting along. Neither one of us is being rational about this mess, and I think we need to settle down and talk about this. I know that this is your room as well as mine. I thought you would understand why I needed to get to sleep early, but I know you also had to get your paper done. Neither one of us wants to flunk out, so let's talk about what to do. Thanks.

RESULTS

Following scoring for level of social cognitive complexity and coding for message design logic and level of goal structure, chi-square and cross-tabulation were used to determine whether or not a significant relationship existed between writers' gender and the type of message design logic they used in their regulative message and writers' gender and the level of goal structure they employed. A contingency table of observed frequencies and percentages of each gender across each level of message design logic was created.

Gender and Social Cognitive Complexity

Following the Crockett RCQ described earlier, female students used an average of 38.72 constructs when writing about a liked and disliked peer. Male writers averaged 29.50 constructs in their messages. Using a two-tailed t test of means for the two groups, with 98 degrees of freedom, $t = 4.9363$ and $p < .001$. Thus, there was a significant difference between male and female writers' levels of social cognitive complexity as measured by the RCQ.

Gender and Message Design Logic

The chi-square results, with 2 degrees of freedom (df), revealed a significant relationship between gender and message design logic ($\chi^2 = 7.523315$ and $p = .0232$ [$p < .05$]). The cross-tabulation table (see Table 10.2) showed that many more men (82.4%) than women (17.6%) used an expressive message

TABLE 10.2
Cross-Tabulation of Students by Gender and Message Design Logic

Gender	Message Design Logic			
	Expressive	Conventional	Rhetorical	Total
Female	3 (17.6%)	27 (48.2%)	16 (59.3%)	46 (46%)
Male	14 (82.4%)	29 (51.8%)	11 (40.7%)	54 (54%)
Total	17 (17%)	56 (56%)	27 (27%)	100 (100%)

design logic and a greater percentage of women (59.3%) than men (40.7%) used a rhetorical message design logic.

Gender and Goal Structure

The study next investigated whether or not there was a relationship between gender and goal structure appearing in writers' regulative messages. Again, relationship existed between gender of writers and the predominant goal structure appearing in their messages. The chi-square test revealed that there was not a significant relationship between gender and writers' use of a particular goal structure (with 2 df, $\chi^2 = .892988$, $p = .639868$ [$p > .05$]). Although the percentage of male writers (66.7%) who used minimal goal structures was twice as high as the percentage of female writers (33.3%) using minimal goal sets, the number of writers displaying minimal goals was relatively small. Moreover, for men and women, the percentages were much closer for the use of unifunctional and multifunctional goal structures and for gender differences across these two levels. Unifunctional goals were written by 48.5% of the female writers and 51.5% of the male writers; multifunctional goal structures were employed by 47.3% of the female writers and 52.7% of the male writers (see Table 10.3).

CONCLUSIONS

Using O'Keefe's (1988) levels of message design logic and goal structure, the present study extends previous work, showing a significant difference between men and women in the likelihood that in regulative writing tasks, women would employ a more complex redefinition of the communicative problem. That is, there was a significant relationship between gender and message design logic. In the present study, many more male writers than female writers used an expressive message design logic. Approximately the same percentage of males and females wrote conventional messages, but a greater percentage of females than males used rhetorical message design logic. Whereas there was a significant relationship between gender and

TABLE 10.3
Cross-Tabulation of Students by Gender and Goal Structure

	Goal Structure			
Gender	Minimal	Unifunctional	Multifunctional	Total
Female	4 (33.3%)	16 (48.5%)	26 (47.3%)	46 (46%)
Male	8 (66.7%)	17 (51.5%)	29 (52.7%)	54 (54%)
Total	12 (12%)	33 (33%)	55 (55%)	100 (100%)

message design logic, in the present study, the relationship between gender of the writer and the goal structure used in the message was not significant. Thus, these results further establish the independence of two features of message production.

Results offer further support for an emerging theory of gender-based differences in communication. One result, here, points to a marked difference between male and female writers with regard to their levels of social cognitive complexity as measured by the Crockett Role Category Questionnaire. Using more constructs than men in their written description of peers, women have further demonstrated an approach to others that tends to be multidimensional and relatively complex.

This complexity is evident also in the likelihood that women communicators, significantly more often than men, employ what is described here as a rhetorical message design strategy. This is a strategy whereby writers incorporate a more complex set of purposes and goals, adapting their individual knowledge structures to accommodate various situations and to negotiate. It is also a strategy that is more precisely negotiative and mutually concessive, and that attempts to recast or reformulate a problem by going beyond conventional politeness constraints (see chapter 6 of this volume). Further, in addition to noting differences in strategies used most often by male and female students in their written messages, this study suggests the relationship between women's higher levels of social cognitive complexity and their choice of rhetorical message design logics.

To the extent that this is the case, these findings support previously cited research exploring differences between men's and women's writing that concludes that women's writing incorporates different stances or rhetorical attitudes from men's, stances that are frequently more cooperative, more negotiative, less competitive, and less autonomous than men's. Thus, there is some evidence for the assertion that women more often than men use rhetorical strategies because this is the message design logic whereby they are able to construct relational, negotiative, other-directed communication.

Finally, results of the present study invite further inquiry. The unambiguous support for the presence and effects of differences in message design logic in regulative communication invites questions about whether or not such differences mark other communicative functions in speech and writing. Results here also point to further questions about the role of gender differences in writers' use and deployment of different message design logics and goal structures. That is to say that further studies in alternative kinds of settings are needed to answer whether or not gender effects here may be related to the particular task or to the message receiver who, in the present study, was assumed to be the same sex as the writer. Additional investigation linking measures of social cognition with writers' choice of communicative strategies is also required.

In general, then, further study is essential to replicate and to extend the parameters of the present study, to continue to investigate the relationships among interpersonal cognitive complexity, message design logics, goal structures, levels of social cognition, and message producers' gender. Such research would necessarily expand the contextual situation of the present study by employing writing tasks that would require types of writing beyond regulative messages, readers and writers who include individuals beyond college classrooms and offices, and means for assessment that would include oral protocols and discrete measures to assess various aspects of the messages' communicative effectiveness. In short, there is much work to be done to better understand interpersonal cognitive complexity and its integral relationship to communication embedded in social contexts, addressing various audiences, and revealing individual processes of solving problems and reaching goals via the composition of texts.

APPENDIX

Writing Task

You are a first-year student who has an extremely important chemistry exam tomorrow morning at 8 AM. You have been studying for days as you know that you have to do well on this exam to get a good grade in the course. At dinner tonight you told your roommate Chris that you plan to go to bed at 11 so you'll be ready for the test. When you said this, your roommate announced plans to stay up late in the room to type a research paper that is due tomorrow. "I'm going to stay up and type until it's done," Chris proclaimed. "Sorry, but I can't move because I've got all my books and notes spread out in order."

When you get back to the room, you tell Chris that you are going to the library to study until 11, and offer to help move the portable typewriter, notes, books, and lamp to the study lounge just down the hall from your room when you get back. But when you return just before 11, Chris again announces plans to stay up, in the room, and type until the paper is done.

"You can sleep," Chris says. "Just don't think about it." You reply that's hard to do, given the noisy portable typewriter (with loud erase function), but you pull the pillow over your head and the bedspread down from the top bunk to block out the light.

Half an hour later, you throw the pillow on the floor. "This isn't working; will you please just move? I'll carry your stuff."

Your roommate answers, "No! It's my room too. I'll move you. . . ."

Hearing the dispute, two neighbors and the floor Head Resident (junior student counselor) come in. Your neighbors tell Chris to type the paper in the morning or move to the study lounge now. The Head Res says that you both should work out your own problems and settle it yourselves—quickly and quietly.

Chris storms out of the room, muttering, "You guys are all out to get me. I'll be back to type my paper in my room!"

Talking hasn't worked well for you . . . so before you try to go to sleep and your roommate comes back to the room, write a note to Chris to see if you can settle things.

REFERENCES

Bereiter, C. (1980). Development in writing. In L. W. Gregg & E. R. Steinberg (Eds.), *Cognitive processes in writing* (pp. 73–93). Hillsdale, NJ: Lawrence Erlbaum Associates.

Bereiter, C., & Scardamalia, M. (1982). From conversation to composition. In R. Glaser (Ed.), *Advances in instructional psychology* (Vol. 2, pp. 197–222). Hillsdale, NJ: Lawrence Erlbaum Associates.

Caywood, C., & Overing, G. (Eds.). (1987). *Teaching writing: Gender, pedagogy and equity.* Albany: State University of New York Press.

Clark, R. A., & Delia, J. (1977). Cognitive complexity, social perspective-taking, and functional persuasive skills in second- to ninth-grade children. *Human Communication Research, 1,* 128–134.

Crockett, W. H. (1965). Cognitive complexity and impression formation. In B. A. Maher (Ed.), *Progress in experimental personality research, II* (pp. 47–90). New York: Academic Press.

Crockett, W. H., Press, A., Delia, J., & Kenny, C. T. (1974). *Structural analysis of the organization of written impressions.* Unpublished manuscript, University of Kansas, Lawrence.

Delia, J., & Crockett, W. H. (1973). Social shemas, cognitive complexity, and the learning of social structures. *Journal of Personality, 41,* 413–429.

Ede, L., & Lunsford, A. (1984). Audience addressed/audience invoked: The role of audience in composition theory and pedagogy. *College Composition and Communication, 35,* 155–171.

Emig, J. (1971). *The composing processes of twelfth graders* (Research Report No. 13). Urbana, IL: National Council of Teachers of English.

Feffer, M. H. (1959). The cognitive implications of role taking behavior. *Journal of Personality, 24,* 152–168.

Flower, L. (1979). Writer-based prose: A cognitive basis for problems in writing. *College English, 41,* 19–37.

Flower, L., & Hayes, J. (1980). The cognition of discovery: Defining a rhetorical problem. *College Composition and Communication, 31,* 21–32.

Flower, L., & Hayes, J. (1981). A cognitive process theory of writing. *College Composition and Communication, 32*, 365–387.

Flynn, E. (1983, March). *Gender difference and student writing.* Paper presented at the annual meeting of the Conference on College Composition and Communication, Detroit. (ERIC Document Reproduction Service No. ED 233 399)

Flynn, E. (1986). Gender and reading. In E. Flynn & P. Schweikert (Eds.), *Gender and reading: Essays on readers, texts, and contexts* (pp. 267–287). Baltimore, MD: Johns Hopkins University Press.

Flynn, E. (1988). Composing as a woman. *College Composition and Communication, 39*, 423–435.

Gilligan, C. (1982). *In a different voice: Psychological theory and women's development.* Cambridge, MA: Harvard University Press.

Hale, C., & Delia, J. G. (1976). Cognitive complexity and social perspective-taking. *Communication Monographs, 43*, 195–203.

Kelly, G. A. (1955). *A theory of personality.* New York: Norton.

Keroes, J. (1986, March). *But what do they say? Gender and the content of student writing.* Paper presented at the annual meeting of the Conference on College Composition and Communication, New Orleans.

Meisenhelder, S. (1985). Redefining powerful writing: Toward a feminist theory of composition. *Journal of Thought, 20*, 184–195.

Newell, A., & Simon, H. (1972). *Human problem solving.* Englewood Cliffs, NJ: Prentice-Hall.

O'Keefe, B. J. (1988). The logic of message design: Individual differences in reasoning about communication. *Communication Monographs, 55*, 80–103.

O'Keefe, B., & Delia, J. G. (1979). Construct comprehensiveness and cognitive complexity as predictors of the number and strategic adaptation of arguments and appeals in a persuasive message. *Communication Monographs, 46*, 231–240.

O'Keefe, B., & Delia, J. (1982). Impression formation and message production. In M. Roloff & C. L. Berger (Eds.), *Social cognition and communication* (pp. 33–72). Beverly Hills, CA: Sage.

O'Keefe, B., & Delia, J. (1985). Psychological and interactional dimensions of communicative development. In H. Giles & R. St. Clair (Eds.), *Recent advances in language, communication, and social psychology* (pp. 41–85). London: Lawrence Erlbaum Associates.

O'Keefe, B. J., & Delia, J. G. (1988). Communicative tasks and communicative practices: The development of audience-centered message production. In B. A. Rafoth & D. L. Rubin (Eds.), *The social construction of written communication* (pp. 70–98). Norwood, NJ: Ablex.

O'Keefe, B., & McCornack, S. (1987). Message design logic and message goal structure: Effects on perceptions of message quality in regulative communication situations. *Human Communication Research, 14*, 68–92.

Piaget, J. (1955). *The language and thought of the child* (M. Gabain, Trans.). New York: World Publishing. (Original work published 1926)

Piché, G. L., & Roen, D. H. (1987). Social cognition and writing. *Written Communication, 4*, 68–83.

Rubin, D. L. (1982). Adapting syntax in writing to varying audiences as a function of age and social cognitive ability. *Journal of Child Language, 9*, 497–510.

Rubin, D.L. (1984). Social cognition and written communication. *Written Communication, 1*, 211–245.

Rubin, D. L., & Piché, G. L. (1979). Development in syntactic and strategic aspects of audience adaptation skills in written persuasive communication. *Research in the Teaching of English, 13*, 293–316.

Rubin, D. L., & Rafoth, B. A. (1986). Social cognitive ability as a predictor of the quality of expository and persuasive writing among college freshmen. *Research in the Teaching of English, 20*, 9–21.

Shantz, C. U. (1975). The development of social cognition. In E. M. Hetherington (Ed.), *Review of child development research* (Vol. 5, pp. 257–323). Chicago: University of Chicago Press.

Spender, D. (1980). *Man made language*. London: Routledge & Kegan Paul.

Swanson, K. H. (1990). *The relationship of interpersonal cognitive complexity and message design logics employed in response to a regulative writing task*. Unpublished doctoral dissertation, University of Minnesota, Minneapolis.

Voss, J. (1988). Problem solving and reasoning in ill-structured domains. In C. Antaki (Ed.), *Analysing everyday explanation: A casebook of methods* (pp. 74–93). London: Sage.

Waters, B. L. (1975). *She writes like a woman*. Paper presented at the Southeast Conference on Linguistics, Atlanta. (ERIC Document Reproduction Service No. ED 115 113)

Werner, H. (1957). The concept of development from a comparative and organismic point of view. In D. E. Harris (Ed.), *The concept of development* (pp. 125–148). Minneapolis: University of Minnesota Press.

CHAPTER ELEVEN

Untapped Resources: "Styling" in Black Students' Writing for Black Audiences[1]

Teresa M. Redd
Howard University

African Americans are heirs to a rich rhetorical tradition, a tradition rooted in the cultures of Africa and cultivated in the streets and churches of Black America (see Abrahams, 1976; Asante, 1987; Labov, 1972; Smitherman, 1977). It is mainly an oral tradition, consisting of such verbal arts as talk-singing, punning, rhyming, and image making. Asante has called these rhetorical strategies "styling," "the conscious or unconscious manipulation of language or mannerisms to influence favorably the hearers of a message" (p. 39). This chapter explores one dimension of styling: the use of African-American rhetorical devices in writing.

Although styling derives from an oral tradition, it has had an impact on writing, especially since the 1960s when many African-American writers began "modeling their work upon styles derived from Afro-American culture" (Turner, 1985, p. 305). Thus, I began to wonder why I had rarely seen styling in my students' writing during 9 years of teaching composition at a historically African-American university. Perhaps my students were too far removed from the tradition: Many of them had grown up in newly integrated neighborhoods, had gone to predominantly White schools, or had attended Anglicized churches. On the other hand, I thought, my students might have assumed that styling was inappropriate in college writing.

---

[1]Throughout this chapter, I use the term *Black* for the sake of accuracy. For instance, I refer to the students' audiences as *Black* and *White* because the students were assigned these abstract racial categories. In addition, I describe my students as *Black* because some were Afro-Caribbean rather than African American.

Yet styling is a useful academic exercise, for it is a form of verbal acrobatics, a way students can exert control over their language. Moreover, as Anderson (1985), and Rubin, Goodrum, and Hall (1990) have pointed out, oral stylistic devices involving imagery, sound, and rhythm are potential tools for making compositions vivid and euphonious—for entertaining, instructing, and moving an audience.

This line of thinking led me to consider the relationship between my students' writing and the cultural background of their audiences. Rhetoricians from Plato (4th century B.C./1956) to Perelman and Olbrechts-Tyteca (1969) have explained how perceptions of one's audience shape discourse. In addition, researchers such as Flower and Hayes (1980) have found that audience considerations play a central role in the composing process of skilled writers. Thus, we would expect skilled writers to adapt their writing to their audience's cultural background. However, even an unskilled writer might invoke the cultural tradition of the audience. As a result of "heteroglossia" (Bakhtin, 1981) and "intertextuality" (Kristeva, 1969), voices of the culture may speak through a writer's text unbeknownst to the writer.

According to rhetorical studies of oratory, many African-American audiences expect to hear these voices, and their expectations influence African-American speakers (Asante, 1987; Brockriede & Scott, 1972; Illo, 1972; Williamson-Ige, 1982). Asante has noted that "Black audiences demand to hear certain expressions, to see certain things, and to enjoy certain kinds of humor" (p. 41). Consequently, African-American speakers may resort to a type of rhetorical "code switching" (Blom & Gumperz, 1972), switching from a mainstream rhetoric to the rhetoric of their African-American discourse community. Of particular interest is Illo's observation that Malcolm X assumed an ornate speaking style in front of an African-American audience: "Before the great black audiences Malcolm adopted a tone and ornament that were his and his audience's but that he relinquished before the white or the academic. The composition was rich in ethnic figuration and humor, in paronomasia, alliteration and rhyme" (p. 172). As Illo noted, for African-American audiences, Malcolm X drew heavily upon the African-American rhetorical tradition. Therefore I wondered, "What would happen to my students' writing style if I assigned a Black audience?" I was not a suitable Black audience because I was a Black *teacher*—an overhearer rather than a rhetorically engaged reader. But if I asked my students to persuade other Blacks, they might draw upon the rhetorical resources of African-American culture. As they began to style in response to the Black audience, I might discover rich resources for writing that—until now—I had not encouraged them to tap.

Previous studies have not explored this possibility. None of the available studies of African-American students' writing compare the impact of Black and White audiences, and only a few of these studies trace the influence of African-American rhetoric. Indeed, most research on African-American students' writing has focused on grammatical, phonological, and lexical features rather than rhetorical features (see reviews by Hartwell, 1980; Morrow, 1985). Surprisingly, some of the researchers who have written about African-American students' rhetorical background have not shown how it affects the students' writing (Honeman, 1990; Linn, 1975; Oliver, 1988). Other researchers have identified African-American rhetorical devices in the writing of African-American children, but not adolescents (e.g., Haas Dyson, 1992a, 1992b).

Thus, little has been done to identify the rhetorical roots of African-American adolescents' writing. One notable exception is a study by Ball (1992), who found that African-American high school students preferred using organizational patterns from the African-American oral tradition—even in academic writing. Another pertinent study was conducted by Noonan-Wagner (1980), who examined essays written by African-American and White students in a remedial writing class. In the African-American students' essays, judges found more instances of "redundancy, the use of quotations, sermonizing and/or moralizing, and references to the Bible" (p. 6). Noonan-Wagner argued that these differences reflect the discourse conventions of the traditional African-American church service. Thus, Noonan-Wagner's study suggests that African-American rhetoric can influence African-American students' writing style, but it does not reveal the impact of Black versus White audiences. The two studies described in the sections that follow examine the role of African-American rhetoric in conjunction with the role of audience.

EXPERIMENT 1

Method

The first study focused on an intermediate composition class that I taught in the spring of 1991 (see Redd, 1991, for a fuller discussion). Among the 17 participants were 14 Blacks from the United States and 3 from the Caribbean. The Caribbean students were included in the study because Black oral traditions in the Caribbean and the United States are closely related (Abrahams, 1976).

All of the students received two audience adaptation assignments. Assignment 1 required students to write two argumentative drafts about affirmative action, one addressed to Black opponents and the other addressed to White opponents. Assignment 2 specified the same target audiences, but this time students wrote two drafts about the causes of poverty among African Americans. For each assignment, I asked the students to "freewrite" (i.e., to compose without editing) so that they could more easily adapt their writing to their audience. Also, to reduce contamination between tasks, I did not return the draft for one audience until I had received the draft for the other audience.

Of the 17 students, 8 submitted all four drafts; 6, two drafts; and the other 3, only one draft. I examined these compositions to determine whether styling occurred in the drafts for Black audiences and, if so, whether it occurred only in those drafts.

The stylistic features that I looked for are rhetorical qualities identified by Smitherman (1977) in *Talkin' and Testifyin': The Language of Black America*. Other scholars (among them Abrahams, 1976; Asante, 1987; Hannerz, 1969; Kochman, 1972; Labov, 1972; Mitchell-Kernan, 1971) have described African-American rhetoric. However, for a stylistic study their categories of analysis are too narrow (e.g., Labov's syntactic categories) or too broad (e.g., Asante's Afrocentric criteria and Abrahams' taxonomy of speech events). To date, Smitherman's is the most useful approach, for she identified stylistic features that apply to African-American discourse in a range of forms and contexts. Many of these features are mentioned in other descriptions of African-American discourse (see, e.g., Abrahams, 1976, pp. 19–21; Asante, 1987, pp. 37–58). As one can see from the following list (based on Smitherman, 1977, pp. 94–100), some of the features overlap with features of classical Western rhetoric:

1. *Exaggerated language* (high-flown words or incongruously formal phrasing). EXAMPLE: "When Jesus walked the face of the earth, you know it upset the high ES-U-LAUNCE." (The speaker accentuates the word *echelons*.)

2. *Mimicry* (imitation of a person's voice, language, and mannerisms). EXAMPLE: "Like he come tellin' me this old mess bout 'Well, baby, if you just give me a chance, Ima have it together pretty soon.' "

3. *Aphorisms* (proverbs and other popular sayings). EXAMPLE: "A hard head make a soft behind."

4. *Word play* (puns and other clever turns of phrase). EXAMPLE: "I don't know Karate but I know Karazor." (The speaker threatens to use a razor as a weapon.)

5. *Image making* (metaphors and other imagery, especially down-to-earth imagery). EXAMPLE: Wig-wearing females "look like nine miles of bad road with a detour at the end."

6. *Braggadocio* (boasts about oneself or heroes). EXAMPLE: Stag-O-Lee was so bad "flies wouldn't fly around him in the summertime."

7. *Indirection* (innuendo, circumlocution, or suggestiveness). EXAMPLE: "Mr. Moderator, Brother Lomax, brothers and sisters, friends and enemies: I just can't believe everyone in here is a friend and I don't want to leave anybody out."

8. *Tonal semantics* (talk-singing, repetition, alliteration, rhyme, intonational contouring, and other lyrical effects). EXAMPLE: "I am nobody talking to Somebody Who can help anybody."

Results

Using Smitherman's (1977) categories, I found significant evidence of styling in the students' drafts for Black audiences. Seven students included exaggerated language, aphorisms, word play, image making, and/or tonal semantics in one or both of their drafts for a Black audience. Because four of these students also submitted drafts addressed to a White audience, it was possible to compare their stylistic choices for Black and White audiences. The comparison revealed that they styled almost exclusively when addressing a Black audience. Next, we take a closer look at their work. (Examples of styling appear in italics.)

Gail Gail's drafts on poverty reveal striking differences in tonal semantics. For example, in her draft for White opponents Gail makes the following statement:

> The Black family, knowledge, and values are the keys to gain financial freedom.

However, in her draft for Black opponents she expresses the idea more rhythmically. Here she employs antistrophe by repeating "the key" at the end of successive clauses:

> *Education is the key, family is the key, values are the key* to economic stability in the black community.

The conclusions of the drafts also offer a striking contrast. In the draft for White opponents, Gail's closing lines are:

> The Black community must fall back on their ancestors strength for the courage to say "Yes I can", regardless of the ever present obstacles that face them such as the stereotypical attitudes of many in society.

On the other hand, in the closing lines of her draft for Black opponents, Gail employs isocolon (repetition of clauses of equal length) and diction reminiscent of gospel songs:

> *It may be hard but it can be done. We can thank our ancestors for showing us the way.*

Nora. In both of her affirmative action drafts, Nora exposes the contradictions between the sacred documents of American democracy and the ugly practices of American society. She tells a Black opponent:

> *Mr. Pendelton, our Constitution may be color-blind, but unfortunately our people are not. Our Constitution may not tolerate classes among its citizens, but our people sure do.*

In contrast, in her draft for Whites, Nora expresses similar sentiments without the rhythm or antithesis that is so prominent in her draft for Blacks:

> The Declaration of Independence proclaims a self evident truth that "all men are created equal". Yet this pronouncement by the Founding Fathers is contradicted by widespread social inequality.

Maria. Each of Maria's drafts for a Black audience displays a talent for word play that is not apparent in either draft for a White audience. For instance, in her poverty draft for White opponents, Maria describes European colonization as follows:

> After colonization and exploitation by Europeans these countries were left bone dry, without resources, impoverished and war torn.

In her poverty draft for a Black audience, she uses antithesis instead:

> When europeans came to explore Africa they immediately found ways to exploit *the many* to create riches for *the few.*

Likewise, in her affirmative action draft for a Black audience, we find word play in the last line: "We do not need *Affirmative* Action, we need an *affirmative* plan to free ourselves!"

Clara. Clara likes to create images. We can glimpse her image-making ability in her poverty draft to White opponents when she writes, "In a society where the fabric of the black family is being torn apart legally it is highly unlikely that we will not improve if discrimination were to vanish." This is the only image in that draft. Yet Clara's draft to a Black audience is filled with images. For example, the draft opens with two vivid scenes depicting the home life of a Black man before and after he loses his job. The draft also ends with a burst of imagery:

> We are poor because we have been raped repeatedly. *Doors are not opened to us, it has been a facade.* We are poor not only economically but socially

as well. We attempt as a people *to climb from this hole, but dirt is constantly being piled on top of us, pushing us farther into our holes of despair.*

In contrast, Clara's draft to White opponents begins with a statistic. It concludes without imagery:

> Discrimination has attributed to our poverty levels especially over the past twenty years. We have been ignored for long enough from the immediate concerns of the government, and we need to realize that our poverty is not self-inflicted but government institutionalized.

Steve. In contrast to the four stylers described previously, one student—Steve—styled only for a White audience: He included an analogy in his poverty draft for Whites but not in the corresponding draft for Blacks. He made the following comparison:

> Rich White America needs to help support the advancement of color people and other minorities because this group of Whites has the largest affect on young Blacks who are to become our nation's future professionals. *It is a lot easier to focus o[n] our Black youth because it is a lot easier to change the growth of a baby tree because it is easier to manipulate than an older tree. The old tree is set in its growth and will break if pressed upon too much.*

Discussion

This pilot study raised more questions than it answered. One wonders why all of the students did not style for Black audiences, and why Steve styled only for a White audience. Skill may be a factor, for research shows that unskilled writers often have difficulty imagining, analyzing, and adapting to audiences (see Redd-Boyd & Slater's 1989 review). However, other factors may also account for the students' performance. Did some students refrain from styling because they were writing instead of speaking? Or were they unable to style because they had grown up outside the African-American rhetorical tradition? Did some students consider styling inappropriate because of the type of Black audience they had imagined—for example, a well-educated Black audience? Or did they hesitate to "rap" to a Black audience because of the academic purpose of the assignments?

To answer these questions, I needed to know more about my students' background, their perceptions, and their intentions. I also needed to control for possible order effects because most of the students had written their draft for Blacks before writing their draft for Whites. Therefore, I designed a follow-up study, incorporating questionnaires, discourse-based interviews, and counterbalanced audience assignments as well as independent coding. The follow-up study focused on two research questions:

1. When Black students write for Black and White audiences, will some students style more often for the Black audiences?
2. When Black students write for Black and White audiences, will some types of styling appear more often in drafts for the Black audiences?

EXPERIMENT 2

Method

The follow-up study explored the writing of 16 students in an all-Black intermediate composition class that I taught in the fall of 1991. The majority of the students had a traditional African-American background: 11 had grown up in African-American neighborhoods, 9 had enrolled in African-American or well-integrated schools, 10 had attended Baptist or Pentecostal churches, and 12 said that they frequently spoke Black English.

During the semester I asked the students to complete the affirmative action and poverty assignments described earlier. To reduce order effects, I assigned students counterbalanced due dates for the "Black" and "White" drafts, adding, "If you believe that something is appropriate for both audiences, you may use it in both drafts." I also asked students to write a brief description of their target audiences. This description would reveal whether the type of White or Black audience influenced styling.

When I announced the poverty assignment (Assignment 2), I also distributed sheets that (a) specified the topic and the target audiences, (b) explained freewriting, and (c) informed students that I would assess how well they adapted their style as well as the content, and arrangement. To prepare them for this assignment, I had conducted three lessons on style—lessons about voice, clarity, wordiness, parallelism, and metaphors. However, I had not discussed ways to adapt style to a reader's cultural background.

Of the 16 students, 15 completed all four drafts, whereas 1 submitted two poverty drafts and one affirmative action draft. (The affirmative action draft was discarded.) As in the pilot study, I did not return the draft for one audience until I had received the draft for the other audience.

After returning the poverty drafts, I interviewed 7 students and asked the rest of the students to fill out two questionnaires. Thirteen students completed Questionnaire 1, and all students completed Questionnaire 2. Questionnaire 1 asked the students to describe their target audiences for the poverty assignment and to say whether they had changed their writing style: If so, how? If not, why not? Questionnaire 2 (filled out a week later) asked students about (a) the ethnic makeup of their neighborhood and schools, (b) the cultural tradition of their church, and (c) their use of Black English Vernacular and Black street slang. This questionnaire also posed the following questions: "What kind of speaking and writing styles are Black audiences most receptive to? What kind of speaking and writing styles are White audiences most receptive to?"

During the interviews, I asked the students the questions from the questionnaires, but before proceeding to Questionnaire 2, I showed the students contrasting passages in their affirmative action and poverty drafts. At this point, I conducted discourse-based interviews, following the example of Odell, Goswami, and Herrington (1983). However, whereas Odell, Goswami, and Herrington asked subjects about variations between unrelated pieces of writing, I asked my students about variations between drafts on the same topic.

Because the focus of the study was styling, I asked the students to explain why they had added, omitted, or replaced any of the rhetorical features identified by Smitherman (1977). To reduce experimenter effects, I took the following precautions: I asked nondirective questions such as "Why did you omit this?" or "Could you elaborate?" and I urged the students to admit when they did not know the answer.

Two graduate students coded the students' drafts, looking for the selected features. (Both coders were African Americans pursuing a PhD in African-American literature, and neither knew the purpose or design of the experiment.) First, the coders read Smitherman's (1977) description of the features and discussed six samples from the pilot study. Then, they coded the rest of the drafts independently, using a coding guide that listed Smitherman's categories and examples (see the list under Experiment 1, the Method section). At first, they achieved a low rate of agreement across categories (41%). However, in conference they resolved all but three disagreements, increasing the rate of agreement to 99%. The three disputed items were excluded.

Results

All of the students indicated on their papers or on Questionnaire 1 that they had tried to accommodate Black and White opponents. Most of the reported audiences (see Table 11.1) were generalized racial categories (i.e., Blacks vs. Whites). Relatively few of either race were described as well educated.

Questionnaire 2 and the interview tapes reveal that most students felt that Black and White audiences preferred different speaking/writing styles. Five students said that Blacks liked a "straightforward" and "down-to-earth" style. Four said that Blacks responded well to "non-proper" English, such as slang or Black English Vernacular. Three other students claimed that Blacks liked a "powerful" or "moving" style, and three suggested that images or stories appealed to Blacks. (Two students gave more than one response.)

These perceptions contrast with the students' descriptions of Whites' stylistic preferences. According to four students, Whites prefer "wordy," "intellectual" discourse that is filled with "big words." The English must be "White English," that is, "proper" or "formal." Whites need no embellishments—just the facts, said three other students. However, three students stated that Blacks and Whites were receptive to similar styles of speaking and writing.

TABLE 11.1
Students' Reported Audiences

Student	Affirmative Action		Poverty	
	Black	White	Black	White
1	Blacks	Whites	middle class & poor	middle class & poor
2	Blacks	Whites	bourgeois & professional	individualist
3	conservative	Whites	successful	White society
4	Blacks	females & liberals	upper middle class on down	White society
5	Blacks	Whites	educated	educated
6	Blacks	Whites	conservative	racist
7	Blacks	Whites	Blacks	Whites
8	Blacks	conservative	conservative	average
9	Blacks	working class	Blacks	most Whites
10	—	—	NAACP	conservative
11	Blacks	Whites	under-privileged	ruling class
12	conservative	most Whites	Blacks	Whites
13	Blacks	Whites	depressed	Whites
14	liberals	liberals & women	lazy	lazy
15	Blacks	Whites	working class	working class
16	conservative	conservative males	middle class	conservative males

Despite their claims, when I questioned all of the students about their strategies for the poverty drafts, only four students said that they had tried to achieve a more "professional" or "formal" tone for Whites or a more "emotional" tone for Blacks. Indeed, some of the very students who differentiated between "Black" and "White" styles admitted that they had not tried to adapt their writing style; they had focused on adapting the content instead. Two students seemed to be confused about what style was, assuming that it was merely a matter of essay organization or the selection of arguments. Nevertheless, as I explain next, there are significant stylistic differences between some students' drafts for Black and White audiences.

Distribution of Stylistic Features

Of the stylistic features associated with the African-American oral tradition, aphorisms, word play, image making, indirection, and tonal semantics were identified in the students' drafts (indicated in italics in the examples that follow).

Aphorisms. Of the eight students who employed aphorisms, four incorporated them exclusively in their drafts for Blacks; three, only in their drafts for Whites; and one, in drafts for both audiences. Following are three aphorisms addressed to Black audiences:

There is a saying that a man must be down before he can get up. Well, Black America it is time to get up. (Alice)

A great philosopher once said for every one door that closes, there are at least ten waiting to be [broken?] down. Behind these doors lies the key from [which] any hope and good life can be obtained. *The road is going to be hard but any[thing] worth having is worth fighting for* and the end result will be a race [that] is worthy of it's culture. (Crissie)

You have to be twice as good just to be considered half as good as a White boy whose only half as good as you. (Giselle)

Word Play. The coders agreed that four students engaged in word play, two for Whites only, one for Blacks only, and one for both audiences. The students' word play is evident in the following examples:

Affirmative Action keeps those who have been discriminated against in *the past* from being mistreated in *the present* and *the future.* (Keisha)

In looking [at] the educational aspect, we find that Blacks aren't *pushed* to succeed as much as Whites are. They are *pushed* into remedial classes. (Selma)

Afro-Americans are too *materialistic* instead of being *realistic.* (Maxine)

Image Making. Image making was the most common styling device. Some images were analogies (e.g., "*Just as the runner needed a head start since he was discriminated against initially, Blacks should continue to receive affirmative action*"). Some were clichés and echoes of Civil Rights speeches, folk sermons, or gospel lyrics (e.g., "*get their foot in the door,*" "*the first hu[r]dling block of a long road ahead*"). Others were highly unconventional ("*Affirmative action is just like potty training is to a child*"). Of the 15 students who invoked images in their drafts, 11 invoked images more often when addressing Blacks; 2, more often when addressing Whites; and 2, equally often for both audiences. The following images appear in drafts addressed to Blacks:

Affirmative action is *like stealing* (taking something that might not be rightfully yours). (Carmen)

A Black man simply cannot make it over *the socio-economic wall* without the help of Affirmative Action. . . . (Raoul)

Indirection. The coders identified only one instance of indirection, a sentence in a draft for Blacks:

As a result, we are being so-called "*rewarded*" by being allowed to hold the unskilled or manual labor jobs many of our people have been granted. (Keisha)

Tonal Semantics.   According to the coders, seven students employed tonal semantics in their drafts. The most common forms consisted of parallel phrases with repeated or contrasting words. Of the seven students, one included tonal semantics equally often for Blacks and Whites. However, four used these techniques more often for Black audiences. For instance, Selma wrote,

> As a result, the race of Blacks are *discouraged and dismayed.*

On the other hand, two students included more tonal semantics in their drafts for Whites, writing, for example,

> *Affirmative Action is not a race issue it is a people issue.* (Keisha)

Only one striking trend emerges from the preceding data: The majority of the students employed more images when writing for Blacks as opposed to Whites.

Styling for Blacks Versus Whites

After examining the data, I shifted my focus to the students. To identify a student's tendency to style for a particular audience, I searched for a consistent pattern in all four drafts of the affirmative action and poverty assignments. Only students with a consistent pattern of styling (indicated in italics) are discussed next.

Styling for Blacks Only.   Three students styled exclusively in their drafts for Black opponents. One was Joetta, a student who had attended a White high school and Catholic church, but had grown up in an African-American neighborhood and home where she had learned Black English. Joetta styled by extending a conventional metaphor throughout the concluding paragraph of a draft for Blacks:

> *Although many African-Americans are at the top or middle of the economic ladder, there are many who are at the bottom.* As long as racism and disunity exists among the African-American community, *many Blacks will fall down the economic ladder* or stay in the same submissive state.

The conclusion of Joetta's corresponding draft for "racist White people" lacks such imagery:

> Although a number of African-Americans are poor for reasons other than racism, there is a larger number of African-Americans who are poor because

of racism. Unfortunately, in our racist American society, the system will continually oppress the Black race as a whole.

Rhonda's concluding paragraphs offer a similar contrast. Rhonda, who said she often spoke Black English, was a product of an African-American neighborhood, an African-American high school, and an African-American Pentecostal church. The daughter of a Pentecostal preacher, Rhonda conjured up religious images in her draft for "black conservatives":

> In conclusion, the majority of African-Americans feel that Affirmative Action is necessary and fair. Those African-Americans who oppose affirmative action have benefitted from it at one time or another & can be considered "sell-outs". They have, in a way, *sold their souls to the devil in which the devil is the White Man or Mainstream Society.* Once again, affirmative action is fair & for the most part extremely necessary for the advancement of African-Americans in these United States.

Rhonda's conclusion for "most Whites" is not only free of the fire and brimstone, but filled with polite jargon such as "advantaged" and "disadvantaged groups":

> In conclusion, Affirmative action is indeed fair. Members of advantaged groups should want to share with instead of take away from those members of disadvantaged groups. Without Affirmative action, progress or advancement is unlikely to happen for someone who is a member of a disadvantaged group.

Rhonda and Joetta reported that they did not consciously adapt their style to an audience. However, during her interview, Joetta insisted that Blacks preferred a "powerful" and "lively" style, whereas Whites just wanted information. Rhonda did not say which styles Blacks and Whites preferred.

One other student, Leroy, styled exclusively for Blacks. Leroy had a traditional African-American upbringing—African-American neighborhood, mostly African-American school, Baptist church—and he claimed to speak Black English "all the time." Leroy styled infrequently, however. An example of his styling appears in his poverty draft for "depressed blacks." Instead of opening with the question "Why are African Americans so disproportionately poor?" as he did in his poverty draft for Whites, he began his draft for Blacks with a simple antithesis:

> In today's society, *there are those people who are rich, and there are those who are poor.* The white race tends more to be those who are rich; while the Black race are the unfortunate poor people.

According to Leroy, Blacks prefer speakers and writers who "get to the point" and "tell it like it is," whereas Whites prefer those who "sound intellectual." Although Leroy seems to "tell it like it is" in the excerpt for Blacks, he indicated that he concentrated on adapting the content rather than the style of his drafts.

Styling for Whites Only.   Contrary to my hypothesis, one student consistently styled for White audiences only. Her name was Faye. She had grown up in a White neighborhood attending White schools. However, she had been a member of a traditional Baptist church and said that she occasionally spoke Black English. Faye's styling for Whites can be seen in the concluding paragraph of her poverty draft for "individualistic" Whites. The paragraph contains a series of parallel phrases and battle imagery:

> African Americans have remained disproportionately poor as a result of racism. Racism has caused black Americans *to loose initiative, to receive inadequate education and to remain in low salary jobs.* Until the war against racism is won, Blacks will remain defeated in the battle against discrimination.

Yet in her draft for "bourgeois and professional" Blacks, Faye's concluding paragraph is unadorned:

> Blacks remain in poverty as a result of racism. Discrimination in the workfor[c]e and in the education system has been the major factor in limiting the economic progress of Blacks. Until attempts are made to eliminate inequalities in the workfor[c]e and in the education system, many Blacks will remain at poverty level.

During her interview, Faye said that she had used the battle imagery in the poverty draft for Whites because she needed to adopt an "aggressive" tone to persuade her White opponents, but wanted to arouse the sympathy of her Black opponents. However, later in the interview, Faye had second thoughts about her strategy for the Black audience. When asked which style Blacks preferred, Faye replied, "A style of writing that motivates them . . . powerful words." Then, after a moment's reflection, she added, "Probably the conclusion that I wrote to the White audience [the one with the battle imagery] might appeal more to the Black audience because they kinda like to hear aggressive things, motivational kinda like things."

Styling for Blacks and Whites.   Four students styled for Blacks and Whites in all four drafts. Two of the students—Greta and Carmen—claimed that Blacks and Whites appreciated the same speaking and writing styles. However, the other two students—Keisha and Maxine—thought otherwise.

Keisha had grown up in an African-American neighborhood and African-American schools, speaking Black English, but she had attended a Catholic church. Although Keisha styled for Whites as well as Blacks, all but one of the images in her writing appear in her drafts for Blacks. For instance, in her affirmative action draft for Black opponents, she explains how "Affirmative Action has *opened doors for Blacks that have been closed or cracked for centuries*" and how affirmative action programs "help minorities *get their foot in the door.*" She also challenges critics who accuse Blacks of taking "*an easy detour*" through affirmative action and speaks of "*the shadow of white America.*"

When I asked Keisha why she had used more images for the Black audience, she could not say. Although she thought about her use of pronouns, in general she did not try to adapt her style. Yet, later, when I asked her if Blacks and Whites preferred different speaking and writing styles, she insisted that Blacks "like more images . . . strong voices" and that "Whites basically don't care as long as the message is comin' across." Surprisingly, she did not notice that this remark could explain her use of imagery in her drafts for Blacks.

In contrast to Keisha, Maxine used the most imagery in her poverty draft for Whites. Maxine, who said she occasionally spoke Black English, had roots in a Baptist church but was a product of White schools and a White neighborhood. In her poverty draft for Blacks ("upper middle-class on down"), she referred to racism as "*this sickness . . . being spread around the United States.*" But in her draft for "White society," she also compared poverty to "*the AIDS of the Black Community*" and affirmative action to a "*vaccine.*" She concluded the draft with the lines:

> . . . White America needs to stop injecting Afro-Americans with *diseases like racism.* The government needs to support the Black community and give economic relief. Black youths are drowning and need to be *saved out of the pool of poverty.*

Maxine said that she had used these images exclusively for Whites because she needed "hard-hitting" images to persuade her "racist" White audience. However, like Keisha, she later described the best style for Blacks as "a writing style that they can relate to . . . images that they can see, those things that they may have experienced, those things that they may have heard about or their ancestors have experienced." Although Whites, she explained, are interested in this Black style, they are used to a "boring style." Why, then, did she include more images in her drafts for Whites than she did in her drafts for Blacks? Oddly enough, Maxine did not notice the contradiction between her remarks and her use of imagery.

Maxine used not only more images but also more tonal semantics in her drafts for a White audience. Yet her comments about the tonal semantics and word play in one draft suggest that her target audience was a moving target. Consider the following paragraph from her poverty draft for Whites:

> The Afro-American feels that he must meet the status quo and were Gucci, Liz Claiborne, and Polo because those are the most expensive tastes of clothing, everyone wants to have the best. However, there's a problem when one does not have a phone or electricity due that leather coat. Due to mixed up priorities, one better sleep in that leather coat to keep warm without electricity. Afro-Americans spend their money on the wrong things and so they suffer. Afro Americans are too *materialistic* instead of being *realistic*.

Even though a similar paragraph appears in Maxine's draft for Blacks, the pairing of "materialistic" and "realistic" occurs only in the draft for Whites. When I queried Maxine about this word play, she blurted out, "You know what? I think I was thinking of a Black audience here! I got my audience mixed up."

DISCUSSION

Like Experiment 1, Experiment 2 offers evidence of styling for Black audiences. For instance, assigning a Black audience elicited certain types of styling that occurred less often when a White audience was assigned. Most notably, image making appeared more often in the students' drafts for Blacks: 11 of the 16 students included more images for Blacks. Consciously or unconsciously, these students may have been adapting to the cultural tradition of their Black audiences. Indeed, the interview and questionnaire data show that some students thought Blacks preferred image-filled discourse.

However, the preponderance of imagery in drafts for Blacks may have more to do with "intertextuality" and "heteroglossia" than with image making. Because some of the images are commonplaces—clichés and echoes of speeches, sermons, or lyrics—the students may have been invoking shared texts rather than inventing images per se. If so, the commonplaces are a sign of audience adaptation, not lack of imagination. As the rhetoric of Martin Luther King, Jr., reveals, commonplaces can be a powerful tool for persuading audiences because they are readymade "audience-approved language" (Miller, 1986, pp. 260–261). Such commonplaces play an important role not only in the rhetoric of African Americans but in the rhetoric of other ethnic groups (Matalene, 1985).

As expected, assigning a Black audience affected the overall *frequency* of styling as well as the type of styling. Three students—Joetta, Rhonda, and Leroy—styled exclusively in drafts for a Black audience. However, contrary to my expectations, one student—Faye—styled for Whites only. Four other students—Greta, Carmen, Keisha, and Maxine—styled for Whites and Blacks.

These styling differences could not be explained by the order of the audience assignments, the students' grades and cultural background, or the nature of their reported audiences.

Nevertheless, three important observations can be made about these styling differences. The first observation pertains to the students' perceptions of their audience. Take the case of Faye and Maxine. Faye and Maxine considered their White opponents more distant and hostile than their Black opponents. Because Faye and Maxine felt that they needed more ammunition for such a hostile and distant audience, they used more images when addressing their White opponents. In other words, they thought that persuading a hostile and distant audience would take "everything they've got." This trend is consistent with previous findings that distant audiences elicit greater syntactic maturity, more contextualization, and stronger refutation than intimate audiences do (Collins & Williamson, 1984; Rubin, 1982; Rubin & Piché, 1979). Likewise, hostile audiences stimulate more argumentation (Hays, Brandt, & Chantry, 1988). However, in this study the White opponents were not always the most distant and hostile. Consider, for example, Rhonda's disdain for Black conservatives whom she brands as "sell-outs." From her perspective, these Black traitors are as bad as—or perhaps worse than—her White enemies. Clearly, how distant and hostile an audience is depends on a student's perceptions, not the audience's race.

My second observation concerns the students' haphazard use of styling. All of the students indicated that they had considered how to adapt the *content* of their arguments to their target audiences. Yet few considered how to adapt the *style* of their arguments, even when they thought that Blacks and Whites preferred different styles. The three students who styled exclusively for Blacks admitted that they had not consciously adapted their style. Keisha too could not say why she had used more imagery for Blacks. In addition, Faye and Maxine styled inconsistently. Although Faye did not style for Blacks at all, she subsequently decided that she should have provided imagery for Blacks. As for Maxine, at times she forgot which audience she was addressing. Moreover, during her interview she did not notice the contradiction between what she said Blacks preferred and what style she adopted for Blacks. In fact, only Greta and Carmen seemed to have styled in a manner consistent with their statements: Both said that Blacks and Whites appreciated similar styles, and both styled similarly for Blacks and Whites.

Finally, my third observation relates to freewriting. In some cases, the opportunity to freewrite may have had a greater impact on the students' style than the assignment of audiences. By releasing the students from most academic constraints, freewriting may have stimulated styling, regardless of audience.

To sum up, Experiments 1 and 2 suggest that assigning a Black audience can elicit styling that may be absent or rare in writing for a White audience.

However, the effect is limited. A few students may style exclusively for Blacks, whereas others may use certain types of styling more often for Blacks. In rare cases, a student might style more often for a White audience if she or he feels that the Whites are more distant and hostile.

Limitations

Experiments 1 and 2 show that assigning a Black audience can influence students' styling, but for several reasons the relationship between the students' styling and their rhetorical background is not as clear. First of all, Questionnaire 2 could not measure the depth of the students' exposure to the African-American tradition, especially within the home. Second, neither experiment included a White comparison group. Third, because of the overlapping and fuzzy coding categories, the coders and I often wondered whether certain utterances should count as African-American styling. After all, some features of African-American rhetoric overlap with features of European rhetoric. At what point, then, are students truly drawing upon an African-American rhetoric?

Implications for Teaching

Despite their limitations, Experiments 1 and 2 suggest that teachers of Black students should learn about African-American rhetoric. Only an informed teacher can make students who style aware of what they are doing and show them how to style more effectively. Above all, teachers should encourage students to style by assigning at least one freewrite for a Black audience. As long as there are students like Gail, Nora, Maria, Clara, Joetta, Rhonda, and Leroy—students who style only for Black audiences—Black students need a chance to write for Blacks. Otherwise, some students may never fully develop their writing potential.

In my subsequent composition classes, I have put into practice what I learned from these experiments, and the results have been encouraging. Just listen to my students' writing about affirmative action:

> It is *insurance* and *assurance*.
>
> Neither does it aim to *exclude*, only to *include*.
>
> The case of affirmative action represents a *contemporary remedy for an age-old ailment*.
>
> Affirmative Action is not *giving handouts*, it is *giving a hand*.

My students are playing with language, and through play they are learning to recognize and utilize their language resources.

ACKNOWLEDGMENTS

I would like to thank Betsy Sanford and Karen Webb for their perceptive comments on earlier versions of this chapter.

REFERENCES

Abrahams, R. D. (1976). *Talking black.* Rowley, MA: Newbury House.

Anderson, E. (1985). Using folk literature in teaching composition. In C. K. Brooks (Ed.), *Tapping potential: English and language arts for the Black learner* (pp. 219–225). Urbana, IL: National Council of Teachers of English.

Asante, M. K. (1987). *The afrocentric idea.* Philadelphia: Temple University Press.

Bakhtin, M. (1981). Discourse in the novel. In M. Holquist (Ed.), *The dialogic imagination* (pp. 259–422). Austin: University of Texas Press.

Ball, A. F. (1992). Cultural preference and the expository writing of African-American adolescents. *Written Communication, 9*, 501–532.

Blom, J., & Gumperz, J. J. (1972). Social meaning and linguistic structures: Code-switching in Norway. In J. J. Gumperz & D. Hymes (Eds.), *Directions in sociolinguistics* (pp. 407–434). New York: Holt, Rinehart & Winston.

Brockriede, W., & Scott, R. L. (1972). Stokely Carmichael: Two speeches on black power. In A. L. Selma (Ed.), *Language, communication, and rhetoric in Black America* (pp. 176–194). New York: Harper & Row.

Collins, J. L., & Williamson, M. W. (1984). Assigned rhetorical context and semantic abbreviation in writing. In R. Beach & L. S. Bridwell (Eds.), *New directions in composition research* (pp. 285–296). New York: Guilford.

Flower, L. S., & Hayes, J. R. (1980). The cognition of discovery: Defining a rhetorical problem. *College Composition and Communication, 31*, 21–32.

Haas Dyson, A. (1992a). The case of the singing scientist. *Written Communication, 9*, 3–47.

Haas Dyson, A. (1992b, April). *Whistle for Willie, lost Presspies, and cartoon dogs: The sociocultural dimensions of young children's composing or toward unmelting pedagogical pots.* Paper presented at the annual meeting of the American Educational Research Association, San Francisco.

Hannerz, U. (1969). *Soulside.* New York: Columbia University Press.

Hartwell, P. (1980). Dialect interference in writing: A critical view. *Research in the Teaching of English, 14*, 101–118.

Hays, J. N., Brandt, K. S., & Chantry, K. H. (1988). The impact of friendly and hostile audiences on the argumentative writing of high school and college students. *Research in the Teaching of English, 22*, 391–416.

Honeman, B. (1990, July). *Rationale and suggestions for emphasizing afrocentricity in the public schools.* Paper presented at the Conference on Rhetoric and the Teaching of Writing, Indiana, PA.

Illo, J. (1972). The rhetoric of Malcolm X. In A. L. Selma (Ed.), *Language, communication, and rhetoric in Black America* (pp. 158–175). New York: Harper & Row.

Kochman, T. (1972). Toward an ethnography of Black American speech behavior. In T. Kochman (Ed.), *Rappin' and stylin' out: Communication in urban Black America* (pp. 241–264). Chicago: University of Illinois Press.

Kristeva, J. (1969). *Semiotike: Recherches pour une semanalyse.* Paris: Seuil.

Labov, W. (1972). *Language in the inner city: Studies in the Black English vernacular.* Philadelphia: University of Pennsylvania Press.

Linn, M. D. (1975). Black rhetorical patterns and the teaching of composition. *College Composition and Communication, 26,* 149–153.

Matalene, C. (1985). Contrastive rhetoric: An American writing teacher in China. *College English, 47,* 789–808.

Miller, K. (1986). Martin Luther King, Jr. borrows a revolution: Argument, audience, and implications of a secondhand universe. *College English, 48,* 249–265.

Mitchell-Kernan, C. (1971). *Language behavior in a Black urban community.* Monograph of the Language-Behavior Lab, No. 2. University of California, Berkeley.

Morrow, D. H. (1985). Dialect interference in writing: Another critical view. *Research in the Teaching of English, 19,* 154–180.

Noonan-Wagner, D. (1980, March). *Black writers in the classroom: A question of language experience, not grammar.* Paper presented at the convention of the Conference on College Composition and Communication, Washington, DC.

Odell, L., Goswami, D., & Herrington, A. (1983). The discourse-based interview: A procedure for exploring the tacit knowledge of writers in nonacademic settings. In P. Mosenthal, L. Tamor, & S. A. Walmsley (Eds.), *Research on writing: Principles and methods* (pp. 221–235). New York: Longman.

Oliver, E. (1988). An afrocentric approach to literature: Putting the pieces back together. *English Journal, 77,* 49–53.

Perelman, C., & Olbrechts-Tyteca, L. (1969). *The new rhetoric: A treatise on argumentation* (J. Wilkinson & P. Weaver, Trans.). Notre Dame, IN: University of Notre Dame Press. (Original work published 1958)

Plato (1956). *Phaedrus* (W. C. Hembold & W. G. Rabinowitz, Trans.). Indianapolis: Liberal Arts Press. (Original work written 4th century B.C.)

Redd, T. (1991). "Styling" in Black students' writing. *CEA-MAGazine, 4*(1), 21–31.

Redd-Boyd, T., & Slater, W. H. (1989). The effects of audience specification on undergraduates' attitudes, strategies, and writing. *Research in the Teaching of English, 23,* 77–108.

Rubin, D. L. (1982). Adapting syntax in writing to varying audiences as a function of age and social cognitive ability. *Journal of Child Language, 9,* 497–510.

Rubin, D. L., Goodrum, R., & Hall, B. (1990). Orality, oral-based culture, and the academic writing of ESL learners. *Issues in Applied Linguistics, 1,* 56–76.

Rubin, D. L., & Piché, G. (1979). Development in syntactic and strategic aspects of audience adaptation skills in written communication. *Research in the Teaching of English, 13,* 293–316.

Smitherman, G. (1977). *Talkin' and testifyin': The language of Black America.* Detroit: Wayne State University Press.

Turner, D. T. (1985). Black experience, Black literature, Black students, and the English classroom. In C. K. Brooks (Ed.), *Tapping potential: English and language arts for the Black learner* (pp. 297–307). Urbana, IL: National Council of Teachers of English.

Williamson-Ige, D. K. (1982). *Shirley Chisholm and women's rights rhetoric.* (ERIC Document Reproduction Service No. ED 247 625)

Author Index

Subject Index